A common sense primer
for your supply chain

Michael J. Stolarczyk

ISBN: 1453737561
ISBN-9781453737569

*To Pamela,*
*who has taught me the most about logistics via three children, spanning three continents, coordinating more than a dozen moves, and navigating through our daily life schedule with drive, determination, and aplomb...not to mention brutal honesty that keeps me focused on the horizon.*

*To Eva Pilar, Nathaniel Jackson, and Maxwell Alexander, my global nomads, whom I hope will each chart a continuing course of discovery and adventure.*

*To my mom and dad, Ted and MaryAnn, thank you for nurturing a desire in me to learn, explore, and lead.*

*To David Rees, for being the brother I never had, and the friend that will always be.*

# Jacket Quotes

"As a change agent, Stolarczyk is an activist determined to change the status quo and make a positive impact."

**Fast Company Magazine**

"For Michael, creating the book and these concepts was easy, as he has used this leadership approach for years!"

**Charles Brown—senior director, Sourcing-Under Armour, Inc.**

"Stolarczyk is motivated to push others above and beyond their known limits."

**J. J. Collier—vice president of Design, Spyder Active Sports, Inc.**

"I had the unique pleasure of being a colleague of Michael's during his time in Europe with the A P Moller / Maersk Group, and I continue to benefit from his leadership style and supply chain knowledge via his board membership with Navismart."

**Ernesto K. Hannya – president of Navismart Hungary Ltd.**

"This is a must read book for any logistician who wants to transcend borders, cultures, and tired common practice as they relate to the international supply chain and global sourcing."

**Herfried Leitner – CEO – HeLogistics Holdings GmbH**

"Michael moves beyond common practices and buzzwords. His strategies embrace the constant need for innovation at all levels of an organization, and the motivation needed to make change successful."

**Daniel Smithson—president and CEO, StarUSA Federal Credit Union**

"In an age when innovation and execution are not mutually exclusive for high-performing organizations, Michael's positive track record in this area speaks for itself!"
**Ken Lyon—chairman and founder, BitLogistics, Ltd.**

"The first touchpoint in positive customer experience is having the product available. Companies who understand that partnering with logistics experts like Michael Stolarczyk to innovate newer, faster and better ways of getting products to the end user will only have a positive impact on their bottom line and enhance customer satisfaction. Michael provides insights to help companies capture greater market share through smarter logistics."
**Matthew Kruchko - managing director, Applied Storytelling**

"Michael's consistent sense of urgency is second nature and contagious... No more waiting for whatever or whenever. Let's get it done, now!"
**Carl Hughes—president and CEO, The Fahey Bank**

"Expert leaders, like Stolarczyk, are not intimidated by change."
**Jack Ricchiuto—author, speaker, DesigningLife.com**

"What I find most instructive is the clarity of his principles and the underlying message that leaders must value people, both internal and external to the company."
**David Hardesty—president (retired), West Virginia University**

"Check mate for Stolarczyk in the Czech Republic"
**Containerization International Magazine**

"For Michael Stolarczyk, it boils down to EI, emotional intelligence."
**The Bottom Line Newsletter**

"I was very excited when Michael joined our organization to continue the rich tradition of fulfillment efficiency, vested collaboration, and mutual profitability that Kontane Logistics facilitates for our partners. His leadership philosophy, and supply chain tenants drive that culture."

**Ed Byrd – founder and CEO of Kontane, Inc.**

"This book provides the reader with a unique insight and an understanding into the future of Supply Chain logistics that even a newbie like myself can grasp. Michael's knowledge about this highly complicated field are presented in a easy to comprehend format and the text is sprinkled generously with Michael's wry humor, which allows you to be pulled farther into this ever changing world of movement, without losing you or the book's message along the way."

**Dennis Schroder – president of Schroder's I.T., Inc.**

# Contents

# Forward

Managers, executives, and people in general, often tell me, "In order to be the best of class, you must work with the best of class."

When I hear these words, I reply: "Best of class may not necessarily mean the best company or, in this case, working with the highest seat in the supply chain." Finding the loose bolt—from either side of the relationship—may result in breaking down the highest of barriers and connecting with people in ways you never thought possible.

Having said this, this very experience happened to me when I was the President of a high-profile Footwear Company. This brings me to my friend and colleague, Michael Stolarczyk. Michael has a magical ability to reach everyone, corporate CEO's, managers, clients, friends, family members and whoever else appears in his path. Finding the loose bolt in every situation is Michael's strength and he is a genius when it comes to reaching the unreachable, and in this book, you will find out just how he continues to do this! His success in the Logistics world is centered on this very skill.

I originally met Michael when our company was searching for an internationally known 3PL solution. My VP of Operations asked that I interview a few candidates by phone and a call was scheduled. I already knew which company I wanted to hire for the job, but allowed for this one interview to happen. Having scheduled the call over the weekend, as time was of the essence, it was a snowy day in Springfield, MA and I really did not have time for a long conversation. I was truly going to "fire" Michael before we even got past the first two sentences. As our conversation passed the "Hello, How are you?" stage, Michael began his passionate plea to give his organization and himself a chance to prove what they could do for us. I was skeptical but intrigued!

As we continued our conversation, Michael asked leading questions and as he closed with his final remarks, he definitely grasped the challenges a 3PL would face in partnering with our company. He grew to understand that this partnership would have to overcome the cultural barriers and build a trust and respect that encompassed not only the C-Suite but also the ranks below them. There had to be an open dialogue and a "give and take" attitude, as a traditional distribution model would not work with our organization. This would require extensive negotiations and the ability to pair the right team members together from both companies. After our conversation was over, Michael went to work. From the time we arrived for the initial tour of their facilities, Michael proved his words true. It was clear to me that he understood each and every point I brought up during our hour long conversation that wintery day in Springfield, MA. He so impressed me, I made the decision to pursue him and we became business partners.

From the jungles of the Amazon, where our product was sourced, and back to the urban jungle of New York City, we embarked upon a journey that led us to creating a door to door logistics solution.

Flash back to the time we had the IT specialists, engineers, B2B (business to business) managers to the DTC (direct to consumer) programmers, present in our showroom to create the platform needed to ship our product from the point of origin, to the 3PL, and finally to either the B2B or DTC end user. Having had the United Nations present, we had to learn to speak in one language (find the common denominator) and attain results in a condensed timeframe.

We created an environment whereby all parties felt the accomplishments; we shipped thousands of products via carriers such as Fed Ex and UPS and then to our business customers whether wholesale, retail, or direct to consumers. We created a solution with an approach that consisted of strategic minds, strong leadership, constant communication, mutual empathy, and respect, all leading to a collective beneficial result for both organizations.

Michael may not have had all the answers but he was clearly one of the thought leaders in their organization and continues to carry this amazing trait with him wherever he goes. After watching him work, I can tell you why everyone pays attention when Michael speaks, he knows how to reach people—the human touch—his techniques, simple as they may sound, really work.

Supply chain is about connecting one end to another. It takes an innovative approach and willingness to compromise. One must seek new ways to reach out through the supply chain process to exude the confidence that their organization can and will be the right solution for the client. Through Michael's forward thinking approach and get-it-done attitude, he was able to break what I considered to be the "Old Boy's Network" to initiate a fresh turn-key approach and solution. As I look back today, what I recognize is that whether you put Michael in an office where everyone's at war, or when management cannot get buy in from the clients, or morale and solutions are not generated on both sides, he'll figure out a way to solve the problem—fast—in a win-win way where everyone comes out ahead.

When you take a moment to read through the following pages, you will find no better guide than Michael. He is brilliant, has a fabulous sense of humor, is kind, inspiring and most of all his he is real, a real human being. His only wish is to bring success to both organizations while achieving the best results for everyone willing to be a part of the journey. So enjoy—and then use this powerful business tool as you navigate the world logically and through Logical Logistics!

**Elaine R. Sugimura**

# Introduction and Acknowledgments

As I walk through the apple orchard on a bright fall morning, I take my grandfather Joseph Stolarczyk's hand to safely cross over the rail line that guides the old Baltimore & Ohio diesel trains to Weirton Steel. I can still feel the rumble of those mile-long hopper cars laboring to carry their coal, the very lifeblood of the Ohio River valley, to fuel the heart of the mill as it methodically churns out steel to build bridges, skyscrapers, and cars for our economy. We sit down on the rocks near the river and wait for one of the barges to quietly float by, riding low in the water... we are on the West Virginia side of the river, so we get a close-up glimpse of the captain and crew of the vessel as they mull about the decks lashing cargo, and checking the draft. I return to the porch, on the side of the hill, with the alley cats in tow, to have my Grandma Mary's freshly baked bread and to share a cold glass of milk with my feline friends as the river's panorama of motion spreads out before me.

Later in the day, I'd be at the kitchen table having lunch with my other grandfather, Louiggi Sanzeri. We would share large portions of eggs, bacon, OJ, and toast before he goes in for a second shift at the mine near Wheeling. Grandma Elsie fills his thermos with coffee blacker than the rocks he pulls out of the ground on a daily basis. He tells me about the conveyors, hoppers, loaders, trams, and tugs he operates that shuttle the coal from deep underground, to the trucks, trains, and barges waiting in constant procession on the mine's perimeter. His face is always a tad bit tight when he advises how thankful he is that his day is now about moving the coal to the mills and power plants, rather than taking the lift down into the void.

I was just eight years old at the time, but I already knew that moving stuff from point A to point B would be in my blood. I loved those big trains, boats, trucks, and machines that transported all of the bulk cargo.

Now it's all about moving information, and that data is even more important than the physical product in today's supply chain. However, the tenants remain the same, get from there to here in the least amount of time, at the lowest cost possible. Not much has changed in the ultimate goal, but the delivery systems and communication, along with the tools that we use to facilitate the modern supply chain continue to evolve.

I've been very fortunate to have had a great many people in my life that have influenced and supported me, so please indulge me a bit of time and space to point out these folks in the next couple of paragraphs.

They have all helped bring me to this moment, and point in my career where I can share with you some knowledge in the sincere hope that it will make your day easier, and give you some comfort and security in knowing your supply chain and transportation world is at one with the logistics' gods.

So, here it goes:

Emily and John Blanda, the best godparents anyone could have. Thank you for always being there for me, and for giving me the support, guidance, and confidence to push beyond what many people believed to be impossible. Both of you have always been the most respected role models in my life, because of your personal beliefs and professional accomplishments.

I'd like to also mention my aunt, Josephine Stolarczyk who always saw the good in people and made me believe that you should always look for the positive in any situation. Lee, Buck, Virginia, Jim, Sophie, Bill, Darlene, Sam, Jean, Bob, Kathy, Karen, Jimmy, Billy, Jay, Rob, David, Don, Zeke, and Ritchie always made going back to New Cumberland and Wheeling, West Virginia, a wild, wonderful experience.

So many people outside of my family also provided me a secure foundation, and challenged me to think beyond just what was in front of my face. First and foremost, Florence Stock; when I was kid she would take me to building sites, and construction zones and we spent many an afternoon having lunch near Marion Power Shovel to catch a glimpse of a new drag-line or the flatcars rolling past with new machinery headed overseas. Rich and Ellen Rees, Matt Rock Sr., Nikki and Emil Rubcich, Bob Webb, Jim Spillers, Herb Samples, Michael Nicolosi, Dr. Charles Hooper, Dr. Margot Racin, Dr. Carolyn Hampson, Dr. Edwin Flowers, Esther Dyson, Ken Lyon, Michael Hassing, Elaine Sugimura, and Steve Douglas all deserve a mention and my sincere thanks.

Finally, I've got to mention all the rogues, friends, colleagues, and ronin that continue to influence my thoughts, observations, and overall snarky viewpoints of everyday life. The list is in no particular order: Doc Searls, Matt Rock Jr., Mark Rubcich, Murray Granger, Kyle Standley, Tim Smiley, Larry Sears, Jay Johnson, Kirby Wisler, Scott Tillet, Ted Simmons, Lance Smith, Darryl Winters, Harold Hightower, Lori Sayre, Todd Carter, Dave Beatty, Dan "Houseboy" Smithson, David "Ohio" Wilkins, Dennis "Gilbo" Gillan, Eric Gregory, Dr. Mike Hess, Dr. Scott "Scooter" Groseclose, Andrew "Whopper" Chatin, John "Chop" Amic, Mark "Amazing" Mazzei, Grant "Overdawg" Overbey, Wes Hines, Stu K, Josh S, Shinya

Mizamori, Dutch Dutcher, Dr. Lynda M<sup>C</sup>, Kenny Evans, Selway and the "Lightweights," Greg Gatton, L Mack, Charlie Brown, Lisa Agona, Pat Kelley, Bill Benincosa, Bob Richardson, Carter Montsinger, Champ Bradford, Kim Ferris, Eric Mo, Big Po, Russell Harvey, Herfried Leitner, Jana Polanska, Imrich Lelkes, Honza Kresl, Mr. Tvrdy, Captain Jindrich Vodicka, Katherine Reed, David Reed, Jeff Baker, Nick Plesich, Jeff Lambert, William Lobkowicz, Ernesto Hannya, Howard Lamb, Henrick Zeuthen, Michael Blach, Jason Bronscheer, Brian Harold, Gary Bull, Greg Moore, David Woodward, Matthew Kruchko, Lee Johnson, Chris Blickhan, Tina Heard, David Heard, Andreas Kemi, Muriel Günhardt, Ed Byrd, Rusty Byrd, Jason "Knighthawk" Essenberg, Jonnny "Storm" Worth, JJ Collier, Shannon Collier, and Chris Jarvis.

# Chapter 1

*My logisticians are a humorless lot...they know if my campaign fails, they are the first ones I will slay.*

**Alexander the Great**

# Locative Solutions and a Brief History of Logistics

Recently, I had the pleasure of hosting Dr. Charles Brown's Marketing Club to a collaborative session to discuss the evolution and development of logistics and transportation within the retail/wholesale global markets. This group is from West Virginia University's Business and Economics School. Since these soon-to-be executives were here to experience the real world, it got me to thinking about the history of logistics and the supply chain...damn! Am I starting to sound like an old man or what?

Logistics has always been a critical part of the four Ps in marketing: product, place, price, and promotion. (Hey, someone tell me...do they still use the four Ps? That's what I remember from my days at WVU's B&E School.) The "place" component ensures the product is at the right place at the right time in the right quantity and the right quality.

The whole premise of logistics is about "place," along with the time and money, impacted by that specific product which is moving along the supply chain continuum. Hmmm, am I starting to sound like Carl Sagan now? Don't worry, this book is all about demystifying logistics, and I can guarantee that is the last time I will use the word "continuum."

So, let's take a stroll back in time to quickly review how the logistics discipline started and how it is evolving today.

**Military Roots**
Logistics received recognition in military operations during World War II. It gained its momentum as it

contributed to the effective distribution of machinery and supplies to troops. A service delivery failure there might have meant an increase in unnecessary fatalities. Peter Drucker (a business guru in the 1960s, whose business acumen never seems to get old) identified logistics as a growing concern within business. This generated more prominence toward the practice of logistics in the late '60s.

**Deregulation**
As the economies in North America evolved in the 1970s and 1980s, transportation deregulation changed the competitive landscape of business. Carriers were free to charge their customers (shippers) a competitive rate for their shipments. Warehousing companies that typically acted as surplus inventory storage locations married up with transportation companies to offer customers full-service solution capabilities. This formed the beginning of the third-party logistics (3PL) business and paved the way for outsourcing logistical activities.

Companies were also starting to lose a ton of money sourcing domestically...hence, the boom to the economies of the BRIC markets: Brazil, Russia, India, and China.

**Globalization**
With the advent of globalization, firms began to seek ways of cutting their production costs. Thus, multinational corporations relocated their factors of production to low-wage countries to gain a competitive advantage. Increasingly, more and more countries are joining the World Trade Organization (WTO) and opening their countries to foreign capital investment. Retail giants like Wal-Mart exploit these new efficiencies and increase their imports from new emerging economies to reduce product prices in their stores. Thus, the new challenge is how to manage the product and information flows around the world. The increased pressure

on managing these operations further underscores the importance of logistics as an area for optimization.

Ha—the advent of 3PLs (organizations like Kontane Logistics) and a drive to create PO to POP (you know, Purchase Order to Point of Purchase) visibility in the supply chain.

## Information Technology
Another contributor that led to an increased presence for logistics was the explosion in information technology and use of computers throughout the 1980s and onward. The cost of computing decreased year after year and computing power rose exponentially. The use of the Internet and increased bandwidth capacity further enhanced and enabled quick connectivity and collaborative relationships that reduced inventories and created a just-in-time operating opportunity for organizations. These efficiencies reduced errors, increased fill rates, and cut overall operating costs for organizations. The '90s created the need for fast info and faster supply chains.

So, where do we go from here? Well, this is when the balance sheet shell game became popular. You know, the Dell model of production and vendor-managed inventory (VMI) that the business world embraced in the late twentieth century. The philosophy of keeping your products off the balance sheet by ensuring that they remain as "work in progress" (WiP) until the moment they are sold.

## Supply Chain Management
As the above factors fueled efficiencies, logistics gained more prominence in organizations. A natural extension was to link the logistical operations from each firm to the entire supply chain. The new paradigm became known as the "systems approach" to supply chain management and introduced the concept of trade-offs. In order to achieve least total supply chain cost, operational integration of the five

5 main areas of logistics must be simultaneously optimized: warehousing, transportation, inventory, order processing, and lot quantities. Optimizing any one of these areas individually will suboptimize the system as a whole. For example, a single warehouse in a network would achieve the lowest warehousing cost. This would create high transportation costs as suppliers ship over greater distances to ship products into the warehouse and, conversely, outbound to its market distribution area. The addition of a second warehouse in the network would reduce transportation costs more than the marginal cost of operating the second warehouse, which would reduce total supply chain costs.

Flow centers, origin management, control tower oversight, and, yes, PO to POP fiscal visibility run rampant. Who is leading the charge to create further supply evolution?

**Future Challenges**
As the business landscape constantly changes with mergers and acquisitions and as globalization grows, there are corresponding changes in the supply chain that need to continuously be optimized to ensure least total supply chain costs. Radio frequency identification (RFID) and other technologies will continue to drive down inventories as better information is made available in a timely manner. Since supply chain activities cross over all functional areas in an organization (such as marketing, finance, and human resources), new metrics must be developed to track true supply chain costs and identify the impact on new costs as corporate strategies change. Organizations that measure and benchmark these costs will have a sustainable competitive advantage going forward.

Yes, RFID, GPS, Smart Boxes, and RF/scan technologies are all evolving. Check this one idea into the back of your mind, though...they will all blend into a new science supporting *LOCATIVE logistics or solutions*. What does "locative" mean?

## Definition of "LOCATIVE"

Locative (also called the seventh case) is a case that in-dicates a location. It corresponds vaguely to the English prepositions "in," "on," "at," and "by." The locative case belongs to the general local cases, together with the lative and separative case.

Further, there is a new usage of the word in "locative media." The Wikipedia definition is: "The term 'locative media' was coined by Karlis Kalnins. Locative media is closely related to augmented reality (reality overlaid with virtual reality) and pervasive computing (computers everywhere, as in ubiquitous computing)."

The technology used in locative media projects is, for example, global positioning systems (GPS), laptop computers, smart phones/iPhones, geographic information systems (GIS), API platforms, and Google Maps. Whereas GPS allows for the accurate detection of a specific location, mobile computers allow interactive media to be linked to this place. The GIS supplies arbitrary information about the geological, strategic, or economic situation of a location. Google Maps give a visual representation of a specific place. Another important new technology that links digital data to a specific place is RFID (radio frequency identification), a successor to Barcode (like Semacode).

William Gibson used this locative media angle in his last two books, *Spook Country* and *Zero History*.

My suggestion to you, though, is this: The same basics (building blocks) of technology will not only drive the media, but also our need to know where products are in the supply chain. **Locative logistics** will be born very soon...and we will need to create "**locative solutions**/platforms" to support the client's needs.

**Definition of "LOCATIVE LOGISTICS"**
A scalable supply chain platform based on API/GIS applications, which supplies specific information about the physical presence, strategic importance, and economic impact of products or cargo in-transit. This is a situational assessment of a location, or locations in a supply chain.

Wow, even my head is hurting from this thought…any further insight would be welcome from my readers and it will be shared in future releases.

# Looking Beyond Rates: Fundamentals of Good Contract Negotiations Go Far Beyond Mere Pricing

Pure data can provide valuable insight, but it doesn't tell a complete story.

Hiding behind pure numbers will only create a one-sided, noncompetitive, zero-sum contract winner—and doom the negotiations to failure.

The recovery is here, and not a moment too soon. Shippers and carriers across all transportation modes that have struggled through the Great Recession, suffering billions of dollars in losses and setting back their business by years, are feeling better about the economy and trade environment than at any point in the past two years. Retail sales are surging, and dramatically depleted inventories are being rebuilt.

And, after a rare high-profile public eruption over winter cargo backlogs wrought by capacity constraints resulting from carriers' survivalist mentality, shippers and carriers appear to have found middle ground in attempting to re-solve their differences instead of bickering about them.

It is, indeed, a new world order—or appears to be. But the true test of how both sides react will come as shippers and carriers wrap up what could be the most important contract negotiations in years, if not more.

Will carriers be true to their word and end the slash-and-burn rate-cutting wrought by their pursuit for market share? Will shippers become true partners in a market where success and speed to market can be determined by the success of their transportation providers?

Will the empathy and collaboration that both sides have long pursued but seldom achieved finally have staying power, or will both sides retreat into their business-as-usual mentality when the inevitable recovery picks up steam?

It is this last point that should be the start of the healing process, and the starting point in the negotiation process, because in an ever-more complex supply chain, a good contract goes far beyond mere price.

Why? Because to be successful in this new economy, empathy and collaboration need to ride on the same vessel toward the mutual destination of profitability. Collaborating creates value, and executive empathy makes money!

To a certain degree, almost everything in business has become data-driven. It's common practice today that if you can't measure it, it doesn't impact the bottom line. Pure data can provide valuable insight, but it doesn't tell a complete story. The news is filled with businesses that have used numbers—real or manufactured—to justify prices and volumes that are no longer with us.

From my perspective, I've noticed some cracks in this data-driven, numbers-only foundation on which our industry used to build and expand profits. Carriers, importers, exporters, and freight intermediaries can no longer base their relationships solely on slot commitments, no-roll clauses, general rate increases, "no show fees," and local charges. Vested collaboration, empathy for both partners' profitability, and efficiency are tantamount to long-term success.

We are moving into the "conceptual age" of business, when the right price is not necessarily the lowest price. It's no longer enough to be a great numbers person. We now expect more of our leaders, and empathy and collaboration are among those qualities.

Understanding the feelings of others is good behavior, but empathy particularly pays off when organizations—that is, the executives who represent companies— understand what their customers and partners are feeling during the decision-making process.

How do empathy and collaboration impact the success of organizations during negotiations? The strongest point to be made is that both qualities involve focusing less on purely statistical internal issues, and more on a collective way to gain mutual benefit. The opposite of collaborative behavior is internally competitive, command-and-control behavior. This is a form of corporate self-absorption that remains from the Enron days of blind selfishness.

It is easy to hide behind pure numbers and cold, hard metrics, but hiding now will only create a one-sided, non-competitive, zero-sum contract winner—and doom the negotiations to failure.

Too often, business leaders focus their attention on rate structures during carrier-contract negotiations while ignoring other important facets of a business relationship. Failure to address the entire scope of the relationship can cause a business to fall short when trying to meet certain goals. Empathy and collaboration will bring to light these more subtle issues that should be addressed to create mutual profits. The following are numerous strategies your business should employ to achieve success in contract negotiations for this year and beyond.

## 1. Pickup Performance

How can your delivery be on time if your pickup isn't? Late pickups cost you more money, sometimes at overtime rates. Before agreeing to a contract, you should know your partner's on-time pickup percentage and how the carrier calculates that measurement on a customer-specific basis. On-time delivery statistics are calculated in a similar way and should be readily available on customer reports—by customer and/or terminal.

## 2. Invoicing Accuracy

This important metric is often overlooked but can be the key to saving a company time and money. Companies that invest in an imaging system allowing them to use information directly from a customer's bill of lading can ensure accuracy while improving invoicing efficiency. If this isn't one of the measurements you expect to receive from your carrier, it should be.

## 3. Claims Structure and Response Time

Getting a shipment to its destination on time doesn't matter much if it doesn't get there in one piece. How quickly are claims settled? What is the percentage of claims-free service? What is the claims ratio of the terminal that will serve your customers? Partners should make these performance statistics available for individual customers and terminals.

## 4. Interactive Web Presence

Examining your partner's Web site can help you determine the availability of customer service when you need it. Is the Web site interactive in a number of ways to provide the information you need? The site should allow you to enter pickup requests and download imaged documents and cus-tomized reports. It should also offer a variety of track-and-trace capabilities, rate quotes, transit times, and terminal information.

## 5. Solid Communication and Open Dialogue

Determining how much customers are involved in their part-ner's decision-making process indicates the level of interest a company has in delivering quality service. Initiating a good communications program and creating collaboration with customers is essential. The open dialogue will reveal posi-tive and negative qualities of each organization.

## 6. Responsiveness

You should be able to talk with experts in each of your partner's departments when you need them. Is the line of communication open and results-oriented? Maintaining a strong communication link goes hand in hand with develop-ing a strong, effective partnership.

## 7. Customer Service

A quick and readily available information resource is invalu-able to you and your customers. This resource should provide an answer to any question you or your customers might have about transporting or tracing your shipments. The debate can rage about whether the customer service presence should be "in the market" and the costs associ-ated with same, or if a centralized approach is more con-sistent and less costly. The mutual goal, however, must be that the core of a long-term, mutually beneficial partnership is excellent customer service.

## 8. Empathy and Proactive Account Management

A partner should know when and why a service failure occurred. If it delivers its shipments on time 98 percent of the time, your partner should be able to elaborate and explain what went wrong with the other 2 percent.

Organizations should follow up on every service failure, not only to find out what went wrong, but also to initiate corrective action plans to ensure the problem does not happen again. Taking this stance will make the company a better partner, and, in turn, provide you with better performance. Ask your supply chain organizations how they analyze service defects.

## 9. Continuous Improvement Mentality and Training

The kind of training available to your partner's employees, how often they are trained, and the degree to which they are trained should be part of any organization's strategy in providing superior service to its customers. Asking questions about the training process will give you an indication of the company's emphasis on quality performance. Does the carrier have an operations training program in place that emphasizes freight handling? Are its drivers trained? Does the carrier offer hazardous materials training to its employees? What about general safety training measures? In addition to these training processes, an organization should have accountability procedures in place at each facility to help reduce costs and waste.

## 10. Multiyear Contracts

More industries are moving toward multiyear contracts, just as the major third-party logistics providers have over the years via "open book" forecasting, budgeting, and costing. A multiyear deal will create an even playing field for each organization to drive out costs (through continuous improvement plans), and increase mutual, long-term profitability. Week-to-week capacity, no rolling, peak-season surcharges, local charges, no-show or dead freight charges become archaic terms of the past, and these tired phrases will become nonissues when looking at the long-term picture of growth, efficiency, and profitability.

## 11. Vested Collaboration

Does your partner organization promote an open, sharing environment or is it merely a transactional workplace? How much does it share with customers via popular social networks such as Twitter and Facebook, or through business-focused networks such as LinkedIn? Creating an atmosphere that has an "open-source" mentality will allow for new ideas to be shared freely and will present an attractive corporate culture to experience. Vested collaboration creates empathy, empathy ensures mutual understanding, and mutual understanding will generate a collective beneficial result.

If you take the time to think critically about these often-ignored aspects of the collaboration process, your company will be equipped with the knowledge and trust it needs to achieve the best possible results far into the future. Consistency, preparation, collaboration, and common sense should be your guiding principles when negotiating with your partners.

Successful partner organizations that build mutual empathy and vested collaboration need to establish a committed leadership structure—creating insight, foresight, and trust, not just oversight of the annual negotiations. By consistently collaborating on budgets, forecasts, and modeling scenarios, with all of the above points taken into consideration, your organization will enjoy long-term fiscal success by being prepared for the best of situations, and being able to forestall the worst. Empathy will create a collaborative atmosphere during the negotiation phase and will chart a course for a lasting, mutually beneficial business platform.

# The IT Factor

The globalization of commerce has made sophisticated logistics technology a necessity for companies large and small.

An apparel company, for example, might source fabric from China, manufacture garments in Vietnam, send them to Italy for customer design work, and then ship the final product to a 3PL warehouse in the USA for delivery to retail stores.

This must be done in time to get a hot fashion item on stores' shelves before "fashionistas" move on to the next trend. It is a huge challenge coordinating this multiparty process via phone, fax, e-mail, and spreadsheets.

The need for advanced solutions may seem obvious, but a surprising number of companies still have a long way to go when it comes to global supply chain technology sophistication.

Many Fortune 500 companies report their global supply chain technology is inadequate to provide timely information required for budget and cash flow planning.

Companies claim that they want supply chain visibility, but what they really need is **fiscal visibility within their supply chains!**

How did companies fall so behind? Who fell asleep at the wheel? Supply chain managers? IT directors? YES and YES...even worse, their CEOs and CFOs are slumbering.

The global supply chain has been relatively ignored because it was traditionally a small part of a company's business mind-set. The world has changed, globalized, and companies now realize their IT systems are not set up to support this...nor are their fiscal models.

With international sourcing growing at a rapid clip, companies have been caught off guard, and are now scrambling to close the technology gap. Without fiscal models to account for costs throughout these systems, and, in most cases, without additional staff, global supply chain managers face a daunting task.

Global supply chains are complex and have many parties involved—contract manufacturers, 3PLs, company-owned factories, custom agencies, brokers, and multiple carriers—plus the sheer distance.

The global supply chain technology void affects logistics managers' ability to deliver crucial financial data. Some CEOs/CFOs have noticed and are now joining the technology crusade. Tying technology investments to a business case outside the supply chain often helps logisticians get the funding for global commerce tools they need.

Once the C-level realizes that a problem impacts financial performance and risk levels, it's easier to push technology requests through the system.

After a company decides to invest in technology, the next question is whether to develop solutions in-house or partner with a technology provider or 3PL. Increasingly, organizations choose to forgo proprietary solutions and seek outside help.

Many companies currently use in-house applications to manage their global supply chains, but those seeking to implement new technology say they favor collaboration with 3PLs. Most supply chain departments don't have budgets to buy external technology, and multiparty, collaborative practices are not a core competency for their internal organizations. They must look outside.

Before 3PL outsourcing, the choice was between building an internal solution or taking eighteen months to implement an enterprise system. Companies that continue using in-house technology solutions face the challenge of keeping up with the speed of developments in both supply chain technology and global business practices. Keeping data (from an increasing roster of partners) connected and synchronized is a labor- intensive challenge and, sometimes, a guessing game.

We are essentially in the early days of reinventing our business processes for globalization. Many companies can't build a technology solution today and be confident it will support their needs five years from now...the landscape is too riddled with uncertainty and risk.

### What can companies do to combat supply chain inefficiencies?

Pinpointing the area of their global supply chain that can benefit the most from a quick technology upgrade is a good place to start. My suggestion is to fiscally account for the total supply chain collectively, not just international inbound or domestic distribution separately...**from purchase order to point of purchase (PO to POP)!**

It is unrealistic to try to solve every problem at once. For most organizations, advanced supply chain visibility, from the fiscal perspective, should be the imminent requirement.

It is an oversimplification to say technology is the magic fix for global logistics problems. **Technology for technology's**

**sake is nothing; it has to have the people and process behind it!**

Imagine that your company created a global *fiscal* visibility tool and, in turn, this platform was able to quicken cycle times and reduce inventory investment. Your CFO is happy with the progress, and he is knocking on your door, asking, "What's next?"

Fiscal visibility, from PO to POP, is the essence of supply chain efficiency. Create it, initiate it, and reap the benefits in the process.

# Logistics 101—RFI/RFP Gets You ROI

So, you didn't get what you wanted when you hired the last third-party logistics firm...hey, don't automatically blame the 3PL. It may be a matter of mixed signals, miscommunication, or lack of a collaborative atmosphere. The key to a successful relationship starts with a clear RFP and excellent communications between your company and the 3PL. Here are ten tips to help you get exactly what you need from your 3PL relationship.

**Send an RFI (request for information) before an RFP (request for proposal).** The RFI will help you collect better data, define your true needs, and involve your 3PL candidates in developing a solution. It can also help you create a "short list" of providers who you think should receive your RFP.

**Be open and honest about issues that could affect your logistics operation.** When creating your RFP and discussing your company with potential providers, include issues that don't necessarily make you look good or that are proprietary. You want, and need, honest assessments.

**Be specific.** Give 3PL providers detailed information about what you want them to accomplish and be extremely careful about making sure the providers fully understand those expectations. Don't just tell them you want next-day delivery; tell them you want delivery by 10:00 a.m. If you want them to bring fulfillment costs down, give them a percentage. The 3PL then has a specific goal to meet.

**Empower your 3PL personnel through training and sharing.** Train your 3PL employees as if they were your own, or have them trained as your own! Have personnel at your provider's fulfillment center attend your proprietary quality training course. Give them extra systems training when you upgrade. Invite key members of the 3PL's account team to the same conferences or training events your own management attends.

**Treat the 3PL as a partner, not just a supplier.** Be realistic about what you expect them to accomplish. Encourage them to be change agents instead of just order-takers, even if it means taking some calculated risks.

**Don't rush responses to the RFP.** Allow four weeks, at least, for a regional warehouse RFP, and six to eight weeks for a national or international RFP. Rushing this process doesn't give the provider time to run multiple iterations and evaluate which solutions will work best for you. Rush the process, and you will get a quick answer...not thorough analysis.

**Ask the 3PL for solutions in your RFP, leaving room for creativity.** Too many companies jump to a rigid solution model instead of putting their requirements and challenges in the RFP and asking the third party for the logistics solution. Experienced 3PLs can add valuable consulting strengths, creativity, and innovations to the equation. Don't miss out on a solution that might be more appropriate than the one you originally had in mind.

**Be diligent about the process you use to collect data from internal locations or departments when putting together your RFP.** Be conscientious about filtering and evaluating the results you receive to avoid a vague or inaccurate RFP that may lead the potential 3PL down the wrong path. A litmus test to determine if your company has made its requests clear is to compare pricing responses. If there is a wide spread, something probably got lost in the translation. Using the RFI as a gauge is also a good idea.

**Take advantage of standard channels to maintain constant communication with your 3PL.** Use e-mail, meetings, and phone calls to accomplish this. Hook providers up to your intranet and Web site; invite them to internal meetings. In this day and age, maybe break out the WebEx platform, or create a logistics-focused "wiki." There are plenty of collaborative platforms out there today...

**Fix the problem instead of looking for a new partner.** If your 3PL provider has been a good performer and has added value to your brand and it happens to stumble, help them fix the problem. Second chances bring out the best in a good logistics provider and that, in turn, will bring out the best in your logistics operations.

If you think you know it all, and are only going to outsource because you have to, think twice about doing it. The last thing a good collaboration needs is a know-it-all. That goes for the 3PL too...sometimes their reps have to be the smartest people in the room. If you get the feeling this is the case, then move on to the next 3PL.

Communication, collaboration, honesty, managed expectations, and realistic goals are essential to make this outsourcing challenge a success. **Go for it!**

# 3PL 101—Outsourcing Strategy

When deployed intelligently, an outsourcing strategy can add strategic advantage to your organization. Whether the value lies in asset efficiency, cost containment, speed to market, customer service, marketing strength, or technological advantage, many 3PL customers can show measurable improvement in one or more of these areas.

Customers dissatisfied with a 3PL, on the other hand, often cite unrealized service-level and technological commitments, cost-reduction goals, nonaligned culture understanding, and lack of strategic improvements as the primary reasons for their discontent.

Typically, outsourcers perceive these failures as a result of a flawed partner selection process. More often, however, these relationships fail because of bad implementation plans and project management (scope creep).

## Start Up Right—Use Common Sense During Implementation

The start-up phase is tantamount to success and how a 3PL relationship will evolve down the road. Yes, the 3PL's implementation team is generally responsible for the start-up execution. However, the customer plays an absolutely critical role in the partnership's initial success.

The customer's first responsibility is to commit to the relationship. A 3PL alliance is intended to last. It is a collaboration of strengths that benefit each partner, and, as in any successful relationship, trust is a fundamental element. During the initiation phase, the customer must show trust by committing to full disclosure of all requested information, and modifying objectives, timelines, and cost expectations as necessary.

For its part, the 3PL should assign a dedicated project manager, with implementation management experience, to coordinate tasks and work with the customer's project manager. If the 3PL does not appoint a dedicated person to handle these initiatives, the customer should ask for one.

The customer must also communicate the role of the 3PL and the objectives of the outsourcing decision. The most diligent 3PL implementation team calls on every department, including sales, accounting, IT, human resources, manufacturing, and purchasing, to gather detailed functional requirements. These internal resources must be available and prepared to offer information in order for the implementation to remain on schedule. The customer's staff should similarly be matched with their functional counterparts at the 3PL and required to share openly.

### Measure, Measure, and Measure Again
One of the most critical tasks during the start-up phase is developing performance measurements and reporting methods. The customer must take the initiative to design measurements that support the company's business goals for the outsourcing strategy. Basic areas to measure include:

- **Service and Activity Costs**
- **Cost Reductions**
- **Customer Satisfaction**
- **Handling and Routing**
- **On-time Delivery**
- **Systems Performance**
- **Productivity Levels per Activity**
- **Staffing Levels (FTE versus Part-time)**
- **Timelines (from Concept to Reality)**

Depending on which functions of the supply chain are out-sourced, companies should decide to tie 3PL performance to many of these strategic business measurements.

In fairness to the partnership, the customer should fully consider input from the 3PL on realistic targets, penalties, and incentives. These targets and metrics should be specific and clear to both sides so there are no gray areas during performance evaluations. Both sides must allow for appropriate flow of information in order to measure performance.

## Conference Room Pilots/Dry Runs/Testing/More Measuring

Before the implementation can be fully operational, the customer must engage in conference-room pilots. These sessions are critical to preparing the customer to understand how its partner will handle orders. The customer should bring representatives from all functions so they can learn how the partnership will impact their respective departments. To make the conference-room pilot most effective, outsourcers should prepare scenarios that are anomalous to everyday business, and challenge the 3PL to illustrate how they will manage these exceptions and create trust!

Outsourcing offers companies great advantages in business effectiveness, but it is difficult and sometimes impossible to recover from a sporadic or an ill-conceived implementation plan. The greatest degree of success will be gleaned if the customer is genuinely active in the implementation plan, trusting of its partner's needs, and aggressive in designing measurements and questioning the readiness of the program before going live.

So, the "school" year is almost over...3PL 101 will conclude next week and I will try to roll out some provocative thoughts to take you into the "real world." So, are you gonna outsource or what?

# Back to Basics—3PL Defined

Organizations want to develop products for global markets. At the same time, they need to source material globally to be competitive. One of today's trends to solve this problem is outsourcing logistics or using third-party logistics (3PL) to manage complex distribution requirements.

Organizations have developed strategic alliances with 3PL companies all over the world to manage their logistics operations network. These alliances are also known as supply chain partnerships or contract logistics (that is Kontane's preferred category).

## Levels of Outsourcing
- **Transactional:** Based on transactions, with no long-term contracts and no bonding between the 3PL and the outsourcing company. Carrier-affiliated organizations are common in this sector.
- **Tactical:** Outsourcing on a long-term basis with negotiated contacts and integrated IT systems to facilitate free information flow and create supply chain visibility (the goal should be fiscal visibility within the supply chain).
- **Strategic:** Based on long-term relationships with successful outcomes, 3PL companies become partners in supply chain management and establish transactional transparency in all facets of the international supply chain.

## Why Choose to Partner with a 3PL?
- **Save Time**: Outsourcing the logistics function can free up resources to focus on core competencies.

- **Because Someone Else Can Do It Better:** Even if you have resources available, another organization within the supply chain may be able to do it better because of its relative position in the supply chain, or they have a certain supply chain expertise, and the 3PL may have economies of scale.
- **Share Responsibility and Risk:** 3PLs can share responsibility (and risk) for managing global supply chains, keeping customers and stores properly stocked, and delivering the perfect order every time.
- **Reconfigure Your Distribution Network:** 3PL outsourcing can be a quick way to reconfigure distribution networks to meet global market demands and gain a competitive edge.

## 3PL Roles in Logistics Success

According to a 2009 Cap Gemini study, apart from a one-point rise in Europe (88 percent), the percentage of organizations reporting that logistics represents a strategic, competitive advantage for companies is compelling leading up to the new decade. The current average for North America is 84 percent, Asia Pacific is 88 percent, and Latin America is 90 percent! What is even more interesting, 94 percent of the 3PLs polled believe that logistics represents a strategic, competitive advantage for their customers (no surprise there)!

These organizations are outsourcing logistics activities and upgrading relationships with 3PL companies from transactional to tactical and strategic relationships.

The report also reveals that respondents devote an average of 47 percent (in North America) up to 66 percent (in Europe) of their total logistics expenditures to outsourcing. This continues a steady positive trend. The percentages differ among the major business centers studied, but all of them expect increases in these percentages in the next five years.

Historically, CEOs of 3PL companies operating in Asia-Pacific expected 15 percent average business growth over the upcoming three years, which is higher than other regions. This figure has tended to be in the high 8 percent or 9 percent range for other markets like Europe and North America.

## Achieving Strategic Outsourcing

Unfortunately, only a few 3PL companies achieve strategic status with their customers. Kontane Logistics is one of them. It is done by constantly innovating and maintaining operational integrity. Some use an open-book costing method to demonstrate their system's transparency, which is being embraced by many Fortune 500 companies.

If you are planning on implementing a 3PL partnership, read my tips about how to successfully implement a 3PL game plan. The tips appear later in the book and are all about collaboration and sharing.

# Chapter 2

*The line between disorder and order lies in logistics...*

**Sun Tzu**

# How Many PLs Does It Take to Get That Abercrombie & Fitch T-Shirt from Fuzhou to Paducah?

What the heck is the difference between a 3PL and a 4PL organization? Their service offerings? Asset ownership versus non-asset ownership? Or is there *really* a difference?

## 3PL

It is normally recognized that any firm that specializes in providing logistics service and is independent from any manufacturer's logistics division can be called a third-party logistics provider (3PL).

## 4PL

The term "4PL" was actually coined by the consulting group Accenture. In fact, they also hold the trademark to the name "4PL." Accenture defines a 4PL in the following manner: "A 4PL is an integrator that assembles the resources, capabilities, and technology of its own organization and other organizations to design, build, and run comprehensive supply chain solutions."

The biggest difference (at least from my perspective) between 3PL and 4PL is the management (ownership) of assets. The 3PL organization has a core offering of one or more of the following services: warehousing, common carrier options (truckload, LTL, Parcel, Ocean, Air, NVO, etc.), forwarding, truck leasing, etc. Most logistics providers originally got into other areas to increase utilization of core products (trucks, warehouses, etc.). A pure 4PL play is mainly technology and integration. They become the knowledge (intelligence) hub that ties together services to meet a client's requirement. This allows the 4PL to, in theory and according to their claims, initiate the best services on behalf of their client base.

It should be noted that the major players in 3PL, like Exel, TNT, DHL, etc., have a much more robust brand acknowledgment than the pure 4PL companies. My company, Kontane Logistics, floats between both of these monikers, successfully, I may add.

Is it this simple? Nah...ask ten people the above question, and you will get ten different answers. The above is my humble opinion...what is your definition?

# To 3PL or Not to 3PL?

Businesses need many qualities to succeed in today's global market, but agility, consistency, and flexibility are the most critical. Strong organizations leverage these qualities to capitalize on the economic benefits of worldwide sourcing and distribution, while satisfying their customers' needs—whether the customer is around the corner or across the sea.

Top-notch 3PLs share the same traits. They have a global footprint, with one-stop solutions that touch every component of the supply chain. They focus on reliable service execution, mindful that today's lean manufacturing processes rely on consistently meeting shippers' time-definite demands.

They are agile, using insight and foresight within an origin market to make proactive, positive decisions on behalf of their clients.

And they are flexible, recognizing the dynamic and global nature of their customers' supply and distribution networks.

## Offshoring Impact

The value of 3PLs has intensified recently because of the increase in offshoring. This creates robust sources of supply and opens up new avenues of distribution as emerging markets gain wealth and buying power.

For now, offshoring's impact is specifically felt on inbound trade to the United States; by some estimates, US import volumes seem to trend at about 5 percent to 8 percent or greater each year. These are robust levels, with no end in sight.

But offshoring is not without risk to the supply chain. As the chain stretches further and further from production source to market consumption, meeting or exceeding a customer's expectations (reliably and cost-effectively) becomes a huge challenge.

Without a well-conceived plan, organizations with offshoring production to far-off locales may discover that the cost of shipping, customs clearance, inventory financing, security, and warehousing—not to mention ill will from customers if delivery performance suffers—erases the savings that drove them to offshore.

Recognizing these hazards, savvy manufacturers have diversified their supply networks and developed multiple production and distribution points to serve their end markets.

Companies manufacturing US-bound products, with variable demand and relatively moderate value, for example, can source in North America or Latin America, position products in domestic distribution centers, and deliver them on demand via low-cost surface transport.

This strategy helps companies avoid the expenses, service disruptions, and delivery delays that can occur when goods move halfway across the globe and through congested US ports. It also allows companies to react quickly to changes in demand in the US market.

The appeal of producing in China or India, therefore, must be balanced against the time and complexity required to deliver finished goods across thousands of miles.

## Global Challenges

As today's businesses expand their global supply and distribution channels, the scope and ability of a logistics provider's infrastructure takes on paramount importance. Helping shippers optimize inventory value by accelerating distribution accuracy and velocity, while also consistently meeting the customer's ultimate delivery demands, are the dual objectives of global 3PLs.

So, say that the twenty-first-century company has become enormously productive and efficient, as the secular decline in inventory-to-sales ratio shows. Yet the absolute dollar value of inventory continues to climb as a result of the escalating value of goods.

Thirty years ago, for example, the typewriter and telex were the office machines of choice. Today, it is the laptop computer, which retails for three to five times their cost. This translates into rising inventory carrying costs, which can be exacerbated by elongated supply chains that can accelerate product obsolescence and erode value.

Unless the trend is reversed, the cost to carry and warehouse inventory will consume over 70 percent of total logistics expenses by the end of the next decade, according to some estimates. To overcome this challenge, 3PLs' physical and IT networks must be more than mere transport facilitators. In fact, the mode and cost of transport is often irrelevant.

Ensuring satisfaction for shippers and their customers through rising service expectations is central to the 3PL value proposition. Delivering this satisfaction means offering near-perfect fulfillment rates and precisely timed deliveries supported by full pipeline visibility—while also minimizing inventory glut and bloat.

The 3PL infrastructures must be aligned to move in concert with the shipper's needs. Not every product will have "made in China" stamped on it; businesses will produce and distribute to, from, and on every continent in the future (and, for the most part, in the here and now).

Ultimately, consignee demands, product value, shifting tariff structures, and logistics partners' ability to reliably hit time-definite delivery benchmarks regardless of distance will dictate supply chain strategy and execution. Logistics providers' networks must reflect those realities.

## To 3PL or Not to 3PL

As commerce extends in reach and complexity, businesses will look for partners that can deliver flexibility as well as goods. Asset-neutral providers, with a wide array of transport services at their disposal, possess powerful competitive tools. They can often strike the optimum balance between price, transit time, and capacity.

And they have the capabilities to expertly manage product and information flow from purchase order to point-of-purchase (yes, my acronym—PO to POP—once again), all through a single point of contact. Asset-based providers' "closed-loop" infrastructures, while formidable in many respects, may not be suitable for all transactions because the flow of goods must fit within their predetermined schedules.

Logistics companies come in all shapes and sizes. The best ones, however, share the common strengths of agility, consistency, and flexibility. Providing proper supply chain management requires meeting delivery targets and reducing costs. A 3PL must strive to align itself with their client, and their client's market(s) of choice.

But only when 3PLs fully understand their customers' business models can they provide and execute the best possible solutions. This must be done by actively listening, sensing, and responding to the origin and destination markets' needs, and ultimately creating a process to meet the customer's challenge.

# Marketing Efforts and Positioning of 3PLs

Growth in the 3PL industry continues to outpace the general economy...and it has become a fragmented industry with many players chasing the same customers. The situation calls for smart, strategic marketing that helps your company break through the clutter and create awareness that leads to more opportunities and more sales.

Here are five common mistakes 3PLs make in their marketing efforts. Avoid these and you'll be a step ahead.

## 1. Marketing from the inside out

The first place many 3PLs look when crafting marketing messages is the mirror. But what they see often reflects most of their competitors as well. For buyers of 3PL services, too much of the same information is confusing. If everyone says "we're quality-focused, we're easy to work with, we can provide visibility to your inventory, etc.," how does the prospect know who to buy from? She doesn't and, for want of helpful information, the message is ignored and some portion of the marketing budget is wasted. The antidote: Get inside the mirror. Look at the buying choice from your prospect's point of view. Is it easy for your best prospects to recognize what sets your company apart?

The process of differentiating your service in the mind of the prospect is called positioning. Create a positioning statement that starts, "We want to be perceived as..." This statement is your marketing destination—the perception your communications are designed to create. If you're thinking from the outside in, the positioning statement will be simple, believable, differentiating, and relevant to the challenges of your best prospects. Before communicating, think about the position you want to occupy in your prospect's mind and be disciplined about reinforcing this perception in all your communications.

**2. Over-investing in sales at the expense of marketing**
Whenever we purchase something, whether a car, a candy bar, or logistics services, we go through the same cycle of buying: **awareness, acceptance, preference, choice.**

While the cycle can be long or short, the buyer does not get to **choice** before going through the other stages. The sales function—characterized by one-on-one interactions—is best designed to create **preference** and **choice** for your service. The marketing function, which uses the Web, media relations, advertising, and other means to communicate to a large target group, is the most efficient way to create **awareness, acceptance,** and broad understanding of your brand's value, and to generate a good percentage of the leads that your sales professionals pursue. The job of the sales department, a time-consuming and challenging one in the 3PL arena, should be to create **preference** and **choice** among the companies most likely to purchase your services. The 3PLs that underinvest in marketing force their salespeople to carry the weight of the entire buying cycle and create a far less-efficient business development process.

**3. Selling as the primary means to drive inquiries**
Most 3PL "lead generation" efforts consist of targeting groups of prospects (via mail, e-mail, or phone) with sales-oriented messages, hoping that their timing is right and that one or more of the recipients will have an immediate need. But hope is not a strategy and such efforts rarely yield a solid ROI. Therefore, 3PLs should place more marketing

focus on creating reasons for the prospect to contact them. Case in point: Since 1990, Gross & Associates, consultants in material handling logistics, has published its "Rules of Thumb" for estimating capital equipment costs associated with alternative layouts, operating systems, and equipment applications. Each year the firm receives about 2,500 requests for this handy reference guide from the very people with whom it wants to build a relationship. With the prospect names and contact information in hand, the firm can continue to cultivate these relationships so that Gross is on the top of their mind when the prospect is ready to buy.

Think about what you are an expert at, then stop selling to cold prospects and start educating. By providing helpful, substantive information, you will draw more people to your message, position your organization as an expert, and generate more leads than typical hard-sell marketing messages.

## 4. Underestimating the power of the Web

While logistics service providers still rely heavily on referrals for new business, buyers of logistics services increasingly look to the Web for guidance. According to WordTracker. com, which tracks keyword searches on the Internet, 205 searches are conducted daily on the term "warehousing" and about 576 on the term "logistics." Add in additional searches on variations of these terms (e.g., value-added warehousing) and other logistics and supply chain-related phrases, and there are thousands and thousands of daily searches relevant to warehousing and logistics. Your prospects are on the Internet looking for help.

The question is, will they find your company during their search? Online marketing includes search engine optimization or SEO (the science of getting your Web site to rank high on search engine queries for specific keyword phrases), as well as keyword purchases, link building, advertising, and other tactics to bolster your online visibility. It has become a complex discipline requiring specialized expertise. Most 3PLs lack the internal know-how to do this well and should seek outside help to assure they are leveraging this critical part of the marketing mix.

## 5. Delegating marketing responsibility

As the 3PL industry has become more competitive, there is a greater need to identify new markets, differentiate the company, and tell its story in a compelling way. But attracting people with the marketing skills to do these things well has not been a 3PL recruiting priority. In fact, the marketing function often is delegated to a manager in another discipline as an add-on responsibility. This may be the only option in a lean organization, and it can work. But don't assume this manager can quickly develop the requisite skills needed to execute programs well. Provide the budgetary support to allow this person to hire communication specialists or source needed talent on the outside.

As a 3PL executive, marketing deserves your attention. Great service at an acceptable price is now table stakes and therefore difficult to leverage as a source of competitive advantage. You'll need smart marketing to help understand the market, identify profitable niches, and create awareness and understanding of your company's unique value among those most likely to purchase your services. But, hey, it is no problem if you keep on doing it the same old way...all the better for Kontane Logistics, DHL, etc.

# To Outsource or Not to Outsource...That Is the Question!

In warehousing and transportation operations, anyone can buy trucks, rent a warehouse, fill it with racking, forklifts, and even the latest logistics systems...and still end up with a dysfunctional and failed operation.

How can your organization dodge this classic ending to a very old story? Here are a few suggestions:

**Foresight:** Taking into account all available knowledge and data, develop a vision and understanding of the task or operation to be planned. Then stick to the vision and communicate it in a collaborative manner throughout the organization.

**Qualify:** Gather all available data to define requirements. They may include volumes, dimensions, weights, item counts, and other related details. Adding up these factors leads to a cost/result, both quantitative and qualitative. Don't get caught up in the current flurry of metrics, measurements, etc...just keep it simple. This will help the communication and buy-in of the vision.

**Planning:** The keystone of successful logistics and supply chain operation planning is based on a close approximation of the end requirement and ensures an optimal cost/result. For example, warehouse space and trucking requirements are directly proportional to the types/volumes of product, required storage/handling, and processing (cross-dock, storage/picking, and so on). Again, common sense and logic will prevail, as they should.

**Change Management:** Changes affect the cost/result. If a warehouse is leased to support a flow-through/cross-dock operation and all products suddenly require storage, a larger warehouse is needed, impacting staffing, materials handling equipment (MHE), fixtures, systems, and supplies. Hence, create an atmosphere of collaboration and embrace the chaos.

**Free Agents:** Most companies don't understand the costs and relationships of all factors relating to outsourcing. However, they can define their needs to an expert, stick with the plan, and create profitability. Careful selection is important, based on previous personal experience or positive recommendations and references from other trusted sources. So, logistics professionals need not understand all the details involved in executing supply chain operations to be successful. Using solid, experienced third-party firms to execute a logistics operation based on a well-defined and accurate requirement is crucial.

Use common sense, let logic be your guiding light, and use an open, honest platform of communication to create a collaborative success!

# Where Do You Want to Outsource?

I recently participated on a few panels at the eyefortransport 3PL Summit in Atlanta that were focused on the inbound supply chain from China. In addition, the GIL's Maritime Supply Chain Council, of which I am a member, is working on a white paper about PO to POP visibility (purchase order to point of purchase, for your review). During the conference, numerous times, the statement was made that retailers should not put all of their eggs in one basket when it comes to sourcing in China. They need to mitigate their risk over a few countries...maybe even "outsource" in the USA. My statement was about the great state of West "by God" Virginia...

The audience did not want to hear negative, derogatory, or dismissive talk about the booming China economy. The listeners were the supply chain counterparts of religious evangelists; nothing could counter their almost mystical faith in the Chinese economy's limitless power and growth.

Certainly, there is much to admire about China. Within a few generations, it has transformed itself from a primarily rural nation into an economic colossus—a feat unparalleled in modern times. Warning signs, however, point to an economy that is turning from white-hot to red-hot to red.

**The Warning Signs**
The signs are plain to see, if people look at reality instead of fantasy. A few facts point to a potential slowdown in the Chinese economy:

Foreign investment in China during the first half of 2010 is level with the previous year. This is the first period without growth in capital investment in almost a decade.

Exports, key to the Chinese economy, have slowed. Today, you can place an airfreight shipment on the next flight out of any airport in China, including Hong Kong. One year ago, cargo shipments were backlogged for days and even weeks—embargoed cargo sat on tarmacs at Hong Kong and Chinese mainland airports waiting to be loaded onto already-full aircraft.

China's domestic economy has cooled. Car sales, particularly luxury models, have collapsed. Consumer electronics purchases for homes and businesses have also dropped appreciably.

Housing prices—always a sensitive barometer of economic health, or lack thereof—have declined with very soft prices. The United States is not the only nation facing a housing crash...it is simply the *reality of realty* in this day and age.

In addition to an economy that is inevitably slowing, China has an overlooked Achilles heel. Its weak spot? China relies almost totally on goods produced to others' specifications. It does almost no product manufacturing, shipping, or marketing for its own products.

As *The Wall Street Journal* recently commented, "The toughest challenge for China is how to transition from low-cost, often no-name manufacturers to respected global brands."

China's contrast with Japan in this area is striking. After World War II, "Japan, Inc.," the informal name given to the partnership between Japan's government and private industry, was determined to produce quality goods. The shoddy merchandise that was the hallmark of Japanese manufacturing in the 1920s and 1930s was erased; they have largely succeeded.

Toyota makes great cars, and has surpassed General Motors and VW as the largest automaker in the world. Apple and Sony sell the best laptops of any manufacturer. Canon produces the best photocopiers. Bridgestone tires are market leaders.

## China's Fate

By contrast, it's hard to name one indigenous, homegrown Chinese product. Instead, Chinese factories seem content to churn out lingerie for Victoria's Secret, computers for Hewlett-Packard, toys for Mattel, and thousands of other products for end users in the United States and Europe.

Making unsuccessful bids for international oil companies hardly solves China's utter lack of brand identification in the West.

China is not immune to the "maquiladora syndrome." Maquiladora plants sprung up about thirty years ago along the US-Mexico border to produce a wide range of low-cost components and finished products for the American market. For a number of years, these factories flourished, with laborers often working twenty-four-hour shifts.

Then came the great sucking sound from China. US manufacturers, always looking out for new, cheap production sources, moved en masse to China. Today, many of the maquiladora plants are closed; some 75,000 Mexican workers living in border cities either lost their jobs or are working part-time shifts. How many have crossed the border to find work in the US? Many of the communities are ghost towns now.

Will China suffer a similar fate? Not completely, because China's industry is far more diverse than in Mexico's and other parts of Asia, where outsourcing is under siege from low-cost competitors (BRIC based vendors).

During the next few years, however, companies will likely start to disengage from production and distribution facilities in China. US transportation companies rushing into China for the first time to create trucking networks or establish large sorting facilities, for example, have missed the boat.

## What Next?
Who will take the production reins from China? I'm betting on the Eastern European nations formerly under Communist rule. The Czech Republic, Slovakia, Hungary, Poland, and now even the Ukraine, Belarus, Croatia, and the "-stans" are poised for their run!

These nations have embraced capitalism and are now hungry for work. They have skilled, experienced, yet low-cost labor forces; offer substantial tax abatements to train workers; and provide other inducements for US and Western European companies to establish production and distribution facilities in the region.

And the similar cultural, political, and historic heritage shared by these nations and the West is an intangible, yet equally important, advantage.

To keep up with the constantly evolving global market, businesses must remove the blinders that have them focused exclusively on China and open their eyes to the other five billion people on our planet.

So, as I said...get ready, West Virginia, Ohio, Kentucky, etc...what goes around, comes around!

# Why Not Outsource in West Virginia?

**US Importers Could Curtail Overseas Outsourcing**

US companies need to think carefully about outsourcing to Asia because the complexity of international trade and extended supply chains means that saving money by outsourcing production to countries with low-cost labor is not guaranteed, logistics experts agree.

Now higher fuel prices and transportation rates, as well as concerns that a terrorist incident or natural disaster can disrupt the continuity of far-flung business operations, may begin to tilt the equation in favor of production in Central America, Mexico, or even the United States itself. Why not outsource in West Virginia? Why not outsource in Ohio and create some jobs and stability in your supply chain that way?

Retailers could look at switching to domestic or regional suppliers, especially when it comes to finding reliable sources for their own brands.

We are closer to that than a lot of people think.

I've got no problem with globalization. But I also respect the opportunity to create some cash flow and create some opportunity here in the United States as well.

# Chapter 3

*Create a culture, empower the believers,
share the success.*

**Michael J. Stolarczyk**

# Create a Culture, Empower the Believers, Share the Success

Utilize the STAR process to create a new culture within your organization, where you can empower the believers, share the success, and ultimately surpass all the fiscal management, organizational development, and commercial achievement goals that have been established.

People are the center of any culture; they drive the STAR process via these four simple words:

SPEED—exude a sense of urgency, thrive on change, desire to meet the situational requirements quickly, efficiently, accurately…every time.

TRUST—facilitate a sense of trust, reliability, and security in a person's mind by being THE consistent, stabilizing factor in their business world.

ACCOUNTABILITY—empower every staff member and with that hold them accountable to reach service, sales, and budget targets.

RELATIONSHIPS—initiate, foster, and expand internal and external relationships through honest, open, two-way communication.

The STAR process was first recognized by *FastCompany Magazine*, in February 2002, as one of its inaugural "Top 50 Innovations." Check it out on www.fastcompany.com.

# Manage Your Life as You Would Manage Your Business

I was going through an old presentation that I made to a group of students and found this thread…

**The greatest risk is never taking one.**
As early as possible, everyone has to take control of his or her career and personal life. Manage your life as you would manage your own business: proactively, diligently, and intensely. Never assume someone will look out for you or manage your life…you have to take the initiative and constantly facilitate your own personal and professional life. Take risks, expand your life experiences, and don't settle for gauging your success or failure on someone else's metrics. Set your own goals, be your own judge, and don't let someone else's career, or what you read, or what you see on television be the benchmark.

In life, and business, superior performance is always the key to independence of action. If you want to manage people, assets, and organizations, you first have to be able to manage yourself. By doing this, you lead by example, which your subordinates and your superiors will recognize immediately.

Treat everyone the same, with respect and loyalty. As your career develops, you will have a chance to make a positive impression on these people. If your career spans many years in the same company, remember that the way you treat people on the way up the corporate ladder will be returned in kind on your way down that same ladder.

Sage advice? Or just wishful thinking on my part? It is my hope that there are a few people out there that live by this creed as well.

# Lose Your Ego to Lead!

Empathy and emotional intelligence are not concepts; they are the two successful pillars of business culture.

Develop "idea practitioners" at every level of the organization, and let them drive the culture.

Empower them—they will be the link between the ideas and the action.

Focus on the people, process, and content—not on a new technology or fad.

Scale up, let go—at some point, you have to get out of the way and let others execute.

Delegate, let your people make decisions, then support them 100 percent.

NOTE 1: They will make mistakes...everyone does.

NOTE 2: As Esther Dyson says, "Always make new mistakes."

# What Is Your EQ?

Emotional intelligence is a way of recognizing, understanding, and choosing how we think, feel, and act. It shapes our interactions with others and our understanding of ourselves. It defines how and what we learn; it allows us to set priorities; it determines the majority of our daily actions. Research suggests it is responsible for as much as 80 percent of the "success" in our lives.

Emotional intelligence is the ability to sense, understand, and effectively apply the power and acumen of emotions as a source of human energy, information, connection, and influence.

In the last decade or so, science has discovered a tremendous amount about the role emotions play in our lives. Researchers have found that even more than IQ, your emotional awareness and ability to handle feelings will determine your success and happiness in all walks of life, including family relationships.

If we lack emotional intelligence, whenever stress rises, the human brain switches to autopilot and has an inherent tendency to do more of the same, only harder. Which, more often than not, is precisely the wrong approach in today's world.

# Idea Practitioners Get Results

As important as the continual search for new concepts is to a company, the task of helping those ideas gain traction is just as critical. Everyone who has seen a corporate change initiative wither on the vine knows that there is often a yawning gap between brilliant new ideas and concrete business results.

Bridging that gap are people sometimes referred to as idea practitioners (IPs). Such managers make it their job to identify business ideas that can make a difference for their companies and make them happen. IPs are not ordained to this work, and they rarely have a formal mandate for what they do.

What idea practitioners share is more than the ability to get excited by an idea's potential. As they scan the horizon for new ideas to bring back to their companies, their finely honed sensibility for what it will take for an idea to overcome internal resistance serves as a filter. Only those ideas that pass this workability test get brought forward. At that point, the IP's skills as cheerleader, viral marketer, ambassador, battlefield tactician, and savvy political insider come to the fore.

The true benchmark of success for an IP, the real reward, lies in seeing that the idea made a difference in the life of the organization. Do you know any IPs? Are you one yourself?

# Chapter 4

*Consistency, preparation, collaboration and common sense should be your guiding principles when interacting with your trading partners.*

**Michael J. Stolarczyk**

# What Should You Share with Your Trading Partners? TRUST!

Should you share important, sometimes sensitive information with your trading partners? When important information is withheld, it leads to enormous inefficiencies or even disasters in the supply chain.

Trust is needed to streamline decision making and interactions in the supply chain.

Before the virtualization of the enterprise and globalization of the supply chain, it was not so hard to be selfish. The boundaries of your "sphere of trust" aligned pretty clearly with the boundaries of the old vertically integrated enterprise. Just keep all that confidential information safe inside your company and you were OK.

HA!
This is simply no longer true. The "sphere of trust" now extends well into the supply chain. We are deeply interconnected. Everything (and everybody) is networked. More to the point, we have outsourced so much that you MUST share confidential information with your trading partners now. If someone else is designing major components of your product, someone else is doing your manufacturing, someone else is servicing your products at your customers' sites, and someone else is running your call centers, then by default you're sharing confidential customer information, product designs, IP, and production information. All the competitive pressures to reduce cycle times and inventory levels, improve service, and innovate products faster

are pushing companies to integrate more tightly and share more information, not less. No longer can you afford the sloppiness inherent to keeping your trading partners in the dark.

So, for today, let's talk about sharing...later we will talk about reducing risk.

## Building Strategic Partnerships (through Building the Relationship)

A clear distinction should be made between strategic partnerships and the more tactical commodity, vendor-buyer relationships. Building strategic partnerships takes time and diligence. It can be accomplished with a small, rationalized set of suppliers. Done right, suppliers become an extension of your enterprise. This requires methodically laying out an agreement on what will be shared, the benefits as well as the consequences of a breach. Building an understanding of the mutual self-interest and interdependence of the relationship is tantamount to its long-term success. In the past, traditional relationships were adversarial; it takes a lot of time to change mind-sets. No matter, you must look to the future...

Many companies use the quarterly business review, generally under strict nondisclosure agreements (NDA), as the primary forum for sharing confidential strategies. These planning sessions at a senior-executive-to-senior-executive level review things like the changes to the market assumptions, scenarios, product roadmaps, transitions (strategy, timing, risks), and supplier performance (goals, actuals, and improvement plans). There are instances when a trading partner abuses this position of trust, but the result is usually bad for the abuser.

Confidential dialogues can be even more challenging when the supplier or customer is also your competitor. Even with a nondisclosure agreement, the sharing of product strategies, roadmaps, and other confidential data is uncomfortable, though it is done every day. Many of the large diversified conglomerates that are likely to be both competitors and trading partners are in the Far East, where IP rights are not as strongly upheld. Another twist: As more and more manufacturing is outsourced to China and elsewhere, it raises the issue of sharing product and manufacturing knowledge with companies that could potentially become competitors of yours.

We all have stories about how IP was sent to China, and was then utilized by the competing vendor "down the street" to build a comparable product at a lower cost. This will continue to happen, unless you establish some principles to reduce your risk.

# So, the TRUST Has Been Established, but You Still Have to Reduce Your Risk

So, now that you have established an open forum to share information and you have created mutual trust, what can you do to ensure its success?

Use the three Ps (policy, process, and performance) methodology as a useful framework to secure value from sharing relevant and useful information while decreasing the risks of abuse.

## Policy

**Segmentation—**The basic foundation for protecting confidential data is the classic technique used by the military to protect secrets: classifying data according to its confidentiality and giving access only on a "need to know" basis. For example, a supplier designing a component that fits in your product usually needs to know only the physical envelope (attachment points and constraints) and electrical interface characteristics for their component, rather than receiving your entire design.

**Actionable Information—**A promising approach is to scrub data into actionable information. Structured contracts, with detailed boundaries, venues, and parameters, are a good example. Instead of sharing range forecasts, companies express future demand via structured contract terms like minimum firm commitments (or MQCs), lead time guarantees with different pricing for different lead times, capacity guarantees for upside flex at a higher price, etc.

**Escrow Account**—At least one company had success with another creative approach: establishing an escrow account that is used if either party violates the agreement. The money is then reinvested in the relationship to fix the cause of the problem, e.g., joint team education, fixing flawed processes, or new technology. This dramatically improved the level of trust in that relationship. (Good luck getting your CFO to buy in on this, but it can be done.)

## Process

It is critical that the policies are backed up by processes and controls to prevent, detect, and correct accidental or deliberate misuse of confidential information, such as:

**Physical Security**—Controlled access to offices, receptionist diligence on who is allowed in the building, badges, questioning unknown people in sensitive areas, not leaving confidential documents out in the open, etc.

**Separation/Rotation of Duties**—For example, having a different person control physical inventory than the one controlling information about that inventory.

**Training and Testing**—Training employees on the procedures and importance of protecting confidential information (yours and others' under NDA); testing awareness and taking corrective steps.

**Logs**—Keeping accurate, tamper-proof records of who accessed what areas/information and when.

**Audits**—Auditing your firm and trading partners to ensure safeguards and proper training. Some companies have computer-assisted "continuous auditing" of compliance.

Particularly sensitive data may require structural organizational safeguards as well. For example, some engineering organizations establish a "clean room" approach that separates the people receiving the highly sensitive design information and restricts their interactions and communications with the rest of their engineering organization to prevent the partner's design information from leaking into their own proprietary designs.

## Performance
Policy and process decisions must weigh trade-offs based on business performance impact:
1) Business value of sharing information
2) Cost of implementing proposed controls
3) Consequences of compromising the information

### Enablers/Technology
There are useful technologies available for implementing these practices. Role-based access controls (RBAC) enable implementation of segmentation, giving access only to specific people only for the specific chunks of information they need. Digital Rights Management systems can protect individual documents even after they are sent outside your company, limiting access to only specific people and certain actions (e.g., no printing, no cut and paste, no forwarding, etc.). Private and industry networks have implemented technologies to protect confidential data between trading partners; for example, the ANS network enables automotive OEMs and their suppliers to securely exchange digitally signed and encrypted confidential design files and business transactions. At the very least, PDF files can reduce some leaks.

### Executive-Level Advocates
This may be the single most important issue to have secured and resolved prior to creating a shared trust environment. To realize the optimum "return on sharing," there should

be advocates for both the sharing and protection of data. Some companies have elevated data protection to a C-level job—the CISO (chief information security officer). Senior supply chain executives must also advocate the benefits of sharing information. These decisions should rationally weigh the trade-offs. The supply chain that maximizes sharing of the right information works like one integrated enterprise, realizing significant competitive advantages over a supply chain whose participants withhold valuable information from each other.

**Be smart when sharing information. Reduce your risk by using the three Ps.**

# Rate Negotiation
# Headaches Averted

Ocean carrier mergers and acquisitions have shaken up the industry, leaving behind a tangled web for consignees and shippers to navigate. So how do you avoid getting snagged in the web of management hierarchy and get the best bang for your buck when negotiating a shipping deal?

1   Use the "big picture" approach to create leverage.
2.  Be creative; offer the package deal.
3.  Control the negotiations.
4.   Let them know what you spend.
5.   Do your homework.
6.  Know the hierarchy in their marketing and sales departments (past and present).
7.  Attend industry conferences and build your personal network.
8.  Know where your freight is at all times; demand to keep the visibility.
9.  Keep trying to negotiate service agreements/levels/KPIs into your contracts.
10. Get to know the local operating personnel in your shipping areas (origins and destinations).

# Chapter 5

*Not everything that can be counted counts, and not everything that counts can be counted.*

**Albert Einstein**

# The Long Tail—Can We Find a Place for It in the Logistics World?

## The Long Tail in Probability Theory

The long tail is the colloquial name given to a long-known feature of statistical distributions (Zipf, Power-laws, Pareto distributions, and/or Levy distributions ). They are also known as "heavy tails," "power-law tails," or "Pareto tails." In these distributions, a vast population of events occurs very rarely in the yellow (or more generally have low amplitude on some scale, e.g., popularity or sales), while a small population of events occurs very often in the red (or have high amplitude). The huge population of rare (or low-amplitude) events is referred to as the long tail. In many cases, the rare events—the ones on the long tail—are so much greater in number than the common events that, in aggregate, they comprise the majority. My question is this: can we find (or take advantage of) this concept within the transport and logistics world?

## "The Long Tail" by Chris Anderson

The phrase "The Long Tail," as a proper noun, was first coined by Chris Anderson. Beginning in a series of speeches in early 2004 and culminating with the publication of a *Wired Magazine* article in October 2004, and subsequent book of the same name in 2006. Anderson described the effects of the long tail on current and future business models. Anderson observed that products that are in low demand or have low sales volume can collectively make up a market share that rivals or exceeds the relatively few current bestsellers and blockbusters, if the store or distribution channel is large enough. Examples of such megastores include Amazon.com, Netflix, and even Rhapsody. The Long Tail is a potential market and, as the examples illustrate, successfully tapping in to that Long-Tail market is often enabled by the distribution and sales channel opportunities the Internet creates. Do these opportunities exist for other retailers of the bricks and mortar type, and can 3PL organizations provide services to support this pursuit of the Long Tail?

A former Amazon employee described the Long Tail as follows: "We sold more books today that didn't sell at all yesterday than we sold today of all the books that did sell yesterday." Yeah, I know it sounds crazy, but read the sentence again...and it's not a Yogi Berra quote.

"We sold more books today that didn't sell at all yesterday than we sold today of all the books that did sell yesterday."

**Question:**
**Can we aggregate market opportunities via reverse logistics service offerings that span multiple markets and multiple customers?**

## Relationship between the Long Tail and Storage and Distribution Costs

The key factor that determines whether a sales distribution has a Long Tail is the cost of inventory storage and distribution. Where inventory storage and distribution costs are insignificant, it becomes economically viable to sell relatively unpopular products; however, when storage and distribution costs are high, only the most popular products can be sold. Take movie rentals as an example. A traditional movie rental store has limited shelf space, which it pays for in the form of monthly rent; to maximize its profits, it must stock only the most popular movies to ensure that no shelf space is wasted. Because Netflix stocks movies in centralized warehouses, its storage costs are far lower and its distribution costs are the same for a popular or unpopular movie. Netflix is therefore able to build a viable business stocking a far wider range of movies than a traditional movie rental store. Those economics of storage and distribution then enable the Long Tail to kick in: Netflix finds that, in aggregate, "unpopular" movies are rented more than popular movies.

**More Questions:**
**Again, what are the most unpopular aspects of the supply chain? Returns? Slow-moving items? Seasonal items? My thoughts are spinning, but a real answer (opportunity) has not become crystal clear!**

## Competition and the Long Tail

The Long Tail is not just a positive economic effect; it can also threaten established businesses. Before a Long Tail kicks in, the only products offered are the most popular, but when the costs of inventory storage, and distribution fall then a wide range of products suddenly becomes available; that can, in turn, have the effect of reducing demand for the most popular products.

## Close

We need to assess the ideas that this topic creates and formalize a game plan. Does your organization have a "Long-Tail Game Plan"? Should it? What do you think? Sooner or later, one of the many logistics organizations is going to grab on to the Long Tail...maybe a carrier-related company (Maersk Logistics, now DAMCO, asset-based), a 3PL (Kontane Logistics, non-asset based), or even a 4PL (Accenture, solutions and integrator). The ultimate question is: When will the industry catch up with the wired crowd by chasing that Long Tail?

# The Square Root Law's Impact on Inventories—And You Thought You Would Never Use Real Math after College!

The square root law states that the total inventory in a system is proportional to the square root of the number of locations at which a product is stocked. The square root law was mathematically proven by D. H. Maister in his 1975 *International Journal of Physical Distribution* article entitled "Centralization of Inventories and the Square Root Law." Whoa! I'm surprised I was even able to type that...

The significance of the square root law is that a company operating five warehouses, which then centralizes into one warehouse, can theoretically reduce inventory carried in stock by 55 percent. This will reduce inventory carrying costs, which may be slightly offset by more costly transport options to meet a customer's service requirements.

Since I am someone who knows just enough to be dangerous on this type of issue, especially when working directly with mathematical minutiae, I am not equipped to review the detailed method of calculation. You simply have to trust the facts as stated.

There are large potential benefits to reducing the number of locations and, on the flip side, also significant inventory increase penalties to adding to the number of stocking locations. However, it is important when looking at such opportunities not to do so in isolation, but to take into account all aspects, including distribution center cost and transport cost, as well as customer lead times and replenishment, before any final decisions are made.

Let's review two of these strategies, specifically slow-moving goods (SMG) and network centralization, just to give you some ideas about where you may begin with direct application to your own organization (or client).

An SMG goods strategy consists of the segmentation and sort of a product range by velocity. Typically, Pareto's law (the 80/20 rule, which, by the way, we need to discuss whether it really is relevant in this day and age) can assist in this regard with the slower-moving 80 percent of products, which might represent 20 percent of sales volume being pulled from the current DC network. These SKUs would then be serviced from one or two more centralized slow-moving distribution centers with the appropriate square root law of inventory applying, depending on how many existing locations at which these products were held. An example would be that these have been pulled back from four locations to one, resulting in roughly a 50 percent inventory reduction, which is significant.

In addition, the picking productivity benefits can accrue, assuming all products were in a consolidated pick line in the previous four full line facilities. By pulling these SMG products out and creating new pick lines, one SMG and four FMG (fast-moving goods) in each of the current facilities, both picking operations will be immediately improved—the FMG by reduced travel times due to not having to pass all of the previous SMG slots, and the SMG by focusing on one pick slot within a more compact picking layout.

SMG network strategies can also be useful in addressing networks that are over capacity and require expansion with the SMG facility, reducing the overall stock holding and space requirement in the existing full line facilities.

Network centralization analysis may often result in significant benefits as well where multiple regional facilities are consolidated to only one or two locations. A determination of the appropriate centralized network strategy for a firm can also be completed by modeling the optimal intersection of number of locations, transportation costs, and inventory carrying costs. This calculation must, of course, be governed by business-defined customer service levels and can vary based on the product density and the relative value of different product lines.

It seems we are returning to the location issue, which again plays an important role in this decision process. How are you dealing with these types of challenges in your organization? How about with your clients?

# Chapter 6

*Technology for technology's sake is nothing;
it has to have the people and process behind it!*

**Michael J. Stolarczyk**

# RFID ROI Rx

With so many companies providing RFID systems, and so many expensive choices, how do you buy smart? Here are ten tips on selecting an RFID system that provides a return on investment:

**1. Get educated:** Learn best practices from early adopters. Attend industry events and EPC global standards meetings, where leading companies openly share their RFID implementation experiences.

**2. Build a cross-functional RFID implementation team:** Include key members from your sales and marketing and supply chain groups to help identify the business processes that can benefit from RFID.

**3. Develop a long-term RFID strategy:** You need a solid understanding of RFID's long-term benefits to design the appropriate first steps. Define an ROI pathway that maps out both near-term opportunities to drive benefit and long-term opportunities to build competitive advantage across the value chain.

**4. Select the right SKUs for the initial program:** Using the ROI pathway as a guide, select SKUs that will accelerate payback from RFID deployment. Don't select SKUs based solely on RF characteristics or the ease of integrating tagging stations into existing processes.

**5. Capture business context:** Create an electronic product code manifest linking key business information to RFID data elements. This builds the business context to support the applications that will drive benefit.

**6. Create an enterprise-wide view of goods movement and inventory:** Integrate trading partners with internal RFID data to create a "single version of the truth" for all goods moving through the supply chain. ROI depends on your ability to recreate goods movement in the physical world from a noisy, incomplete, error-laden RFID data set captured at many points across the supply chain.

**7. Collaborate with partners in the value chain:** Share RFID data with trading partners and develop active communication to identify opportunities for jointly driving efficiencies across the value chain—for example, automating shipment verification among trading partners.

**8. Share RFID data with internal teams:** Provide internal teams with access to enterprise-level RFID data. Long-term success of an RFID rollout requires carefully prioritizing opportunities to modify business processes to drive benefit. This requires insight from internal stakeholders across the business.

**9. Avoid custom development:** Every business needs to tailor RFID-centric systems to fit its products, business processes, and facilities. Custom development is expensive and difficult to support, and increases long-term total cost of ownership (TCO). Minimizing TCO requires the ability to configure scenarios within a supported platform.

**10. Integrate RFID with existing systems:** In the long term, enterprise applications such as ERP (Enterprise Resource Planning) and CRM (Customer Resource Management) will capitalize on the inventory visibility and goods movement that RFID provides. Devise a strategy for integrating the RFID data management platform with existing enterprise systems.

# What Are the Three Most Important Issues Surrounding RFID Technology? Location... Location...Location!

In retail, a store's location impacts sales performance more than any other factor. Quite often, great managers, great marketing programs, great price points, and even great products do not matter as much as a great location!

The quantifiable value of location is distinct. However, the ability to tap into location as a meaningful component of new business intelligence platforms or systems is a relatively new concept altogether.

Some estimates purport that 85 percent of all data used by businesses today contains some type of location component. In other words, somewhere the data holds information that is tied to a geographic location.

Sometimes a location component is quite specific and spelled out...essentially "metadata." An example would be an organization storing the latitude and longitude of its assets, customers, and so forth in a database. Other times, the geographic metadata may be an address that can be pinpointed on a map, either manually or through a process called geocoding to determine longitude and latitude.

Location indicators can also be less obvious—for example, some companies can use the first six digits of a phone number (that is, the area code and the three-digit prefix) to designate a record to a specific place.

A natural fit for location metadata, which is easily accessible, is needed and required. By decentralizing analytics and distributing decision-making tools to a large number of users, organizations work to break the bottleneck between inspiration and insight. The goal must be for systems users, and decision makers in every strategic unit of your organization, to have access to the data they need quickly, without the need to be experts in the use of legacy or distributed system-based platforms.

Location awareness (intelligence) goes one step further and provides an easy way for users to quickly analyze and visualize critical spatial relationships among data that, unless the user is a technical expert, would not be apparent.

In a hyper-competitive market (like retail), where every investment must generate a return, smart organizations realize that location turns out a fast, high-benefit reward. Early adopters of business intelligence software (supply chain visibility or demand planning) saw that, by publishing the data that defines their business across the organization, they could gain an advantage over the competition. Similarly, progressive users of this type of technology realize that, by revealing location within their core databases, they can positively alter the way they do business and never look back.

Obviously, the new technology currently taking hold in retail and manufacturing supply chains stands out as a great example of location metadata in action. RFID tags can solve critical problems related to supply chain management, store-level inventory, intuitive displays, homeland security, and other important processes. While the issue carries some controversy relative to privacy, and industry standards, RFID also has great potential. Organizations as diverse as the Department of Homeland Security and Wal-Mart are deep into their pilot programs and have full-scale strategies to take advantage of RFID.

Hence, RFID is creating vast amounts of location metadata. For some who manage large volumes of data, the advent of RFID technology creates the need to develop a whole new set of analyses. The process of creating data for tracking product shipments, inventory, and even a customer's buying patterns begs for a powerful business intelligence tool. It must be powerful enough to allow analysts and operations managers to monitor and measure the status intuitively. Since every record in an RFID database also has a geographic component, the right business intelligence solution for the job should incorporate location metadata.

The fact that manufacturers and retailers desire to share data about inventory and supply causes location intelligence to gain even more importance. Using a location-enabled platform, retailers will allow suppliers to view and query reports describing the movement of product through warehouses and outlet centers. The supplier may require access to or need to view a map that breaks out the volume of shipments of a product by location. The map would show the location of warehouses and inventory in those warehouses, as well as outlets where shipments have already been delivered. It could even show the presence of shipments at indeterminate waypoints throughout the supply chain. Ocean carriers and air carriers will no doubt embrace this (many already have, to some degree).

Location metadata is positioned to be a modern-day "lighthouse" that will unlock geographic understanding, extract the value of place (during a specific time, at specified waypoint), and integrate it with business intelligence systems. Its singular goal is to give organizations greater return on their investment in forecasting and demand planning, and to provide all staff with a means to interact with the meta-data in a manner not previously available or even barely acknowledged.

There are only a few fundamental ways to measure, understand, and analyze information, and several tools already exist to maximize the level of understanding. However, these tools often altogether ignore the critical components of location, location, location...and many organizations stand to gain great efficiencies by enabling location technologies through RFID, GIS, social networks, and locative logistics solutions.

# Are You Managing Reverse Logistics or Reversing Logistics Management?

If Europe is any harbinger of things to come, US businesses are on only the periphery of properly addressing and reaping the true value of reverse logistics. Europe's ratification of the Waste Electrical and Electronic Equipment Directive legislates that electronic equipment and appliance manufacturers are accountable for end-of-life disposal of their products, including refrigerators, computers, TVs, and cell phones.

This will give product lifecycle management a whole new spin and greatly shift the way global manufacturers approach concepts and designs, even to the point of specifically manufacturing products with recycling in mind.

It's no longer simply a matter of pushing product to the consumer then managing returns; it's a matter of managing a product's entire lifecycle. As such, corporate strategies must support this holistic vision.

This trend is a pivotal watershed in how enterprises embrace reverse logistics by placing the twin imperatives of reverse logistics and recycling targets together, and it doesn't take much to imagine the challenges involved. This is evident for both manufacturers and retailers; reverse logistics and recycling are outside of what might realistically be considered their core areas of competence. Even if the skills could be recruited or acquired, challenges remain to initiate, manage, and measure success.

Take materials handling, just as an example, where supply chains are used to managing brand-new, neatly packaged goods through highly automated distribution centers—not rusting washing machines or old refrigerators.

Retailers do not have (and will not have) the space to store end-of-life goods. Retail space is expensive, and is consequently devoted to goods for sale rather than goods for recycling, but also significant image and safety problems exist in mixing the two flows of goods—one heading to consumers, and one heading to the trash heap.

The unique challenges will be here soon, but companies will continue to focus attention on their core strengths and outsource reverse logistics management to a growing cadre of service companies dedicated to the task. The advantages of rethinking reverse logistics will extend well beyond corporate citizenship and responsibility as retailers and manufacturers build a more dynamic and fluid supply chain.

While fiscal pressures may ultimately compel some to seek cost-cutting measures, paying attention to returns management makes good business sense regardless of the economy.

The reverse logistics business is really not cyclical or based on good or bad economic times. In lean times, companies have a need to take surplus product and convert those assets into cash as quickly as possible. In good times, these same companies will manufacture more product. The rate of returns rises as volume grows, hence the same value applies.

Companies may still be conflicted by the complexity of returns management, but where there is pain there is also opportunity for gain. In the broader scope of global supply chain management, reverse logistics is starting to make more sense. It's just a matter of time before more organizations will take advantage of this opportunity.

# Chapter 7

*Leaders win through logistics. Vision, sure. Strategy, yes. But when you go to war, you need to have both toilet paper and bullets at the right place at the right time. In other words, you must win through superior logistics.*

**Tom Peters**

# Assess Risk. Manage Risk. Do It Now...Then Repeat.

While enterprise risk management (ERM) continues to gain acceptance in the financial services industry as a means to address credit, market, and operational risks, and improve performance of business operations, other industrial sectors have lagged behind in adopting a true enterprise-wide view of risks. Companies are now realizing that global sourcing and just-in-time lean manufacturing, while yielding significant cost savings, may have also increased their exposure to global risks. Now, with minimal inventory levels and efficient utilization of production capacity, the traditional buffers against disruptions are no longer available. To respond to this new competitive environment, businesses are beginning to enhance their current capabilities in managing global risks and mitigating impacts of disruptions. Here are some thoughts on how organizations can get started in rapidly identifying and assessing manufacturing and supply chain risks to enhance their operational awareness and responsiveness to said risk events.

**1) Nominate a Cross-functional Team of Risk Experts**
An extended team of experts from across an organization should be selected to help with rapid and thorough identification of risks. Team members can be chosen from among risk managers, statistical analysts, operations research analysts, manufacturing engineers, purchasing staff buyers, commodity experts, supply chain and logistics managers, operations IT systems experts, etc. Each team member is expected to represent his or her business unit and assist with identifying and gathering quantitative and qualitative

risk data. Traditionally, in most large organizations, risk management as an expertise has a corporate home in insurance and risk financing or audit services. However, the real risk owners for manufacturing and supply chain risks are in operations. Thus, we advocate that the team must include subject matter experts from business operations who have handled many of these supply chain and manufacturing disruptions in the past. These operations specialists can contribute significantly in identifying risks and explaining event severity from an operations perspective.

Among the team, there has to be a core team of "risk evangelists," who must take up the challenge to promote risk awareness across the entire enterprise, share risk management and mitigation successes, document and convey lessons learned, and leverage knowledge and experience to embed risk management in operations business processes. Early on in the process, the team should also obtain top management support and a management champion to help overcome organizational roadblocks, and drive improvements in operational awareness and responsiveness to risk events.

## 2) Convene the Cross-functional Team for Brainstorming to Identify and Map a Portfolio of Enterprise Risks

The portfolio should include financial, strategic, hazard, and operational risks. These four categories are chosen, as they are typically how risk management responsibilities have been divided and assigned to different business units in many large corporations. A simple high-level risk categorization used in the map allows executives and mid-level managers to readily engage in the process of editing the map as well as identifying or taking ownership of some of the risks from the portfolio. This portfolio is an excellent starting place for manufacturing engineers and supply chain analysts to begin identifying risks that would affect their work, or they could impact through their operations responsibilities. The portfolio must include all possible enterprise risks that the team can identify. Capturing this full portfolio is important, for it demonstrates to top leadership that the team has been as thorough as possible in identifying risks. The portfolio will be a key tool for risk awareness discussions, for it encourages groups to talk openly about risks they can control, manage, or mitigate, and those risks that are outside their spheres of influence.

### 3) Filter, Assess, and Prioritize Risks

Once the risk portfolio is defined and agreed upon, the next step is to have the team filter down the broad portfolio to those risks that are relevant to manufacturing and supply chain operations. They could be boiled down to manufacturing and supply chain risks. This exercise can generate valuable discussion on ownership of some of the risks, recognition that some risks do not have clear owners, and help the team to build a common understanding of the breadth of the company's portfolio of risks.

Once the subset portfolio of manufacturing and supply chain risks is identified, the next task is to construct a subjective risk map or "heat map" for the manufacturing and supply chain risks, and classify risks based on probability of occurrence and loss severity. Without collecting much statistical data, the team can subjectively place risks in the quadrants, and openly discuss which risks could most impact manufacturing and supply chain operations. Lastly, the loss severity assessment should also intuitively include how difficult and costly each risk is to mitigate.

Further division of the probability of occurrence into four categories (such as very unlikely, improbable, probable, very probable) and the loss severity into four categories (such as insignificant, minor, serious, catastrophic) can help clarify and distinguish among the different manufacturing and supply chain risks in terms of their overall impact. This refined classification will help the team to recognize the relative difference across all risks in terms of occurrence and severity, and help them arrive at a prioritized list in view of organizational metrics.

This subjective risk map can guide allocation of scarce resources (people, time, money) to subsequent risk modeling and analysis efforts. Once the prioritized risk map has been developed, the team can naturally create a top ten priority list of risks. The exercise of constructing a top ten list is important. As your team starts to form the top ten priority list, the team may have to revisit and adjust their probability and severity assessments on the risk map as well.

## 4) Work on All "Actionable Risks" and Integrate What Has Been "Learned" into Business Processes

Leaders can use this proposed approach to prioritize manufacturing and supply chain risks that can be strategically influenced or managed over time. We note that some risks are "out there," but nothing can be done about them. Managers should acknowledge these risks, and move on to other risks that are actionable. Secondly, enhancing risk management in manufacturing and supply chain operations amounts to changing organizational culture and priorities. This type of change has the promise of making operations more resilient and responsive to the dynamic environment, but cannot be achieved overnight. The risk maps and models can help multiple stakeholders visualize and comprehend cost-benefit trade-offs of various mitigation efforts and impact on the overall enterprise. Risk management for manufacturing and supply chains is adopted in an evolutionary (rather than revolutionary) manner because manufacturing and supply chains typically evolve over time, and sudden interruptions for the sake of better risk management can affect morale of the organization significantly. Management should consistently revisit the prioritized heat map of risks along with the top ten risks to update actionable and urgent risks, and monitor how the firm is doing in enhancing operational responsiveness to manufacturing and supply chain risks. What do you think the take-aways will be from this exercise?

**Key Issues for Leaders and Supply Chain Professionals:**
1) Do it now!
2) Utilize a cross-functional team to identify risks.
3) Be thorough in identifying enterprise risks.
4) Don't get lost in too much data to assess probability and severity risks.
5) Subjective risk assessment is a quick way to get started with ranking risks.
6) Prioritize focus to the key manufacturing and supply chain risks.
7) Empower business units to take ownership of managing risks.
8) Work on actionable risks and integrate into operational business processes.
9) Repeat on annual basis.

## Top Ten Risks—Priority List (Example)

To close our discussion on risk assessment, let's look at a top ten list:

1) Supplier Problems: Financial, Quality, Missed Deliveries
2) Loss of Key Supplier (Due to Natural Disaster or Catastrophe)
3) Logistic Route or Mode Disruption
4) Building or Equipment Fire
5) Logistics Provider Problems

6) Labor Issues
7) IT System Failure(s)
8) Terrorism
9) Computer Virus/Denial of Service Attacks
10) Loss of Key Equipment, Facility, or Staff

What do you think? Do you have any risks to add?

# Contingency Plans—Hope for the Best, Prepare for the Worst

Can your company weather a logistics disaster, such as a terrorist attack, airport closure, or worker strike? Sudden disruptions will create possible long-term disconnects with your customer—along with your customers' freight. Here are some commonsense tips on planning for a crisis and handling emergency transport changes when a major disruption happens:

**1. Designate business continuity (crisis) managers.** Because any disruption to your business can be extremely costly, it is imperative to make managers within your organization responsible for your continuity planning. Give your point people the authority to carry out the job and make them responsible for all actions and outcomes, including emergency shipments.

**2. Define all possible disruptions to your business.** Business disruptions come in all shapes and sizes—from natural disasters, fires, and chemical spills to system failures and call center outages, work stoppages, and unforeseen airport closures. Think through the gamut of scenarios that could present a shipping emergency for your company.

**3. Hope for the best but plan for the worst**. Outline the steps that need to be taken to remedy each disruption scenario. This includes making sure that everyone involved—technology, operations, purchasing, transportation—knows his or her role, as well as who is responsible for what actions.

**4. Know where to get help.** Because it's almost a sure bet that you'll need to expedite shipments in an emergency, talk to carriers about their capabilities before a crisis arises. While all expedited carriers are in business to speed shipments, they offer different types of services and have different service records. As with any purchase, you need to select carefully. Do your shopping in advance so that you've already identified your mission-critical carriers and will know whom to contact immediately during a crisis.

**5. Understand all your transportation options.** There are numerous cost- and time-related issues to consider in choosing how you want to expedite your emergency shipments, including exclusive use of vehicle, two-way tracking ability, twenty-four/seven/three-sixty-five availability, special handling requirements, and domestic versus international capabilities. Your final carrier choice will depend a great deal on the nature of the emergency and your recovery needs.

**6. Test your plan and get professional training.** It helps if you test your recovery plan with your carriers up front to uncover any problems with the process. The cost of a test run will likely be minimal compared to the effect on your bottom line if your expedited transportation plans fail in a real emergency. Solicit training from professional risk assessment/training organizations.

**7. When an emergency strikes, stick to your plan that was tested.** Keep a cool head and follow the actions you've already outlined. Make sure everyone involved in the recovery effort maintains constant communication with each other to help ensure that your efforts run as smoothly as possible.

**8. Even the best laid plans can go wrong..so be ready to improvise.** Unfortunately, Murphy's law has a way of creeping into emergencies. Be prepared for last-minute glitches that may cause you to alter your plan. For instance, if you planned to use a ground expedited carrier to transport a new generator for your facility but a flood has washed out the main road, you'll need to go to Plan B. The best advice: Be flexible with your contingency planning. You might need to explore more than one option to resolve the crisis.

**9. Stay current on factors that could change your plan.** Contingency planning is an ongoing process because many factors can change your requirements. For instance, since the September 11 attacks, security measures for cargo tendered to commercial aircraft have not increased, but the scrutiny has. According to FAA regulations, only "known" shippers who have customer records with the broker and either an established shipping contract or an established business history can tender packages or freight to commercial airlines. The ocean industry is another matter with C-TPAT, etc.

**10. Believe in your plan, and believe in the people that will facilitate the steps.**
If you don't have a contingency plan, **call Kontane Logistics!** Even if you don't have a formal business continuity plan, you can still help resolve your transportation emergencies by getting help from a quality organization that can handle multiple modes of transport.

## Ten Steps for a Safer Warehouse
Injury prevention starts with leadership, training, communication, risk assessments, and metrics.

### 1. START AT THE TOP
While everyone is responsible for his or her individual safe behavior, the company's leadership team must own, lead, and participate in safety management. It's not enough for leadership to merely support safety; they must exhibit

behavior that clearly demonstrates to all associates that safety is critical to the success of the organization.

## 2. TRAINING IS PARAMOUNT
From the first day of an employee's tenure with a company, training is key to safer warehouse operations. Educate all associates on safety-related practices, requirements, and responsibilities. Once the organization's vision and safety requirements are explained, the groundwork has been laid for continuous training.

## 3. OBSERVE ASSOCIATES IN ACTION
After associates receive basic safety training, reinforcing workplace safety behavior is ongoing. Managers should observe, for example, how an employee drives a forklift during the first few days following forklift training, and be prepared to offer immediate and meaningful feedback. Good managers point out the positives of safe behavior and coach areas that need improvement, often on an ongoing basis.

## 4. GET EMPLOYEES INVOLVED
Create cross-functional, in-house safety teams that meet at least monthly to focus on preventing accidents and injuries by identifying hazards and unsafe conditions in the warehouse, and ensuring proper controls are in place to bring all hazards within acceptable levels of risk. Teams should include warehouse workers, forklift drivers, supervisors, vendors, and customer liaisons.

## 5. WORK SCHEDULES TO MATCH DUTIES
It is important for employees to be safe, and for employers to create a reasonable workday and safe workplace to facilitate their duties. To avoid unsafe behaviors caused by fatigue, consider implementing ergonomic improvements; rotating job assignments; supplementing shifts with temporary or part-time employees; adding a shift; and providing adequate rest and beverage breaks, especially in hot and humid conditions.

## 6. ASSESS RISK

Identify individual job activities, the potential hazards associated with each activity, and their existing controls. Then assign a risk rating to each activity by using a numeric formula that considers the probability of loss, the severity of loss, and the frequency of each activity. The risk rating will determine if additional controls are needed.

## 7. PERFORM SITE ASSESSMENTS

A group of health and safety professionals should work hand in hand with site management to seek out unsafe conditions and hazards, and create action plans to bring risk within acceptable levels before employees are injured or property is damaged.

## 8. INVESTIGATE ACCIDENTS

After an incident, identify immediate and upstream root causes, and implement better controls to prevent a repeat occurrence.

## 9. COMMUNICATE

Frequent and consistent communication among all levels of management and associates regarding safety processes, performance, and expectations is critical to building an effective safety culture and successful safety performance.

## 10. GATHER MEANINGFUL AND TIMELY METRICS

Create metrics that reflect the presence of safety (leading indicators), not just the absence of safety (trailing indicators). Metrics must also be designed based on their intended audience. For example, metrics for safety managers will need to be very detailed and facilitate analysis of correlations and trends. Metrics for operating managers need to be at a higher level and help identify deficiencies the team can address.

# Chapter 8

*If you don't like change, you will
enjoy irrelevance even less.*

**E. Gordon Gee**

# King of Chaos

A few quick thoughts on change, chaos, and managing them both in the here and now seem to be appropriate. Today, change is not the issue and chaos is, well, CHAOS!

Businesses, industries, and markets are experiencing massive restructurings, reengineerings, and redirection. Skills and tools are needed for the appropriate responses to various impacts to help us create rather than react. We are spinning faster, and the same old change tools do not always seem to work. We need to incorporate an actual chaos management strategy!

Whether it's your workplace or your personal relationships; whether you run a large organization, a small business, a tiny team, or simply your own life—the tools you need now are for managing chaos.

## 1. Be the "eye" of the storm.

Let's consider a hurricane, or a cyclone...utter chaos, causing great devastation. Think of the center. Calm, peaceful, quiet. The eye. Think of it as yourself. Be the eye. You may not be able to stop or even control the wind and the noise around you. But you can retain your own center. Find your strength, your capabilities, your power, and your value, and stand quietly in your own ability to respond to each situation with courage and wisdom. We all have it. We just forget it sometimes when the winds of change are howling around us.

## 2. Know what matters.

The first rule of success is to have positive energy. It is important to know how to concentrate it and focus it on the important things, instead of frittering it away on the minutiae. The most powerful thing you can do at any moment is refocus. What do you want to achieve? Why is this important? Then, make it happen.

## 3. Nurture your network.
No one person is an island. We operate best when interdependent. Not leaning, but supported. It may be time to revalue family, to reassess social contacts, to reenergize team consciousness in the workplace. One of the keys to managing chaos is the ability to tap into support facilities. Productivity almost invariably increases when we delegate, leverage, and pull together. Find those idea practitioners as well (the Trojan mice).

## 4. Have the courage to tell the truth.
This may not be so for you, but for many people an enormous amount of time and energy is wasted in developing and maintaining the mask. There's no time anymore to do that—have you noticed? It's time for empowerment, accountability, and ownership. Take it, and make it happen!

## 5. Learn to live with less.
This is a strange concept for many of us in business who have spent much of our working lives running after "more." When life moves fast, the less baggage we have to carry, the better. Traveling light, in many ways, becomes more effective. We're discovering that a simpler life can be a lot less stressful. I am not down on wealth and its pleasures—just to eliminate the desperate struggle for it!

## 6. Rejoice regularly—don't be afraid to express yourself or an emotion.
A behavioral researcher visited a kindergarten. "How many of you can sing?" he asked. All hands went up. "How many of you can paint?" Again, all hands were proudly thrust in the air. "And how many can dance?" "Me, me, me," was

the answer. The researcher asked the same questions in a university lecture hall. "How many of you can sing?" Two hands. "How many of you can paint?" Not one. "And how many can dance?" Fingers were pointed at others, with comments and laughter, but not one claimed the ability. What happened? Why did we forget, or decide our own self-expression was not good enough? It's just about a joyful release of stress hormones—good for the mind, the soul, and the body.

## 7. Choose care over fear.

There are only two fundamental emotions: love and fear. Anything that isn't one is the other. Until recently, we didn't talk about this in the corporate arena. Now we know that tough love builds good teams, and chaos is exacerbated by fear. This is not about being soft and gooey—you know that. It's about finding a way to address issues head-on with an intelligent mix of courage, commitment, and compassion.

## 8. Do the right thing!

Always do the right thing and with strong beliefs and conviction. So I'll use two quotes:

Harry S. Truman—"To do what is right, is the right thing to do…and let the rest of them go to hell!"

Vaclav Havel—"Hope is not the conviction that something will turn out well but the certainty that something makes sense, and is right, regardless of how it turns out."

Chaos is inevitable. In the sense that perturbation is evolutionary, it's also desirable. But managing it is essential. It is no use for any of us to hope that someone else will do it. Take charge! Do you have your own personal strategies in place? What are they? Can you lead other people to the task? Will you do the right thing?

# The Final Mile...or Is That "Miles"?

For US retailers with broad global supply chain operations, "last mile"—the portion of transit from the final delivery center to the customer's door—is really the last hundreds of miles from the destination port to the store. This crucial part of logistics, which accounts for the majority of a shipment's cost and complexity, is becoming increasingly difficult for retailers to manage.

To a certain degree, retailers are victims of their own success. As global sourcing expands and companies become more proficient at managing inbound supply chains, container trade between Asia and the United States continues to explode. This places a growing burden on the US intermodal transportation infrastructure.

This burden will create more frustration for retailers, according to trade forecasts. Inbound container traffic will continue to grow, congestion at and around ports will pose larger delays, and transporting product—and, ultimately, revenue—from the ports to the shelf will be increasingly difficult, particularly during peak season. How well retailers manage the last mile inside the United States plays a critical role in their ability to compete.

As the importance of last-mile distribution excellence increases, so does the value of US logistics assets: trucks, distribution centers, land, people, technology, and anything else that helps cargo move smoothly and efficiently. You know me...people and process are the most important factors!

Just look at what companies are willing to do to buy and protect US logistics assets. The Dubai ports deal was only the latest example of a foreign company accepting a large price tag for US assets.

Deutsche Post's multimillion-dollar acquisitions of DHL, Airborne Express, and Exel forced UPS and FedEx to spend millions on Capitol Hill to protect their US markets. And Netherlands-based APM Terminals, the terminal management division of Maersk, built a costly new facility in Virginia that is one of the world's most advanced marine terminals.

Foreign companies realize the importance of last-mile logistics control inside the largest consumer market in the world. Why? They know that what occurs after containers are dropped at US ports can make or break a logistics strategy. Retailers that have control over this portion of their supply chain will be market winners...but this does not mean that it has to be controlled in-house.

A responsive last-mile supply chain allows retailers to meet demand, manage seasonal peaks, and drive hot merchandise to the shelf quickly and efficiently.

Information technology is essential for providing last-mile visibility, control, and flexibility. But technology by itself is only a tool. People and effective business processes drive results. To get those results, retailers need real-time control of various assets on the ground to maximize sales and reduce logistics costs as much as possible.

**Keep Your Options Open**
Three critical factors control inbound last-mile logistics today: options, options, and options. Can you feed imports quickly into your distribution network from ports on both coasts? Do you have the right crossdock and consolidation facilities in the right places to build cost-effective truckloads?

Do you use pool distribution to streamline store delivery? Can you bypass your DCs and go right to the store to move hot merchandise if necessary? Do you have a 3PL that can capitalize on all of these opportunities?

As the importance of last-mile logistics control grows, the answers to those questions will continue to have a great impact on retailers' overall competitive position. Look around…see what the major retailers are doing. They are looking to the outside for more flexibility and productivity, which means cash flow velocity—not just supply chain speed!

# SRFM? Yes, Another ACRONYM (or, YAA)!

The planning, execution and partner collaboration processes of nearly all companies today are driven by a "plan," itself typically part-forecast, part-performance target. Together, the plan and these core processes are at the heart of almost everything a company does—from MRP output, to commitments, to customers and suppliers, to internal performance targets and the bonuses that depend on them, to the financial projections delivered to Wall Street.

The day-to-day activities that absorb the majority of working hours, however, and through which things ultimately get done, often seem to occur in a reality almost separate from the plan and the core systems that support it. The reason? Actual supply and demand rarely match the plan. Uncertainty, whether about supplier performance, market conditions, a delayed product transition, or one of the many other drivers of supply and demand, leaves companies facing actual circumstances that differ from those planned for. Firefighting ensues: e-mails, voice mails, renegotiations, spreadsheet work-arounds. Stress is placed on relationships, and performance fails to live up to expectations.

What can be done? We can continue to hope for and work toward better forecasts and plans. But forecasts will never be perfect as long as there are factors that impact our business that are outside our control. Which is to say forever, particularly as more key activities are outsourced and business becomes increasingly global.

We can also invest in being able to better react to actual events as they occur—to the actual circumstances that differ from the plan—as soon as we learn about them. But response lead times aren't zero, and flexibility isn't free. Supply chains that win invest in responsiveness, but also acknowledge, and work to minimize, its costs and liabilities. And they choose to operate at a point where the incremental cost of further responsiveness rises to the level of the value it delivers. Which isn't infinite flex at zero lead-time—in most cases, it is far from it.

There is a solution to the plan versus reality gap—one supported by systems and processes that enable advance planning for the range of supply and demand outcomes that can occur—and which enables efficient execution and effective performance management in response to the outcomes that actually do occur.

**It is called supply risk and flexibility management, or SRFM.**

SRFM begins by acknowledging that trying to run a business in an uncertain environment, using systems and processes design to execute a fixed plan, is like trying to manage a construction project in quicksand. If the one thing we are sure of is that the forecast will be wrong, using it as the foundation of our core systems and processes makes consistent and efficient performance equally unlikely.

The appropriate foundation for planning and execution in an uncertain environment is the range of possible future supply and demand conditions. Using "range forecasts" allows us to capture and utilize all we know about prospective supply and demand conditions, whether from historical experience or from the market information currently available to sales, marketing, and procurement. In contrast, "point" forecast systems are only able to capture a single "best guess."

Information about the range of potential outcomes—clearly critical and valuable—is excluded from core systems as a result, forcing "informal" manual processes to attempt to cover it.

Two processes form the core of SRFM, both of which are built on supply and demand range forecast foundations. The first process quantifies the impact of supply and demand uncertainty on prospective future operating and financial performance. The second enables supply chain strategies to be defined and executed—both internally and with key supply chain partners—to manage the range of future performance outcomes and risk factors identified to best meet business objectives. These two processes, and the transformation of supply chain planning, execution, and performance they enable, are best illustrated with this example:

Consider supply management. Under traditional processes, negotiations focus on price. Lead times, along with flex terms that outline performance responsibilities in the event of inevitable forecast changes, may also be discussed. Data about how these terms impact future cost, value, and risk is rarely available, however, nor will commitments that quoted terms be honored under the adverse supply and demand conditions when they matter most.

In contrast, under SRFM procurement, teams enter negotiations armed with data that quantifies how specific price, lead time, and flex terms for the product or material in question impact future cost, availability, and liability across the range of potential supply and demand outcomes. The data covers both key operating variables, such as inventory and service levels, and key financial variables, such as liability, margin, and revenue, and summarizes expected levels, risks, and trade-offs across potential outcomes.

Drawing on this information, procurement identifies the specific lead times and flex terms for the material or product that best meet the company's objectives. Procurement requests that suppliers provide quotes on commitments to perform to these lead times and terms. Suppliers respond with terms that summarize—in advance—their ability (and, where relevant, the ability of their suppliers) to honor the requested performance commitments across the range of potential future supply and demand conditions, and the costs, lead time, and liabilities they must incur to do so. Potential capacity constraints are surfaced in time to be efficiently addressed, and information about other key supplier costs, objectives, and constraints can be evaluated and balanced against buyer objectives and benefits from the supply capabilities they enable.

Through the negotiations and counterproposals, the two parties identify the price, lead time, and flexibility terms that best prepare the supply chain for the material or product in question to meet the business objectives of both firms across the range of potential future supply and demand conditions. The requirements and commitments in the final agreement clearly define who has committed to do what and get what across possible future outcomes, and on what terms. Rather than firefighting, execution over time is an efficient process of optimally leveraging the assets and options put in place to best meet actual supply and demand conditions as they unfold, regardless of what they may be.

Parallel benefits accrue within the company. Procurement can now put clearly specified alternatives for performance across prospective supply and demand outcomes on the table, gain consensus with other functional leaders on the alternative that best meets the company's objectives, and commit to deliver the quoted performance across potential supply and demand outcomes with confidence. The discussion at a cross-functional planning meeting for a new product introduction may go something like this:

Cross-functional management team asks procurement: "Should we secure the more flexible supply? Why or why not?" Procurement's SRFM answer: "With the additional flex, our availability increases to a level that will enable us to hit peak demand, at locked-in pricing and lead times. Our liability if the product launch underperforms is also reduced by fifty percent. However, the incremental cost of the additional flexibility reduces margins by two percent. We can commit now to deliver either type of performance risk and return. Marketing and finance, the choice is yours— which alternative do you think best meets the company's objectives?"

Companies implementing SRFM today are realizing 5 percent to 10 percent improvements in performance by managing and executing—both internally and externally—SRFM processes able to address the uncertain reality of their business environment.

Now, we all have informal versions of the above...but does your organization have a formal SRFM game plan in place? Should it? Will it? What of it?

# Chapter 9

*Logistics must be simple—everyone
thinks they're an expert.*

**Anonymous**

# The Intelligent Trade Lane—Is This an Oxymoron or Just Insane Logic?

IBM and Maersk Logistics have jointly launched Intelligent Trade Lane, a new wireless supply chain security platform that will serve as the first plank of the soon-to-be-announced Global Movement Management, a wider supply chain security initiative now under development at IBM.

IBM and Maersk, a division of the A. P. Moller-Maersk Group, have already started land-based testing of Intelligent Trade Lane, a platform aimed at providing security as well as supply chain efficiencies to customers shipping products beyond national borders.

The technology combines tamper-proof smart cards, wireless sensors for measuring such things as location and temperature, and satellite, cellular, and mesh wireless networks for worldwide communications with customers over the Internet-based Global network.

Future plans call for starting a technology pilot, to be followed by a much larger test with retail, manufacturing, and CPG (consumer packaged goods) distributors. At this point, commercial availability was set for the second half of 2006 (to be honest, it always sounded very optimistic) and is only now being implemented.

In the pilot, the non-RFID wireless tracking technology will move from land-based testing to deployment aboard ocean vessels, trains, and trucks. Specific technologies to be implemented include the Iridium satellite network (well, you knew sooner or later all those Iridium satellites were going to be used for something...do you remember when Iridium made the claim some years back that they would change the face of cell phone communication?), Zigbee wireless mesh networks, smart-card encryption from IBM, and, on the epcGlobal network, RSA authentication and directory services from VeriSign Inc. Damn, to this point, that has to be the most difficult paragraph produced in this book.

IBM will also work with national customs agencies throughout the world to seek standardization of the Intelligent Trade Lane technology (good luck on that).

Intelligent Trade Lane also represents the first implementation of GMM, an initiative IBM expects to unveil over the next few months.

Intelligent Trade Lane will revolve around cigar box-sized devices, dubbed TRECs (Tamper Resistant Embedded Controllers), which will attach to shipping containers.

Each TREC device will house a full-fledged computer, smart card, and sensors. Identification and location environment will be stored in the smart card and secured with the use of IBM's encryption technology.

If this initiative becomes a reality, it will give Maersk Logistics, now DAMCO (IBM Solutions?) a laser-focused level of data collection (i.e., the dreaded "visibility" word), while also allowing communications to customers in real time, or near real time, to become a true industry benchmark.

The skeptic in me wants to say that this is just as much hype as it is reality. However, the concept is solid. The creative use of existing technology lends itself to be a more realistic alternative to all of the RFID claims being thrown over the wall the last few years. So, let's take a cold, hard look at this platform…and grade it on the results, not the hype.

# GE and Siemens to Partner on Container Security Device

General Electric's security subsidiary said it has signed an agreement with German conglomerate Siemens to market its security device for detecting unauthorized openings of ocean container doors.

Under the agreement, Siemens' Building Technologies Group will have exclusive marketing and distribution rights in Europe, and will take a minority stake in CommerceGuard AB, the GE Security subsidiary that is developing the container security device. It will also be the preferred company to integrate the product with other systems.

US Customs and Border Protection is testing Commerce-Guard as part of its Smart Box initiative expected to become the centerpiece of the agency's "Green Lane" effort to eliminate container security inspections for pre-vetted shippers that belong to the Customs-Trade Partnership Against Terrorism.

The partnership is noteworthy because GE and Siemens are two of the largest diversified companies in the world, and compete in areas ranging from industrial machinery and appliances to medical equipment and lighting. *Fortune* ranks GE as the world's ninth-largest company and Siemens the twenty-first.

The previous October, GE Security struck a similar deal with Mitsubishi Corp. to sell, distribute, and support the

CommerceGuard product to terminal operators, ports, exporters, and transportation companies in Japan and Asia.

The GE device magnetically attaches to the inside of the container and uses an electronic proximity sensor to detect and record when the door is opened. Fixed and handheld readers used at ports and other locations can pick up the signal with the identification number and status from the internal transmitter.

GE Security officials say they have corrected problems with nuisance alarms and that the false positive rate now falls well below the 1 percent threshold required by CBP and its parent agency, the Department of Homeland Security.

GE Security officials say they are moving ahead with plans to commercialize CommerceGuard, and that the Siemens endorsement indicates there is interest in the product from shippers and carriers with or without approval from CBP.

What's next?

# Smart Box Tests Show Low False Alarm Rates; Other Problems May Arise

Department of Homeland Security officials disclosed that the manufacturer of a security device for detecting door breaches on shipping containers has reduced the false positive alarm rate below the 1 percent threshold required by the US government for its "smart box" program, but other technical difficulties remain to be corrected.

Testing conducted last year by Johns Hopkins University's Applied Physics Laboratory for DHS's Customs and Border Protection division determined that nuisance alarms only occurred on three of one thousand containers—an error rate of 0.3 percent, said Randy Koch, general manager for GE Security, the maker of the container security device (CSD). That is a significant improvement from the 5 percent rate for false alarms the device experienced a year ago. Before GE Security began taking over the product in 2004 from Swedish vendor All Set Marine Security, error rates were as high as 40 percent, according to industry sources at the time.

The third-party testing by CBP validates results GE officials previously reported from their own testing of shipments on GE's internal trade lanes.

"The big news is that the false positive rate has been fixed. We have a 99.7 percent success rate," Koch told Shippers

NewsWire. "That's the most complex function of the CSD. That's the toughest part of the CSD to crack."

About a dozen major importers, who participated in the tests by letting CBP and GE outfit their shipments with the device, were briefed by DHS and GE officials on the results during a meeting at Johns Hopkins' Washington campus. The companies all belong to the Customs-Trade Partnership Against Terrorism, and have a vested interest in the results because CBP has made the development of a tamper-evident "smart box," a key component of its plan to create a no-inspection "green lane" for its trusted shippers who use the device and take other supply chain security measures.

But CBP and GE still aren't out of the woods. Koch said 4 percent of the container devices had problems with their internal clocks used to place a time and date stamp on each electronic status message transmitted by the device.

The GE device magnetically attaches to the inside of the container and uses an electronic proximity sensor to detect and record when the door is opened. Fixed and handheld readers used at ports and other locations can pick up the short-range radio frequency signal with the identification number and status from the internal transmitter.

Koch said GE has identified software fixes for the clock drift and resetting problems, and plans to have corrections in place in time for CBP to run additional tests.

Another 1.7 percent of container security devices had various problems, such as arming and disarming the devices, that will be corrected by manufacturing improvements when GE moves from the prototype stage to commercial-grade manufacturing with rugged components, Koch said.

GE Security plans to commercially launch its CommerceGuard product this summer, Koch said. The General Electric Co. subsidiary said German conglomerate Siemens will market and distribute its CommerceGuard device in Europe and other markets. Koch said customers are demanding the device for their own purposes ahead of any government standards for securing containers.

"We probably will not use it anytime soon. We have to see what is going to happen," said Sandra Fallgatter, a customs compliance manager for J. C. Penney, who attended the smart box briefing.

So far, CBP has limited testing to the CommerceGuard product, but CBP officials indicated that their goal is to evaluate multiple devices, Fallgatter said.

"It sounded like they were not committing to the GE CommerceGuard program," she said.

CBP officials indicated they are considering giving a similar update on the smart box issue during the agency's C-TPAT seminar in Costa Mesa, California, Fallgatter said.

How smart is that?

# Secure Freight, Michael Jackson, and Puke?

Believe it or not, the below press release is from real sources, not *The Onion*...

The United States is boosting the concept of a neutral global shipping database that international trading partners could draw on to improve supply-chain security. Michael Jackson, deputy secretary of homeland security, laid out the broad terms of a so-called secure freight initiative at Customs and Border Protection's Sixth Trade Symposium.

The initiative would charge a private-sector entity with gathering shipping data covering the supply chain from purchase order and fulfillment to delivery. International trading partners could then draw on the common operating platform "data fusion center" for their own risk-management needs.

The database would build on existing programs such as Customs' Automated Commercial Environment, Jackson said. He said a for-profit or nonprofit private entity is preferred, because the US government "is no good at developing new, nimble technology."

Jackson proposed an initial pilot program to be set up between two or more counties, and said he has talked to other governments about the project. He would not identify the countries. "This is a fundamental philosophical jump from where we are today," Jackson said. **"But we can't do it as a bunch of government pukes on our own nickel."**

I'm not really sure what concerns me more...the fact that there may be one, for-profit, entity out there that could be the gatekeeper for every last bit of supply chain metadata? Or the fact that a senior US government official actually used the term "puke" in an official press statement!

# Chapter 10

*When you consider supply chain solutions, that are within physical fulfillment platforms, the right price is rarely the lowest price.*

**Patrick Kelleher**

# Spend Money to Save Money!

**Short-term Perception:** Today's lean manufacturing environment, shaped by just-in-time stocking and razor-thin margins, has made the use of premium freight a daily reality for manufacturers.

Though once used only on occasion to protect plants, shipping goods via premium freight is now a regular occurrence. While this shipping method can be expensive, manufacturers that incorporate premium freight as part of their overall logistics plan are able to create new efficiencies and cut costs.

For years, the use of premium freight was viewed as a "the last resort" of the supply chain. Even today, many manufacturers see utilizing premium freight as an admission of inefficiencies.

As efforts to eliminate the practice have revealed, premium freight is not always a by-product of poor manufacturing processes or inefficient supply chains. Logistics challenges currently facing manufacturers—including rapid product launches, an ever-increasing focus on lean inventories to reduce warehousing costs, and the need to develop efficient global supply chains—confirm premium freight's position as a necessary business practice.

Companies that include premium freight as part of their overall logistics strategy develop solutions that enable the supply chain to function seamlessly without forcing significant spending on a small amount of premium shipments. Using premium freight in this way gives companies a unique competitive advantage because it helps cut costs and ensure projects are completed near- or under-budget, and on time.

**Long-term Strategy:** Using premium freight should be viewed not as a day-to-day tactical decision, but as part of a long-term transportation strategy. Decisions regarding premium shipments that were made on the plant floor now garner the attention of top executives, who look closely at expenses and strategize with plant-level decision makers on cost-cutting methods.

In addition, the impact of premium freight has significantly changed these executives' views on whether or not to keep their plants running at all times. In the past, the mantra was: Whatever the cost, keep the plant running. With a strategic focus on premium freight as part of the long-term logistics strategy, executives are on top of issues that previously may have forced a plant to shut down to preserve cost efficiency.

Premium freight expenses are often contained within general inbound or outbound freight budgets, and are not singled out as separate line items. Looking at these budgets in a holistic fashion, however, reduces manufacturers' ability to identify fixes that ultimately reduce costs and create efficiencies.

By investigating premium freight occurrences, and taking the time to break out the causes and expenses associated with these shipments, companies often find an untapped area for cost savings. Because a premium freight strategy enables transportation flexibility, manufacturers increasingly view their outsourced logistics providers as partners. Openly sharing information and examining ways to eliminate inefficiencies within an ubiquitous supply chain has become commonplace.

This heightened level of trust has brought about strategic and collaborative efforts among manufacturers, suppliers, 3PLs, 4PLs, and service providers.

The result? More effective process planning, system design, and integration, which culminates in uninterrupted supply chains and hard cost savings.

# Supply Chain Visibility
# Not Just for Cargo

The globalization of commerce has made it necessary for companies both large and small to have a worldview—a big-picture, global perspective that helps them see the possibilities for their business in their entirety. It's particularly essential for manufacturers whose markets demand that they source from overseas.

A US apparel company might source fabric from China, manufacture garments in Vietnam, send them to Italy for customer design work, then ship final product to a stateside warehouse for retail delivery. There's no pulling off that complex, unbelievably urgent piece of multiparty commerce without a worldview—and some fairly sophisticated logistics technology.

Pulling it off in an economical way—and I mean economical in *every* sense—comes down to far more than technology. It comes down to having a worldview of the supply chain, a view that extends well beyond the physical means of moving products and considers the impact the supply chain has on corporate finance.

Technology is a good place to start, though. The need for advanced IT solutions may seem obvious, but The Aberdeen Group's research suggests that a surprising number of companies still have a long way to go when it comes to having the kind of sophisticated global supply chain technology that can help them make crucial and timely financial decisions.

According to *EyeForTransport*'s 2010 "*Fortune 500* Supply Chain & Logistics Challenges Report," many *Fortune 500* companies report their global supply chain technology is inadequate to provide the kind of timely information required for budget and cash flow planning. They've got cargo visibility but no fiscal visibility, if you will.

The global supply chain has been relatively ignored because it traditionally has been a small part of a company's business mind-set. The world has changed, though, and companies now realize that neither their IT systems nor their fiscal models are set up to support globalization.

With international sourcing growing at a rapid clip, companies have been caught off guard and are now scrambling to close the technology gap. Without fiscal models to account for costs throughout these systems, and, in most cases, without additional staff, global supply chain managers face the daunting task of managing this activity using makeshift systems, faxes, and phones.

Because the supply chain technology void affects logistics managers' ability to deliver crucial financial data, some CEOs and CFOs have noticed and are now joining the technology crusade. This may open a window of opportunity for logisticians who can tie technology investments to a business case outside the supply chain in order to secure needed funding for global commerce tools.

After a company decides to invest in technology, the next question is whether to develop solutions in house or partner with a technology or logistics provider. According to The Global Institute of Logistics Global IT Council, organizations are increasingly choosing to forego proprietary solutions and seek outside help.

Up-front investment and implementation costs are primary factors. Maintenance is another. So is speed to market. Most supply chain departments don't have the budget to buy external technology, and multiparty, collaborative practices are not a core competency. They also can't be confident that the technology solution they build today will support their needs five years from now. They need to be able to combat supply chain inefficiencies now and into the future.

How do they do it? By having fiscal visibility *within* their supply chains.

It's unrealistic to try to solve every problem at once. For most organizations, achieving fiscal supply chain visibility should be both the immediate and ultimate goal, and it can be accomplished in steps.

First, pinpoint the area of the global supply chain that can benefit the most from a quick technology upgrade and make that change. Keep in mind that technology is not the magic fix for global logistics problems. Technology for technology's sake is nothing. It has to be accompanied by skilled people and efficient processes in order to work. That may make it a larger investment, but it will reduce risk and improve return.

The next and most important step is to fiscally account for the total supply chain—not just international inbound or domestic distribution, but every aspect from purchase order to point of purchase (PO to POP). Fiscal visibility, from PO to POP, is the essence of supply chain efficiency. It quickens cycle times and reduces inventory investment. It also draws interest and excitement from CFOs, who invariably come knocking on logisticians' doors asking, "What's next?"

# Bean Counting and Logistics Costs Don't Add Up!

Does your company actually have true fiscal visibility throughout the supply chain? Many claim they do...very few really do...what should you do?

Supply chain management (SCM) is one of the key drivers in today's business world with offshore sourcing, foreign competition, and global markets. The responsiveness required to keep the inbound supply chain flowing with materials and products and to keep store shelves filled is demanding. SCM requires reducing costs, increasing inventory velocity, and compressing cycle time; and some say these three may not be compatible or consistent.

Doing all this and "doing it well" takes creativity and management skill. However, there is a factor that limits the design, development, and implementation of such supply chains. That factor is **accounting** (i.e., bean counting), and how it recognizes, and treats, logistics costs.

My view is that accounting is an impediment for logistics, whether for supply chain management, both international and domestic, for lean, or for outsourcing. This is a fact, not because of accountants, but because companies simply do not understand how to fiscally account for their supply chain!

Generally accepted accounting principles create the foundation so that every company reports its financial data the same way. Or so they say...

This financial snapshot is consistent, then, from firm to firm (or it should be). Hence, this makes possible the analysis of the data and comparisons.

These accounting standards have a long history. They date back to Henry Ford and the Model A. Companies then may have been vertically integrated with a primary focus on domestic sales, sourcing, and production. This business model has become nearly extinct, especially for large companies that source internationally. As a result, accounting rules have not kept up with present business operations and practices.

Some differences with supply chain management and accounting are:

**Process versus Transactions**
SCM flows across the organization. As a process, it flows across many of the organization's departments and boundaries. Accounting is transaction oriented, with its focus on identifying and summarizing vertical sales and make-or-buy activities.

**Organization Direction**
Supply chain management is horizontal and crosses departments and organizational boundaries. Transactions are vertical and are consistent with organization silos.

**Scope**
SCM extends into suppliers and logistics service providers to gain inventory velocity and to reduce cycle time. Accounting stays within the company facilities and boundaries, and looks inward.

**Outward or Inward**
Supply chain management looks both inward and outward to deal with suppliers, transport firms, warehouses, and other

logistics service providers. Collaboration is important when managing the complex, global supply chain. Accounting is traditional and focuses within the corporate boundaries.

## Continuous versus Discrete
SCM is ongoing. Product is always flowing. Accounting looks at different summaries, which create supply chain disconnects. Logistics costs are organized individually, not recognized at all, or recognized in different places.

For example, freight and warehouses show on the income statement and are recapped monthly.
Inventory appears on the balance sheet and is presented annually.

**ARRRGH! I am already driving myself nuts with this topic! Just think what it's like in a multinational organization!**

So three key logistics elements are dissected and shown in different financial reports!

And nowhere does "actual time," a vital business driver and the action that creates inventory and service, appear on any financial statement. Add time and, to a great extent, this view of logistics costs makes accounting obsolete for supply chain management.

## Dynamic versus Static
Supply chain management is constantly changing—as suppliers, customers, plants and warehouses, shipment sizes and order mix, and store locations change. This contrasts with accounting, which has the historical perspective of what has already happened.

As a result, accounting does not understand changes in transportation costs, for example, because of changes in the distance inbound and outbound shipments must travel, or in the shipment size or in the mix of commodities being shipped. Or, for the time it takes...

These differences make it difficult to develop meaningful performance metrics for supply chain management that are recognized in the board room and that are aligned with the company strategic plan. Financial metrics, while commonly used, have limited application to supply chain management performance improvement.

For example, inventory velocity, inventory turns, and inventory yield maximization (all time related) are important to achieving the best returns on inventory and on the capital that it represents.

Cycle time, from purchase order to sale or time within the total supply chain, is a measure of company performance with strong bottom-line implications. Yet none of this is part of traditional accounting measures, which are rooted in the past. What about the present? What about the future?

Today's business world is focused on the customer. The perfect customer order is a key performance metric for gaining and maintaining customers and for achieving deeper customer penetration. These are not standard, traditional financial measures!

Similarly developing unique supply chain programs that differentiate by A versus B versus C inventory, or by customer, or by product family segment, or any other delineator are not supported by accounting!

**Financial standards do not readily recognize such stratifications.**
Sourcing right decisions are also restricted by accounting, which has blinders as to the potential impact of the

outsourcing decision on the company and transforming its processes, operations, and results.

These limitations also impact the success of lean program development and lean success. Waste and non-value-added actions do not conform to traditional accounting. As a result, time and inventory waste identification run counter to how accounting sees these manufacturing and supply chain processes and subprocesses.

Incremental and continuous improvement with its flow and pull are part of adapting to the new business model of faster and better…even less expensive. Unfortunately, cost accounting practices are enablers of the old ways, not the new ways of business and business models.

Accounting professionals have recognized the limitations of accounting in today's business. Activity-based costing is one way they try to adjust to the new world. But ABC is not incorporated into income statements and balance sheets, which still reflect an antiquated way of summarizing business financials and performance. Frankly, most of the old boys on the board wouldn't know how to read or interpret this new fiscal game plan anyway!

At some point, **accounting** must step up and stop band-aiding a bad system. It must redefine, reinvent, and reinvigorate itself…so it can be part of the global business world.

Until that happens, companies will continue not to properly measure and improve their performance, operations, and results. Their supply chains will be fragmented…just as their outdated financial documents are.

# Total Landed Cost Versus Supply Chain Reality

Total landed cost is the sum of all costs associated with making and delivering products to the point where they produce revenue—usually your customer's door.

So, if you employ tactics to reduce costs in all discrete functions from manufacturing through delivery, you'll have a lower total landed cost, right? Theoretically, yes. But in the real world, cost savings in one area often result in cost increases in another.

Raw materials and freight are cheaper in volume, for example. But warehousing and inventory costs go up when that volume lands on your dock. Conversely, show me a warehouse that operates on just-in-time deliveries, and I'll show you a high freight bill.

To find the lowest total landed cost, you have to think strategically. Rather than view your supply chain as a series of discrete functions, think of it as a whole. Your goal is to reduce the cost of that whole.

This approach helps you think outside the box. Rather than focus on lower warehouse costs, for example, you begin to wonder if you need that warehouse at all. That idea, in turn, sets off a chain of thoughts: transportation changes, stable inventory, different sources of raw material, origin warehousing, EC versus WC flow centers…you get the picture.

Once you've conceived a strategic approach for lowering total landed cost, it's time to model it. Spreadsheets are cumbersome, and modeling software is expensive and has a steep learning curve, so outsourcing the development of your model is often your best bet. Yeah, being from Kontane Logistics, I like that option the best!

When choosing someone to develop the model, look for an expert in supply chain design and operations, not just a techie who knows how to drive the software. You need someone who can create solutions from practical logistics experience—i.e., find a solid organization with lots of real-world experience.

It's good to run various "what-if" scenarios. Don't simply model a preconceived solution and accept the result. If you have a supply source in China, for example, run a model that compares it to a source in the United States. This tests and quantifies the trade-offs between a longer chain that has lower unit costs but greater inventory, and a shorter chain with less inventory but higher unit costs. (Yep, going back to my "outsource in West Virginia" quote.)

It's also good to run sensitivity analyses to determine how robust the model's design is. Test it by modeling transportation costs against oil prices, or a total disruption in your supply chain, such as a port strike. What are your options in those situations? In these times, be as creative in the doom and gloom scenarios as possible. Seems reality is scarier than our collective imaginations now.

As you might guess, a model's quality depends on the quantity and quality of the data it is built upon. Models are also time-dependent: The more complex your supply chain, the longer it takes to develop a model. The potential savings, however, are great; typical companies save 6 percent to

12 percent. Let me rephrase that: Most companies could save around 5 percent.

Adapting the model with a successful process in hand, and continuing focus on the total landed cost, you can put on your tactical hat and fuss over discrete tactical functions. Work the supply chain backward from the customer, one function at a time—keep in mind that every supply chain process or function you compromise from the model affects other processes, either positively or negatively.

Remember that supply chains are perpetually changing, so the right model today can easily be wrong tomorrow. A new product introduction, a different vendor, increased freight costs, new sourcing areas—these all impact your total landed cost strategy.

The good news is that a strategy is easier to modify than to create. The model you used to finalize the first approach will still be there to tinker with. It is ever-changing, but why not select a 3PL to sort this out under a continuous improvement program that is always driving out costs? The 3PLs have IT, operations, and engineering professionals that are at the ready to model, create scenarios, and tweak your supply chain! Give them a chance by sharing some info and an idea for the future. See where they can take it.

# Chapter 11

*There is an art and a science to supply chain logistics.*

**Christopher Jarvis**

# Automate Your Warehouse!

Competitive business environments require companies to lower their operating costs and increase productivity just to survive. However, many companies are reluctant to upgrade their computer system because of a past bad experience, and/or to not incur additional expenses.

Great tools and technologies exist, but fear of change prevents some manufacturers, distributors, and retailers from making the cultural change that's needed to use a new technology and to improve their operation. What they fail to realize is that having an aging platform will result in higher operating costs, along with excess inventory in the warehouse. This will decrease the bottom line profit of your organization.

The story goes like this: A company will not trust software houses due to previous bad experiences, and will inform most providers that the only reason they will see your organization is because a consultant recommended the meeting.

Discussing real business issues resulting from this outdated platform can be summarized via these three major issues:

**1. Wrong credit issued:** Rather than invoicing one million dollars to a major chain store, the computer issued a credit instead. The accounting department did not catch the mistake in time and it took nine months to get the money credited back and the invoice paid.

**2. Inventory issues:** Having an unautomated warehouse resulted in poor inventory control, incorrect shipments, and massive returns. When new inventory was received, shelves were consolidated and the computer records were not properly updated. This resulted in inventory being misplaced and new inventory being bought. As a result of these issues, the company ended with two million dollars in excess inventory that cannot be sold. This inventory will have to be sold on the Web in a "fire sale," trying to salvage as much as possible.

**3. Charge backs:** It's common to get fifty thousand dollars for "charge backs" from major department stores due to incorrect shipments and EDI errors.

If any of the above business problems seem all too familiar to you, don't worry—there is light at the end of the tunnel. Poor invoicing, excess inventory issues, charge backs, and many other unnecessary business consequences can be a thing of the past. But you must first learn to embrace a cultural technological change and invest for the future. This includes automating your warehouse.

## Upgrade Your Warehouse—This Will Reduce Operating Costs and Improve Your Bottom Line Profit

Computer software in the warehouse is one of the most crucial areas of investment and opportunity for savings. Not having an automated warehouse will result in additional personnel, higher labor costs, misplaced inventory, incorrect shipments and high rates of returns. Often the misplaced inventory will not be found until the next physical inventory. This will result in excess inventory that may be obsolete when found, and will be bound for the outlet store or clearance retailer.

## Positive aspects to automating your warehouse:

1. Newly received inventory is scanned and your computer files are updated in **"real-time mode,"** resulting in instant data availability.

2. **Consolidating shelves** will be easier and more efficient as your "real-time" computer files will reflect both the consolidated and new inventory location and quantity. **Dynamic slotting**...if you don't know the term by now, you better read up.

3. You will be able to **find misplaced inventory** and prevent it from "collecting dust," and get some inventory to the discounter quicker.

**4. Shipping mistakes and returns will be reduced,** as picked inventory gets scanned for accuracy. At the staging area, before being packed, it gets scanned and verified, confirming that the correct products and quantities are being shipped to the right customer.

**5. Labor costs will be dramatically reduced.** Since automating your warehouse will create a more efficient and effective inventory environment, you can quickly reduce the size of your inventory management department.

**6. Forecasting** can finally be done, so your order quantities will be based on real historical data, not wild guesses.

Nobody likes change, but today's reality dictates being as efficient as possible. As we have discussed before, the tools and technologies exist to make your business life easier. You must also add to this mix good people and solid processes.

Higher operating and labor costs, poor invoicing and mismanaged inventory operations, and other unnecessary business disruptions that affect your bottom line can be a thing of the past.

# Rockin' Your DC with Pick Zone Punches!

Nothing is more frustrating for DC managers than seeing unused, dust-covered pallets wasting away in a prime picking zone.

Those one thousand Rock 'Em, Sock 'Em Robots your buying department purchased a decade ago, for example, take up valuable space. Being greeted by the blue and red robots every morning for the past ten years is a reminder that proper storage slotting is essential.

Here are some strategies to consider for maintaining a lean storage profile in your DC operation.

### Eliminate the Cause

Work with your organization's buyers regularly and strengthen communication—make them partners in the inventory storage process. Have buyers visit the DC at least once each quarter and show them the wasted space devoted to unused products. Buyers often better understand the process after seeing the raw storage space their items require.

Another effective trick is to do a quick study on the buyers' behalf. (They are often too busy ordering the next "hot" item to look back on previous bad purchasing decisions.) Run a report on how many Rock 'Em units were sold during a three-month peak season, and extrapolate that across all the units stored in the DC.

Present buyers with a graph showing the number of units and the years of inventory those units represent. Use decades or even centuries if years don't cut it! Then, forecast how many future generations of Rock 'Em, Sock 'Em Robots enthusiasts you'll need to serve (by the way, I am one, if you must know).

Add captions to the graph highlighting compelling factors about how the products will hold up over time. Use boldface type with words like **"POW!" "BANG!" "SMASH!" and "CRASH!"**

### Smart Slotting

Classically trained DC managers have been taught to focus on reducing travel time for pickers when slotting inventory. But some key considerations are absent in this philosophy.

DC managers typically have insufficient open slots to profile product the way they desire; more than 60 percent of DCs were operating at greater than 95 percent capacity during their three busiest months, according to a 2005 industry survey. Instead, managers choose the best available open slots.

At their peril, few warehouses have proactive reslotting programs that continually shuffle pick locations. Sales constantly change and your facility has to be a living, breathing reflection of that fact. The less open space you have, the more critical it is to achieve. Reslot inventory in the off-peak season if you don't have time for a regular reslotting routine.

### Strategies That Work

One company, for example, freed up several hundred active carton pick slots by keeping one unit in each bin and palletizing dead carton stock mixed onto bulk pallets in remote locations. The labor to potentially break the pallet for future picks—which may never happen—was more than offset by gaining valuable prime picking slots.

Many warehouses use product velocity codes—a value of the inventory turn, or cube and turn of a product—but few have location velocity codes or zones. To keep it simple, DC managers should assign location velocity codes within prime picking areas, such as the first rack in the shipping zone, away from dead storage areas such as a mezzanine overhead location.

But that's not the only element to consider when assigning slots. Basic rules such as utilizing prime pick areas—fondly called gold zones—with high-volume picks and placing rarely ordered products deep within your storage dungeon are basic rules of engagement on the war against inventory fluff. "Gold zone" is a tired term…can we not find a better one in the twenty-first century?

Many operations slot inventory based on "cubic velocity." The concept is sound and works well for some warehouses.

Using the dimensions of each SKU—length, width, and height—establish a product's cube and multiply that result by a "pick velocity" factor, or the number of trips a picker makes to a product's location. Cubic velocity may differ from sales volumes if you bulk pick or run multiple waves. Just use sales numbers if you want to keep it simple.

The next step is to sort SKUs and assign them to location velocity codes. Don't forget about clustering products that are ordered together—keep the Rock 'Em, Sock 'Em Robots with, say, Twister close by.

### Don't Forget Handling
The most common factor omitted in slotting strategies is material handling—too many companies forget to evaluate

downstream handling. Companies often store heavy, dense products next to light, crushable products with comparable product velocity codes. The result? DC workers have to lift and move heavy products multiple times before orders can be shipped.

Workers have to rehandle heavy products to build symmetrical, stable pallets that protect fragile products from being crushed. The solution to this challenge is inspired by, of all things, the Jolly Green Giant.

Case-picking operations performing pallet picks should build a theoretical Jolly Green Giant pallet—a giant pallet with every SKU in the distribution center that does not have to be rehandled before shipping.

Assign SKUs within zones based on this theoretical pallet build. Heavy items go in primary pick locations, lowest to the ground. Though this setup might increase travel time, it offsets that by reducing handling during labeling, quality control, packing, and shipping.

Finding the right balance between location maintenance, material handling, and optimizing cube is a fine line. Integrate slotting as part of your weekly goals and you will be amazed at the productivity gains you can accomplish each month.

If you don't, you may just feel like one of those Rock 'Em, Sock 'Em Robots when he takes a good punch on the chin! BAM!

# You Can Pick Your Friends, You Can Pick Your...Why This Is All About Picking Operations!

Companies often think their picking operation is efficient as long as products roll out on time and customers are happy. But most picking operations in warehouses across America could use a reorganization, and it's all about the process you know...and training and people and systems!

**1. Profile your orders.** Your most popular SKUs likely change with the seasons, so reslot your warehouse to accommodate your business model, and review the setup at least once a year. This ensures that your "A" SKUs are in the correct storage media and physical location, reducing unnecessary travel for your order pickers. A good WMS should have a dynamic "slotting" tool within its platform.

**2. Analyze your current picking methodology.** Make sure your picking methodology suits your organization. Whether you choose single order, multiorder, batch picking with a single picker, or zone picking, the correct picking methodology is critical for optimizing productivity. Hey, you can always ask Kontane Logistics to analyze it!

**3. Use software to sequence orders.** Sequencing your orders by pick path, and batching together single lines, same-zone orders, and difficult picks—such as nonconveyable picks—saves tremendous time on the DC floor. Software can help organize the workflow and optimize system performance.

**4. Create a warehouse within a warehouse.** You can gain tremendous efficiency by grouping together the 20 percent of your SKUs that complete 80 percent of your orders. This cuts down on travel time for your pickers. Be sure, however, that the 80/20 area or zone is properly designed to accommodate high-volume activity. You know, this is kind of old-fashioned BS…in this day and age of the Long Tail, you may not have the ability to utilize the 80/20 rule because you may be selling "few of many," instead of "many of few"!

**5. Evaluate your storage equipment to ensure proper application.** Placing slow-moving, low-cube items in bin shelving, and fast-moving items in carton/pallet flow—or other appropriate storage options—improves storage density and picker productivity. This also allows you to better utilize the DC's cube. Seasonality and promos can mess with this idea, so be aware.

**6. Create "wheelhouse" zones in your picking area.** You can increase picking productivity and improve order picker ergonomics by slotting your fastest-moving SKUs in the waist-to-shoulder or "wheelhouse" area of your storage media.

**7. Designate only two or three standard shipping cartons.** With only two or three boxes to choose from—plus a few custom sizes, if necessary—pickers will put orders together faster. Cutting down on sizes optimizes freight expenses and reduces corrugated spending. It also makes it easier to support a pick-path methodology.

**8. Consider automation.** Order pickers spend about 60 percent of their time walking product or moving product around. Consider an automated solution, such as conveyance, to reduce their extensive travel time. Multilevel pick towers could also save travel time.

**9. Understand your technology options.** Plenty of options are available to increase efficiency, including bar codes, RF, pick-to-label, pick-to-light, and voice-activated technologies. These technologies are designed to provide different levels of increased picking productivity and improved accuracy.

**10. Implement an incentive program for pickers.** Incentive programs can be extremely valuable to an organization. To ensure your program is effective, you must guarantee that productivity measurements are accurate, fair, and equitable. Use the KPIs to drive productivity.

Lastly, outsource with a 3PL. We've got all of the above covered and more...it's just a phone call away!

# Garbage in, Garbage out—Data Formats Are Crucial

The purpose of any automatic identification and data collection (AIDC) system is to provide a quick and accurate way to enter data into an IT system. But the old maxim, "garbage in, garbage out," still applies. Without a consistent means to represent data within a bar code, RFID tag, XML, or other form of data exchange, there's no check on the quality of the data entering the system, i.e., technology for technology's sake is a load of wasted time and money!

**You have to fine-tune the process and get your people invested in said process!**

The proliferation of data standards appears to make trading partner data exchange more complex, but standards actually simplify it by establishing known formats that can be easily integrated into your own IT system. Here are ten tips to ensure that trading partner data meets your organization's needs, as well as your upstream and downstream sources.

1. Investigate the data format and structure standards that pertain to your industry and your customers' industries. You have to understand what these standards are before you move forward with your trading partners.

2. Determine whether your customers are aware of existing standards, and if they are capable of using them. Meet with them (duh!); see what they are doing internally and discuss how you can work together to make this happen.

3. Recognize that customers in different industry sectors may require different data standards. GS1 (formerly EAN/UCC), health care, automotive, government, defense, and other industry standards define the structure, content, and special features that are to be used in representing data. This is a maze full of pitfalls...be careful, be aware, be flexible.

4. Learn about the standards that pertain to your data-entry method. Bar codes, for example, are covered by symbology standards that define how a bar code is to be printed. ISO/IEC standards apply to specific applications, and RFID standards are currently being developed. Because these standards may affect the data stream coming from a reader, your organization needs to understand them...as do your clients. Don't take this for granted.

5. Understand that most data standards contain "overhead" characters. These characters are used to ensure that the correct data is entered into the system. Overhead characters should be stripped off before entering the data string into your IT system.

6. Educate IT personnel on the importance of conforming to existing standards. Make sure they are on top of this. Continual training is necessary and required.

7. Insist that your suppliers conform to these standards. You want your IT system to be streamlined and standardized. Compliance is important and required.

8. Become active in all relevant data synchronization activities and AIDC committees. Standardizing product descriptions facilitates data exchange at every level. Knowing what's on the horizon is important both for planning and to help ensure that new standards are in harmony with exist-

ing high-level standards you've implemented. Get engaged, get active!

9. Develop corporate policies to ensure compliance internally and among trading partners. This must come from corporate, or it will be difficult to enforce and implement a streamlined data collection and identification system.

10. Once you've completed #9, **REPEAT!** Be prepared for the evolution of standards as new capabilities and technologies become available.

The evolution will never stop, and your ability to guide your organization is tantamount to long-term success. Get it done! Good luck!

# Warehouse Speed—Forecast, Train, Document, and Communicate

If speeding warehouse operations is one of your goals, obtaining more accurate inventory information should be your first step. It is easier to quickly move orders out of the warehouse if you have accurate, high-quality data on inbound shipments.

**1. Manage inbound orders prior to execution within the warehouse.** This eliminates unnecessary steps. Think beyond merely storing goods and moving orders out of the facility, and develop or implement a system to process customer requirements, carrier requirements, and delivery specifications in advance.

**2. Forecast correctly for demand planning.** Make sure you have the necessary data to plan warehouse operations according to demand. Staffing your warehouse to meet inbound and outbound shipment volume is critical for maximizing warehouse speed.

**3. Slot inventory properly.** Understand which products move frequently through your system, and slot inventory based on demand planning and actual use. This is key for improving warehouse productivity. Having the right product in the right storage media close to receiving and/or shipping locations maximizes operations efficiency.

**4. Consider hiring a logistics engineer.** To best achieve proper storage media and warehouse layout, seek the expertise of a logistics engineer when designing your warehouse, or sign a small consultancy agreement with a reputable 3PL.

**5. Coordinate with your carriers.** Be sure your warehouse management team coordinates with inbound carriers and drayage companies, among others, to ensure staffing is properly aligned with inbound receipts. It is important to have the ability to efficiently move products through your facility and directly into the correct transportation mode.

**6. Train a core group of employees in all warehouse processes.** Having the right employees in the right department to process time-sensitive receipts and/or shipments is crucial.

**7. Document processes.** Managers should document warehouse execution steps so all employees know how to perform their jobs effectively. Create a training manual—it can be either an electronic or paper document, whatever works best for your company.

**8. Utilize a warehouse management system (WMS).** Choosing the right WMS is critical. Make sure the system is not overly robust, which can bog down operations with unnecessary requirements, or too simple, requiring additional manual processes to overcome deficiencies. Research different solutions, solicit RFPs, and make an educated investment.

**9. Invest in radio frequency (RF) equipment.** Placing RF guns throughout the warehouse is key to increasing throughput. Make sure you have the correct number of devices in receiving, putaway, picking, and shipping, as well as ample backup guns for temporary workers to use during busy times.

**10. Make teamwork and communication a priority.** Make sure team members are well informed and prepared to achieve daily goals. Consistent and frequent communication about upcoming events, as well as feedback from front-line leaders and management, is key for responding to the operational changes required to meet customer demands.

You know, you could also **hire yourself a top-notch 3PL** to manage all of the above as well. That may be easier...and when it's all said and done, maybe just a bit cheaper too!

# Chapter 12

*The essence of flexibility is in the mind of the leader;
the substance of flexibility is in logistics.*

**Rear Admiral Henry E. Eccles, US Navy**

# Big Box or Scattershot?
# 3PLs Can Help Both

Companies that are considering outsourcing warehouse operations for the first time should keep several issues in mind. Most important is ensuring that customer service is enhanced, rather than diminished.

Another important consideration is what logisticians call optimized network design—or, more simply, "Where should I locate my outsourced warehouse, how many should I have, and how will this impact the flow of my products?"

**Won't I Lose Control?** An important psychological barrier that any first-time outsourcer must cross is the fear of losing control if internal employees are not running the warehouse.

Let's analyze the "control" issue. If you don't outsource, and it's a slow time at the warehouse, your employees are drinking coffee on your dime. Not so in a cross-utilized third-party logistics (3PL) environment, where labor can be shifted to other contracts during periods of slower activity.

If a major screwup occurs, you can do two things with your own warehouse employees: Scream at them and fire them.

In an outsourced environment, however, you can still scream at the 3PL and fire them but you also have the option of building penalty clauses and gainsharing programs into your contract to ensure that the 3PL pays you if anything out of the ordinary happens. That option is not available using your own labor. In fact, most companies that outsource warehousing operations find they gain more control than they ever had.

**What Kind of Warehousing Should I Outsource?**
Warehouses come in many shapes and differ in their design and operation. Some common warehouse operations include:

**Finished goods**
**Raw materials**
**Direct-to-consumer fulfillment (often for catalogs and Web sites)**
**Vendor-managed inventory (VMI)**
**Returns (reverse logistics)**
**Inbound flow center products (seasonal or slow movers)**

Each type of warehouse is fundamentally different from the next, but in most cases, companies can consolidate several of these functions into one location, rather than operate numerous warehouses around the country.

Although every company's requirements are different, many opt for the "warehouse-within-a-warehouse" function—replenish across the aisle, rather than across the country—to keep customer satisfaction high while avoiding ballooning facility costs.

And, remember, there is a fundamental difference between "public" (multiclient) warehousing for small footprint and/or short-term users, and contract (single-client) warehousing for larger companies with multiyear demand.

**Costs versus Client Happiness**
Two standard examples of the types of companies ripe for outsourcing warehouse operations for the first time are:

**1. Big Box:** These companies operate one or more large warehouses or distribution centers, but don't realize they are using more labor than they need. Big-box companies often use order picking, rather than more efficient zone or wave picking algorithms typically employed by 3PLs to dramatically cut down the required head count.

These companies are delighted to discover that the 3PL needs only eighty workers, instead of the hundred workers the company employed, and that the 3PL will hire their best eighty people. These big-box companies get the best of both worlds: They significantly reduce costs and maintain a trained and right-sized warehouse team.

**2. Scattershot:** These companies scatter inventory around the United States with impunity—placing inventory in a small, public warehouse every time they get a new customer. Then twenty years go by, and now they operate thirty warehouses.

Sound familiar? Sales has told corporate management that they'll lose customers if they don't operate this way. Operations hasn't realized that with the advent of modern logistics concepts, customers can still receive one- to two-day delivery service with a consolidated, optimized small warehouse footprint.

Thirty warehouses can be consolidated into five without disrupting customer deliveries, and costs can be rationalized.

### Will Freight Costs Rise?

Companies now often handle will-call demand with a "hold for pickup" option at the local truck terminal, at a fraction of the cost of expensive public warehousing. Customers are just as happy to go to address A instead of address B.

Third-party logistics providers are standing by to help both big-box and scattershot organizations. Remember, they do this for a living.

Frequently those considering outsourcing will ask: "If I consolidate my warehousing network, won't my freight costs rise because some customers will now be farther away from a warehouse?" Yes, some costs will rise, but others will fall.

Remember, three costs are involved: the freight, of course, but also the capital warehouse expenses, and the labor component to move merchandise to your customers.

Third-party logistics providers are trained to combine all three costs, rather than look at only the cost of transportation, to give you a lower total distribution cost than before you outsourced.

For companies trapped in the "we've always done it this way" mind-set, a whole new world of cost-avoidance opportunities are waiting for you.

And your customers will be right there with you...so will your 3PL. Good luck!

# DC Sites—Location Is Key, but Don't Forget about the People in That Location!

The decision to build a distribution center comes with expectations that it will help a company reach key markets, hire an appropriate workforce, and maximize profitability while minimizing operating costs. Finding that ideal location in a community that embraces the company's operations, however, is more difficult than merely choosing any site within a targeted region.

Location decision is crucial for the long-term success of a business. Factors such as infrastructure, labor costs, proximity to customers and suppliers, and community and site characteristics need to be part of an acceptable model that supports the company's goals and objectives.

**Finding the Right Site**

If a company selects a less-than-optimal site, it may have labor availability problems, ongoing transportation issues, and yearly recurring costs. These issues can be resolved by paying close attention to site selection.

Companies choosing a distribution center location need to consider three key factors to site selection success:

**1. Locating near delivery points cuts transportation costs.** Transportation is one of the most important factors in distribution center logistics. The cost of hauling products from a distribution center to customers and consumers

is based on fuel prices as well as driver and truck maintenance costs, which usually increase annually.

Being in the right location is vital for minimizing transportation costs from a distribution center to retail stores, or
wherever a company's final destination is. Generally, costs
are associated with shipping from the distribution center
to the end user, as opposed to vendors shipping into the
distribution center.

**On the Rail Trail**
Although trucks are often the standard method for transferring goods, many companies desire a location with rail
access to cut shipping costs on large volumes of heavy products that do not require precise delivery times. Businesses
should be prepared for a timing trade-off because delivery
times via rail often are slower and less predictable.

An optimum distribution center location for a major retailer,
for example, needs to best serve its delivery points. Analyzing
its network of existing and planned distribution centers is a
good way for the retailer to determine optimal location. In
the retail business, on-time delivery is crucial, so proximity
to clients and suppliers through highly accessible highways
or rail lines saves time and cuts costs.

In addition to a site's physical location, its internal functions—rack and conveyor systems, and pick-and-pack
solutions—are important. When designed and located
effectively, these systems help increase product flow and
shipping efficiency.

**2. Labor and community acceptance can make or break
a project.** While various markets may meet a company's
transportation needs, it may be harder to find a reliable
and productive labor force. As such, labor force is the foremost community characteristic to identify in site selection.

Firms should also analyze turnover rates because retraining employees increases operating costs.

Most communities will provide a survey outlining the area's wage and benefit rates, which are impacted by geography and the presence of organized labor. Often, incentive packages are offered to businesses that meet or exceed community wage averages.

**Getting a community's support is vital.** When a community is behind a project, everything from permit approvals to the plan's review processes moves faster. Selecting a pro-business community is a definite plus.

The likelihood of increased truck traffic and noise in the area are the most common concerns raised by citizens when firms build new distribution centers. Companies can mitigate these concerns by locating off an interstate and away from residential areas.

The best way to counter misperceptions is to have community leaders speak with officials in an area where the company has successfully located other operations.

**3. Site characteristics impact initial investment and beyond.** Carefully selecting a site location with ideal characteristics minimizes up-front development costs. A fairly flat site that is not environmentally challenged is the best location for a distribution center. Blasting large rocks and mitigating wetlands is expensive and time-consuming. Choosing sites that are free of environmental issues also reduces initial site development costs.

The time it takes to study and resolve environmental issues may influence companies to search in another market. Sometimes, however, they have no choice but to build in an environmentally sensitive area to serve customers.

Companies with short development time frames need sites with existing water, sewer, power, and roadways, but these sites are usually more expensive. If businesses plan far enough in advance, they can leverage communities to provide free or discounted land, and find government incentives that deliver infrastructure at no cost to the company—and can potentially benefit the community.

Increasingly, organizations require fiber optics to receive and transfer data. New technologies run through fiber optics allow companies to set up inventory systems that automatically order items from the distribution center when they are purchased from a store.

From available properties to workforce data to economic development incentives, the Internet has put valuable information at the fingertips of those seeking optimal distribution center locations. Yet attaining the appropriate mix of site characteristics is still complicated by time-consuming research and approvals.

The time and money spent planning and building a distribution center is accurately viewed as a major investment, but choosing the right site will reap positive business performance for years to come.

# Last Chapter—Odds and Ends

*I don't want to sell anything, buy anything, or process anything as a career. I don't want to sell anything bought or processed, or buy anything sold or processed, or process anything sold, bought, or processed, or repair anything sold, bought, or processed. You know, as a career, I don't want to do that.*

**Lloyd Dobler**

# People, Process, and Productivity—Simple!

OK, yes, I know…this is going to sound like a broken record… You don't need the latest ERP package or other SCM software to improve your distribution center operations. True, technology plays its part as an enabler; however, the majority of the savings are found in area often overlooked: **processes (and don't forget those people behind them)!**

As you add on more suppliers, SKUs, and customers who generate more complex order requirements, your organization often works around the complexity that these challenges bring, leading to inefficient processes. The result? Higher error rates, lower productivity, and late orders. Here are three process areas that can improve the situation, and they can be implemented using your current staff.

**Process area #1: Inbound—everything begins here**
Is your inbound area a constant bottleneck? Why? Lack of appointment scheduling, poor pre-receipt planning and documentation, and incorrect purchase order information will bring any dock to a halt.

This is the source of problems that, if not corrected, will precipitate and multiply their effects throughout your operation (exponentially), creating inefficiencies and ultimately affecting your end customer. Eventually, you have to fix the problem (e.g., wrong item shipped) later—adding even more cost. Why not fix the problem the first time around? Do you have documented processes for the following areas?

– **Appointment scheduling**
– **Pre-receipt planning and document preparation**
– **Vehicle arrival and unloading procedures**
– **Quality control procedures**

How well are they followed? Investing time to ensure that your associates are trained and aware of these processes will pay dividends later in the form of decreased credit invoices, fewer damages/returns, and higher profitability.

## Process area #2: Picking—the most costly activity in your operation

Since approximately 50 percent of labor hours are attributed to picking in a typical distribution center, even incremental improvements will have a significant bottom-line impact. The largest component of picking time is travel time (the time it takes for the picker to get to the next pick slot). By reducing the travel time, the picker spends more time picking and less time traveling, thus improving picking productivity. A number of solutions will facilitate this:

– **ABC analysis to identify fast, medium, and slow SKUs to reprofile layout**
– **Introducing flow rack for smaller items to free regular pallet slots**
– **Multilevel picking and shelving for very slow items**
– **Batch picking for small volume orders**

How are new items slotted in the distribution center? Unless there is a defined process, usually everyone is "too busy" to do it properly with the end result being large traveling distances for pickers—and a corresponding loss in productivity.

## Process area # 3: Realistic work productivity standards must be set

One operation I have visited measured productivity as cost per case. While this is an important managerial-level metric, it does not translate well to the distribution center associates. For example, when ten receivers are scheduled in inbound but only seven are available due to illness or holidays, the cost per case will increase (full-time absent workers are still being paid) for that period; however, the productivity may actually increase due to fewer associates dealing with more volume. Thus, management will observe a decrease in productivity when it actually increases during that period. Simple logic that is often ignored, or just plain missed! Consequently, this does not motivate the team to improve.

Instead, it is important to measure cases per hour and set a target for the month. Compare this to last year's actual productivity and year to date. These are meaningful numbers that can, when tied to an incentive program, motivate the team to increase productivity. If you currently use a time and attendance system (TMS), you can easily modify the reporting outputs to include departmental productivity, whether it is inbound, putaway, replenishment, picking, or shipping. Once again, by having a process to measure and monitor productivity properly, realistic expectations can be communicated to all associates.

**Don't forget about your people, people!**
By implementing processes for the above three areas, distribution center operations will run more smoothly despite all the complexity that exists and continues to develop.
You know, it always comes down to people and process

"Lose your ego to lead." Michael J. Stolarczyk

# Value? Technology, People, Process, and Profits!

What primary value do logistics operations by 3PLs bring to their clients? Technology! Building technology capabilities to outsmart traditional logistics competitors within supply chain planning and executing logistics operations will remain center-stage and THE focus in the future.

This subject is also a question that remains in the minds of 3PLs: How do we choose a cost-effective yet productive technology that can serve our company and our customers better?

So, yes, don't worry; I still maintain that people, and process, and then technology drive this equation (don't forget the STAR process)!

Working with asset and non-asset-based 3PLs, 4PLs, carriers (TL, LTL, specialty transportation as in bulk goods in energy, automotive, etc.) and railroads to improve visibility and supply chain integration, we find the need to deliver shipper-facing solutions on the rise substantially.

Taking a tailored-solutions approach also requires that such applications are reliable and can sustain consistent value from operations.
Such strategies yield results and early ROI (return-on-investments) for 3PLs' technology investments.

The next technology application that is critical are tactical tools like 24/7 (shipper portals) tracking, events management, online signed PODs/BOLs, and shipper communication for marked improvements in customer service. All these tools remain factors that help achieve successful business outcomes using technology implementation.

**Some of the most preferred 3PL applications and their advantages include:**

- **Automate rating and bidding to maximize benefits** for your shippers' benefits—on-time deliveries, service levels/price points, and reduced cost per lane. Internally, your operations are transformed to an automated platform that can electronically receive RFQs from shippers, send out bids to carriers and receive their quotes, select/commit to carrier partners for specific lanes upon receiving your authorization—using an integrated workflow for approvals.

- **Optimizing for profitability** while enabling maximum capacity utilization of carrier/fleets and ensure shipper's demand (delivery reliability) fill full truckloads even in LTL situations, helping reduce unused miles and cost-to-serve.

- **Web portals for shipper/carrier management** provide a simple yet universal view of events that happen within your supply chain network, and partners with a logistics planning-to-execution cycle for increased visibility to monitor and control movement of your shipper's freight.

- **Load planning, building, and routing optimization** based on a mathematical modeling technique that delivers assured profitability gains and improved asset utilization for lowering costs, including personnel (workload management) in warehouses/DCs, pools, etc.

- **Automated dispatch to manage on-time deliveries and performance** indicators while reducing operational congestion to absorb impact propagated due to uncertainties or delays. Automated dispatch and scheduling systems offer tremendous productivity, compliance, and efficiency gains for 3PLs.

- **Lower transportation and logistics costs for your customers** by increasing supply chain visibility, inbound and outbound costs from improving operation effectiveness, and maximizing revenue margins from improved utilization of your capacity and fleet.

- **Delivering continuous move** opportunities that help implement supply chain network optimization and attain a supply chain flawless execution to evaluate private fleet decisions.

Some 3PLs say, "Show me the money."

**3PLs can realize returns from technology in the following areas:**

- **Improvements in ratios of their logistics operations**
- **Real-life dispatch productivity**
- **Capacity utilization**
- **Shipper demands serviced online**
- **Costs and revenue management**

Additionally, using an optimized (mathematical model) technology to elevate drivers in key performance improvements can help unlock value (cost savings or increased revenues) and flexibility within 3PL operations while mitigating risks.

**Summary:**

The 3PLs can identify processes and automate them, optimize them within their operations, and firm up on possibilities to realize a step-level business transformation to lead the pack in delivering supply chain benefits to shippers and their businesses using technology.

Oh, yeah...don't forget the people! Hire, train, develop, and foster your people by creating a culture, empower the believers, and SHARE THE SUCCESS!

# Addendum—Geographic Considerations

*Lean forward. It's always better to fall on your face than on your backside.*

**M. Cox**

# Inland Ports versus Coastal Ports

Are you considering using an inland port instead of the usual coastal port? That's a decision many companies are analyzing as they face high fuel and transportation costs, as well as congestion at larger ports. Choosing an inland port may not work for every company, but it can help achieve greater supply chain management success through the use of multiple transportation modes.

**Here are ten tips for evaluating inland ports.**

**1. Consider your transportation needs.** How do you ship your product? Do you use rail, road, water, air, or a combination? See if the inland ports are well connected to these transportation modes. For instance, consider how far the port is from the airport or railway. Align your needs with the port's location.

**2. Do a transportation analysis.** Calculate what you spend now, then project what it would cost to use barge in an inland port system. Moving inland and shipping via barge could save money in the long run. In addition, check out the carrier service offered at the inland port. What kind of barge lines or short-line railroad carriers operate from the port you are considering? Evaluate the carrier service the port offers, whether you have contracts with those carriers, and if they can meet your freight-handling needs.

**3. Analyze the port's location.** Understand the markets you serve and if the port is within close proximity to those markets. Get to know how the port's location can offer both north-south and east-west transportation options. If the port is located along the Inland Waterway System, for example, does it provide access to both the Gulf and the Great Lakes? Does it offer access via road and/or rail to the increasingly popular north-south NAFTA corridor? The inland port could also offer important east-west connections that give your business access to booming coastal freight activity.

**4. Check out the financial incentives.** Many inland ports are attracting business through incentives. Find out if the city or port offers attractive lease rates, bonding ability, or Foreign Trade Zones. Such incentives might make choosing an inland port a good business decision.

**5. Make sure the inland port can meet your delivery needs.** If you run a just-in-time inventory operation, you need to be particularly sensitive to the fact that it could take additional efforts to schedule product inflow and outflow, especially if you use barge transportation. Shipping via barge means you most likely will use several lock and dam systems, which will translate into slower transportation times, despite cost savings. Carefully plan your inbound and outbound transportation. Consider how critical timing is for your operations. How will your delivery method affect your supply chain? Can you efficiently meet your customers' needs? How often will you need expedited freight to handle emergency situations? Will an inland port be the best area from which to service customers and distribute product?

**6. Consider the port's capabilities.** Check if the inland port has the ability to expand and the labor to execute your logistics needs—onloading and offloading products, for instance. Ports are often landlocked. Find out if the inland port can offer adequate space to expand if necessary. Know what freight-handling options are available at the port and their costs. For example, what type of cranes or onloading/offloading capabilities does the port have? Can the equipment already in place be easily used to handle your products? What will it cost? If equipment is not in place, will the port allow you to use the necessary equipment? At what cost? It is vital to know how you can leverage the freight-handling system the port currently uses.

**7. Enlist the help of trade associations.** Utilize existing networks to find help and best practices. The place to start is a trade association or port-focused organization. Check out Inland Rivers, Ports, and Terminals Inc.; the National Waterways Conference; the American Association of Port Authorities; or the Upper Mississippi, Illinois, and Missouri River Association. These organizations offer insight into the port industry and can help you stay abreast of current issues.

**8. Review port management and operations.** Take time to fully assess the port's lease rates and terms. Also determine if the port favors short- or long-term leases, or if you can purchase property at the port and build to your specifications. Investigate what types of shared services—trucking/rail lines, large conference rooms—might be available to your company. Check to see if the port includes you in its marketing materials, and/or gives you a presence on its Web site.

**9. Evaluate the region where the port is located.** Fully examine the business climate—cost of doing business, available workforce, and quality-of-life issues—that you and your employees will find valuable.

**10. Examine the companies currently operating at the port.** Are they satisfied with the port and its operations? Note which companies could complement your business, and vice versa. Having a location in a port, which is often an industrial maritime development park, could serve as a catalyst for your company.

# Will Your China Strategy Get Stung by ASP Technology?

"High-performing Chinese supply chains of the future will integrate today's legacy and server-based applications with future technologies inherent to the Internet..."

## Logistics Technology in China

### Infrastructure Chokepoints and Investments

FY 2009, container volume in China's ports increased over 28 percent (from the previous year) to over 59 million TEUS. The crush of traffic and cargo volume led to massive delays in Shenzhen, Ningbo, and Shanghai, with a spillover effect in all Chinese ports (including, to some degree, Hong Kong).

Annual growth of containerized traffic is expected to be between 20 percent and 30 percent for the next several years (through 2015). It should also be noted that, in 2004, China's import/export containerized volume was over 60 percent of the total volume shipped in Northeast Asia (including Hong Kong), Southeast Asia, and the Indian subcontinent. This means that every China gateway will be a chokepoint, where fast, accurate, and flexible TMS platforms will be needed to stay ahead of the cargo avalanche.

Government officials in Beijing are committed to spend eighty billion US dollars, over the next five years for its "Go West" plan to develop the infrastructure network. They have also committed to expand their national rail network to sixty-two thousand miles, from its current forty-five-thousand-mile level in the same period! Matching investments in the barge and river gateways will also keep pace.

Over the next seven years, more than 150 new vessels will be built, with the majority of them topping the eight thousand TEU capacity. Just three years ago, the top capacity ship on the market was a measly sixty-five hundred TEU!

## Logistics Technology Blueprint for the Future

High-performing Chinese supply chains of the future will integrate today's legacy and server-based applications with future technologies inherent to the Internet. These future platforms will have to manage the movement of product and information from origin to destination.

Collaboration across a network of trading partners, along with empowering individuals to quickly make informed and intelligent decisions on behalf of their clients, is tantamount to long-term success. To accomplish these goals (with speed and reduced cost) will require a strategic technology framework that embraces multiple systems and can readily incorporate new partners, vendors, suppliers, locations, and services.

For the China market, the only way will be an ASP or API solutions, which is the most expedient, cost-effective entry for most vendors and China-focused 3PLs. The core building blocks include:

1) A global data model that uniquely reflects the supply-chain network will provide a single version of "the truth" for customers, suppliers, vendors, and employees worldwide.

2) Future TMS platforms must provide the China market with distinct features and functions (not clones of what is being used in Germany or the United States) to manage

shipment-related tasks like booking, asset management, track and trace, freight auditing, etc.

3) The TMS platform must provide integration technology that ensures the automatic flow of critical information, which triggers processes across applications and partners.

4) The end-user experience must be one of user-friendliness, speed, and accuracy...along with after-sales support that is unmatched and attuned to the China market specifically.

Finally, a Capital Consulting & Management study this year determined that only 20 percent of companies that made investments in supply chain-related software in the last three years were satisfied with their return on investment!

The Chinese market is growing and ready for more ASP solutions as they relate to TMS and logistics. Containerized export/import volumes will continue growing, over 20 percent on an annual basis, for the next ten years. The Chinese government is going to spend billions of dollars to keep pace from an infrastructure perspective as well. The China client base is rich and diversified, with many industry cornerstones (3 PLs, ports, carriers, and vendors).

Everyone has a China strategy, but does it include easy access to all that data via an Internet-based platform? Is your company willing to take the risk? Or will it get stung by the ASP!

# The European Union—A Distribution Primer

So, it's time for a little look at European expansion. Your company is global, and because it is no longer cost-effective to reach international customers from your US operation, you need to open a European distribution center. Finding the best place to locate that hub is key.

The European Union is made up of twenty-five countries, all with their own laws and regulations, some of which are imposed on a European level. You also need to consider language barriers; unique employment, transportation, and warehouse rules; and directives from the European Economic Community.

Before making any decisions, you must carefully weigh a variety of factors that will ultimately focus your decision. Here are some issues to contemplate:

**1. Analyze your company's needs.** The first step in the process is understanding your requirements. Be sure you can answer these questions: How much product is flowing and where is it flowing to? Where is the majority of your European customer base? What are your shipping needs? What products are you shipping: medical, pharmaceutical, food, hazardous materials, garments, or fragile items?

**2. Become familiar with the European Union's demographics and currencies.** The original fifteen EU countries have more mature economies than the ten that joined in May of 2004. Bulgaria and Romania are in discussions to join the EU in the future. Many of the original EU members use the euro, but not all. The United Kingdom and Sweden, for example, use their own currencies.

**3. Check out national employment laws.** Employment laws differ from country to country, which makes it challenging to manage your labor pool. This is especially so under the difficult trading conditions that exist in some countries, such as the employment protection and redundancy costs in France and Germany. Countries such as the UK, with more flexible laws, attract a greater number of companies. The cost of employing the staff also varies among countries, given different pension costs and vacation time, which makes a difference to your total labor amount. This employment information may be difficult to obtain.

**4. Make sure you understand the country's planning laws.** Building regulations change from country to country. In some nations, such as France, a different permit is required for storing chemicals, and new consent is required for storing metals or paper. In most other countries, general storage consent applies. In addition, modern DCs need twenty-four-hour operation, but in some countries, facilities located near a residential area will have restrictions. The inability to operate twenty-four hours a day can substantially inhibit your business.

**5. Learn the EU transport initiatives.** The EU is working to get freight off roads and onto rail and water systems. It has a number of initiatives, such as Marco Polo, TEN-T, and Motorways of the Sea, to encourage this idea. There is also a discussion about charging tolls (mainly in Germany, Belgium, and Holland). It is important to understand these initiatives and how they impact your business. Your decision should favor a location that offers different transportation modes and has access to ports.

**6. Examine transport connectivity and infrastructure.**
Infrastructure is not consistent across Europe. Using rail transport, businesses face track gauge changes entering Spain and Russia as one challenge, but most national railroads are still comfortable in working with their European neighbors. Consider how well your distribution center will link into the transportation system, specifically rail and water.

**7. Know your potential exit strategies.** You must understand the property's sale and leaseback value, and whether or not you will be able to exit the property if your circumstances change. Is the site attractive to another potential buyer? Issues such as remoteness, labor availability, specialization, and connectivity must all be examined. These factors affect the future sale or lease of the DC if you choose to move or leave the country.

**8. Ask about available grant incentives.** In certain economically disadvantaged regions, the government may encourage economic activity through grants, which boost financial investment in the country and its economy. These grants are definitely worth considering, but should not solely drive your location decision.

**9. Understand the European drive time directives.**
Similar to the United States, the EU is reducing the number of hours truck drivers can work before taking a break, and putting limits on the number of hours a driver can work in one week. This substantially limits labor in the market and affects the number, size, and location of the distribution centers companies establish.

**10. Check out property pricing and local taxes.** Rents and investment yields differ across Europe to reflect market maturity. These dynamics change all the time. Countries have different ways of taxing property, which can impact your operations costs.

This is pretty straightforward advice. So, use it as a guide. Right now, the push to source and distribute product from some of the new EU countries is all the rage. The Czech Republic provides one of the best locations (in the heart of all European countries), matched with excellent labor talent and costs. Add the Czech Republic's robust transport infrastructure and you have a well-situated alternative to distribute your product into all of Europe.

The bottom line is do your homework up front, and find people who know the market and understand the complexities to manage your foray into the EU market.

# GLOSSARY

## A

**Abandonment:** The decision of a carrier to give up or to discontinue service over a route. Railroads must seek ICC permission to abandon routes.

**ABB:** *See Activity Based Budgeting*

**ABC:** *See Activity Based Costing*

**ABC Classification:** Classification of a group of items in decreasing order of annual dollar volume or other criteria. This array is then split into three classes called A, B, and C. The A group represents 10 to 20% by number of items, and 50 to 70% by projected dollar volume. The next grouping, B, represents about 20% of the items and about 20% of the dollar volume. The C-class contains 60 to 70% of the items, and represents about 10 to 30% of the dollar volume.

**ABC Costing:** *See Activity Based Costing*

**ABC Inventory Control:** An inventory control approach based on the ABC volume or sales revenue classification of products (A items are highest volume or revenue, C—or perhaps D—are lowest volume SKUs).

**ABC Model:** In cost management, a representation of resource costs during a time period that are consumed through activities and traced to products, services, and customers or to any other object that creates a demand for the activity to be performed.

**ABC System:** In cost management, a system that maintains financial and operating data on an organization's resources, activities, drivers, objects and measures. ABC models are created and maintained within this system.

**ABI:** *See Automated Broker Interface.*

**ABM:** *See Activity Based Management*

**Abnormal Demand:** Demand in any period that is outside the limits established by management policy. This demand may come from a new customer or from existing customers whose own demand is increasing or decreasing. Care must be taken in evaluating the nature of the demand: is it a volume change, is it a change in product mix, or is it related to the timing of the order? *Also see: Outlier*

**ABP:** *See Activity Based Planning*

**Absorption Costing:** In cost management, an approach to inventory valuation in which variable costs and a portion of fixed costs are assigned to each unit of production. The fixed costs are usually allocated to units of output on the basis of direct labor hours, machine hours, or material costs. *Synonym: Allocation Costing*

**Acceptable Quality Level (AQL):** In quality management, when a continuing series of lots is considered, AQL represents a quality level that, for the purposes of sampling inspection, is the limit of a satisfactory process average. *Also see: Acceptance Sampling*

**Acceptable Sampling Plan:** In quality management, a specific plan that indicates the sampling sizes and the associated acceptance or non-acceptance criteria to be used. Also see: *Acceptance Sampling.*

**Acceptance Number:** In quality management, 1) A number used in acceptance sampling as a cutoff at which the lot will be accepted or rejected. For example, if x or more units are bad within the sample, the lot will be rejected. 2) The value of the test statistic that divides all possible values into acceptance and rejection regions. *Also see: Acceptance Sampling*

**Acceptance Sampling:** 1) The process of sampling a portion of goods for inspection rather than examining the entire lot. The entire lot may be accepted or rejected based on the sample even though the specific units in the lot are better or worse than the sample. There are two types: attributes sampling and variables sampling. In attributes sampling, the presence or absence of a characteristic is noted in each of the units inspected. In variables sampling, the numerical magnitude of a characteristic is measured and recorded for each inspected unit; this type of sampling involves reference to a continuous scale of some kind. 2) A method of measuring random samples of lots or batches of products against predetermined standards.

**Accessibility:** The ability of a carrier to provide service between an origin and a destination.

**Accessory:** A choice or feature added to the good or service offered to the customer for customizing the end product. An accessory enhances the capabilities of the product but is not necessary for the basic function of the product. In many companies, an accessory means that the choice does not have to be specified before shipment but can be added at a later date. In other companies, this choice must be made before shipment.

**Accessorial charges:** A charge for services over and above transportation charges such as: inside delivery, heading, sort and segregate, heating, storage, etc. *See also: Upcharges*

**Accountability:** Being answerable for, but not necessarily personally charged with, doing specific work. Accountability cannot be delegated, but it can be shared. For example, managers and executives are accountable for business performance even though they may not actually perform the work.

**Accounts Payable (A/P):** The value of goods and services acquired for which payment has not yet been made.

**Accounts receivable (A/R):** The value of goods shipped or services rendered to a customer on whom payment has not yet been received. Usually includes an allowance for bad debts.

**Accreditation:** Certification by a recognized body of the facilities, capability, objectivity, competence, and integrity of an agency, service, operational group, or individual to provide the specific service or operation needed. For example, the Registrar Accreditation Board accredits those organizations that register companies to the ISO 9000 Series Standards.

**Accredited Standards Committee (ASC):** A committee of the ANSI chartered in 1979 to develop uniform standards for the electronic interchange of business documents. The committee develops and maintains U.S. generic standards (X12) for Electronic Data Interchange. Page 3 of 167

**Accumulation bin:** A place, usually a physical location, used to accumulate all components that go into an assembly before the assembly is sent out to the assembly floor. *Syn: assembly bin*

**Accuracy:** In quality management, the degree of freedom from error or the degree of conformity to a standard. Accuracy is different from precision. For example, four-significant-digit numbers are less precise than six-significant-digit numbers; however, a properly computed four-significant-digit number might be more accurate than an improperly computed six-significant-digit number.

**ACD:** *See Automated Call Distribution*

**ACE:** *See Automated Commercial Environment*

**ACH:** *See Automated Clearinghouse*

**Acknowledgment:** A communication by a supplier to advise a purchaser that a purchase order has been received. It usually implies acceptance of the order by the supplier.

**Acquisition Cost:** In cost accounting, the cost required to obtain one or more units of an item. It is order quantity times unit cost.

**Action Message:** An output of a system that identifies the need for and the type of action to be taken to correct a current or potential problem. Examples of action messages in an MRP system include release order, reschedule in, reschedule out, and cancel. Synonym: exception message, action report.

**Action Plan:** A specific method or process to achieve the results called for by one or more objectives. An action plan may be a simpler version of a project plan.

**Action Report:** *See Action Message*

**Activation:** In constraint management, the use of non-constraint resources to make parts or products above the level needed to support the system constraint(s). The result is excessive work-in-process inventories or finished goods inventories, or both. In contrast, the term utilization is used to describe the situation in which non-constraint resource(s) usage is synchronized to support the needs of the constraint.

**Active Inventory:** The raw materials, work in process, and finished goods that will be used or sold within a given period.

**Active Stock:** Goods in active pick locations and ready for order filling.

**Activity:** Work performed by people, equipment, technologies or facilities. Activities are usually described by the "action-verb-adjective-noun" grammar convention. Activities may occur in a linked sequence and activity-to-activity assignments may exist. 1) In activity-based cost accounting, a task or activity, performed by or at a resource, required in producing the organization's output of goods and services. A resource may be a person, machine, or facility. Activities are grouped into pools by type of activity and allocated to products. 2) In project management, an element of work on a project. It usually has an anticipated duration, anticipated cost, and expected resource requirements. Sometimes "major activity" is used for larger bodies of work.

**Activity Analysis:** The process of identifying and cataloging activities for detailed understanding and documentation of their characteristics. An activity analysis is accomplished by means of interviews, group sessions, questionnaires, observations, and reviews of physical records of work.

**Activity Based Budgeting (ABB):** An approach to budgeting where a company uses an understanding of its activities and driver relationships to quantitatively estimate workload and resource requirements as part of an ongoing business plan. Budgets show the types, number of and cost of resources that activities are expected to consume based on forecasted workloads. The budget is part of an organization's activity-based planning process and can be used in evaluating its success in setting and pursuing strategic goals.

**Activity Based Costing (ABC):** A methodology that measures the cost and performance of cost objects, activities and resources. Cost objects consume activities and activities consume resources. Resource costs are assigned to activities based on their use of those resources, and activity costs are reassigned to cost objects (outputs) based on the cost objects proportional use of those activities. Activity-based costing incorporates causal relationships between cost objects and activities and between activities and resources.

**Activity Based Costing Model:** In activity-based cost accounting, a model, by time period, of resource costs created because of activities related to products or services or other items causing the activity to be carried out.

**Activity Based Costing System:** A set of activity-based cost accounting models that collectively define data on an organization's resources, activities, drivers, objects, and measurements.

**Activity-Based Management (ABM):** A discipline focusing on the management of activities within business processes as the route to continuously improve both the value received by customers and the profit earned in providing that value. ABM uses activity-based cost information and performance measurements to influence management action. *See also Activity-Based Costing*

**Activity Based Planning (ABP):** Activity-based planning (ABP) is an ongoing process to determine activity and resource requirements (both financial and operational) based on the ongoing demand of products or services by specific customer needs. Resource requirements are compared to resources available and capacity issues are identified and managed. Activity-based budgeting (ABB) is based on the outputs of activity-based planning.

**Activity Dictionary:** A listing and description of activities that provides a common/standard definition of activities across the organization. An activity dictionary can include information about an activity and/or its relationships, such as activity description, business process, function source, whether value added, inputs, outputs, supplier, customer, output measures, cost drivers, attributes, tasks, and other information as desired to describe the activity.

**Activity Driver:** The best single quantitative measure of the frequency and intensity of the demands placed on an activity by cost objects or other activities. It is used to assign activity costs to cost objects or to other activities.

**Activity Level:** A description of types of activities dependent on the functional area. Product-related activity levels may include unit, batch, and product levels. Customer-related activity levels may include customer, market, channel, and project levels.

**Activity Network Diagram:** An arrow diagram used in planning and managing processes and projects.

**Activity Ratio:** A financial ratio used to determine how an organization's resources perform relative to the revenue the resources produce. Activity ratios include inventory turnover, receivables conversion period, fixed-asset turnover, and return on assets.

**Actual Cost System:** A cost system that collects costs historically as they are applied to production and allocates indirect costs to products based on the specific costs and achieved volume of the products.

**Actual Costs:** The labor, material, and associated overhead costs that are charged against a job as it moves through the production process.

**Actual Demand:** Actual demand is composed of customer orders (and often allocations of items, ingredients, or raw materials to production or distribution). Actual demand nets against or "consumes" the forecast, depending upon the rules chosen over a time horizon. For example, actual demand will totally replace forecast inside the sold-out customer order backlog horizon (often called the demand time fence), but will net against the forecast outside this horizon based on the chosen forecast consumption rule.

**Actual to Theoretical Cycle Time:** The ratio of the measured time required to produce a given output divided by the sum of the time required to produce a given output based on the rated efficiency of the machinery and labor operations.

**Adaptive Control:** 1) The ability of a control system to change its own parameters in response to a measured change in operating conditions. 2) Machine control units in which feeds and/or speeds are not fixed. The control unit, working from feedback sensors, is able to optimize favorable situations by automatically increasing or decreasing the machining parameters. This process ensures optimum tool life or surface finish and/or machining costs or production rates.

**Adaptive Smoothing:** In forecasting, a form of exponential smoothing in which the smoothing constant is automatically adjusted as a function of one or many items, for example, forecast error measurement, calendar characteristics (launch, replenishment, end of life), or demand volume.

**Advance Material Request:** Ordering materials before the release of the formal product design. This early release is required because of long lead times.

**Advanced Planning and Scheduling (APS):** Techniques that deal with analysis and planning of logistics and manufacturing over the short, intermediate, and long-term time periods. APS describes any computer program that uses advanced mathematical algorithms or logic to perform optimization or simulation on finite capacity scheduling, sourcing, capital planning, resource planning, forecasting, demand management, and others. These techniques simultaneously consider a range of constraints and business rules to provide real-time planning and scheduling, decision support, available-to promise, and capable-to-promise capabilities. APS often generates and evaluates multiple scenarios. Management then selects one scenario to use as the "official plan." The five main components of APS systems are demand planning, production planning, production scheduling, distribution planning, and transportation planning.

**Advanced Shipping Notice (ASN):** Detailed shipment information transmitted to a customer or consignee in advance of delivery, designating the contents (individual products and quantities of each) and nature of the shipment. May also include carrier and shipment specifics including time of shipment and expected time of arrival. *See also: Assumed Receipt*

**After-Sale Service:** Services provided to the customer after products have been delivered. This can include repairs, maintenance and/or telephone support. *Synonym: Field Service*

**Agency Tariff:** A publication of a rate bureau that contains rates for many carriers.

**Agent:** An enterprise authorized to transact business for, or in the name of, another enterprise.

**Agile Manufacturing—**Tools, techniques, and initiatives that enable a plant or company to thrive under conditions of unpredictable change. Agile manufacturing not only enables a plant to achieve rapid response to customer needs, but also includes the ability to quickly reconfigure operations—and strategic alliances—to respond rapidly to unforeseen shifts in the marketplace. In some instances, it also incorporates "mass customization" concepts to satisfy unique customer requirements. In broad terms, it includes the ability to react quickly to technical or environmental surprises.

**Agglomeration:** A net advantage gained by a common location with other companies.

**Aggregate Forecast:** An estimate of sales, often time phased, for a grouping of products or product families produced by a facility or firm. Stated in terms of units, dollars, or both, the aggregate forecast is used for sales and production planning (or for sales and operations planning) purposes.

**Aggregate Inventory:** The inventory for any grouping of items or products involving multiple stock keeping units. *Also see: Base Inventory Level*

**Aggregate Inventory Management:** Establishing the overall level (dollar value) of inventory desired and implementing controls to achieve this goal.

**Aggregate Plan:** A plan that includes budgeted levels of finished goods, inventory, production backlogs, and changes in the workforce to support the production strategy. Aggregated information (e.g., product line, family) rather than product information is used, hence the name aggregate plan.

**Aggregate Planning:** A process to develop tactical plans to support the organization's business plan. Aggregate planning usually includes the development, analysis, and maintenance of plans for total sales, total production, targeted inventory, and targeted customer backlog for families of products. The production plan is the result of the aggregate planning process. Two approaches to aggregate planning exist—production planning and sales and operations planning.

**Aggregate Tender Rate:** A reduced rate offered to a shipper who tenders two or more class-rated shipments at one time and one place.

**Agility:** The ability to successfully manufacture and market a broad range of low-cost, high-quality products and services with short lead times and varying volumes that provides enhanced value to customers through customization. Agility merges the four distinctive competencies of cost, quality, dependability, and flexibility.

**AGVS:** *See Automated Guided Vehicle System*

**AI:** *See Artificial Intelligence*

**Air Cargo:** Freight that is moved by air transportation.

**Air Cargo Containers:** Containers designed to conform to the inside of an aircraft. There are many shapes and sizes of containers. Air cargo containers fall into three categories: 1) air cargo pallets 2) lower deck containers 3) box type containers.

**Airport and Airway Trust Fund:** A federal fund that collects passenger ticket taxes and disburses those funds for airport facilities.

**Air Taxi:** An exempt for-hire air carrier that will fly anywhere on demand: air taxis are restricted to a maximum payload and passenger capacity per plane.

**Air Transport Association of America:** A U.S. airline industry association.

**Air Waybill (AWB):** A bill of lading for air transport that serves as a receipt for the shipper, indicates that the carrier has accepted the goods listed, obligates the carrier to carry the consignment to the airport of destination according to specified conditions.

**Alaskan carrier:** A for-hire air carrier that operates within the state of Alaska.

**Alert:** *See Action Message*

**Algorithm:** A clearly specified mathematical process for computation; a set of rules, which, if followed, give a prescribed result.

**All-cargo Carrier:** An air carrier that transports cargo only.

**Allocated Item:** In an MRP system, an item for which a picking order has been released to the stockroom but not yet sent from the stockroom.

**Allocation:** 1) In cost accounting, a distribution of costs using calculations that may be unrelated to physical observations or direct or repeatable cause-and-effect relationships. Because of the arbitrary nature of allocations, costs based on cost causal assignment are viewed as more relevant for management decision-making. 2) In order management, allocation of available inventory to customer and production orders.

**Allocation Costing:** *See Absorption Costing*

**Alpha Release:** A very early release of a product to get preliminary feedback about the feature set and usability.

**Alternate Routing:** A routing, usually less preferred than the primary routing, but resulting in an identical item. Alternate routings may be maintained in the computer or off-line via manual methods, but the computer software must be able to accept alternate routings for specific jobs.

**American Customer Satisfaction Index (ACSI):** Released for the first time in October 1994, an economic indicator and cross industry measure of the satisfaction of U.S. household customers with the quality of the goods and services available to them—both those goods and services produced within the United States and those provided as imports from foreign firms that have substantial market shares or dollar sales. The ACSI is co-sponsored by the University of Michigan Business School, ASQ and the CFI Group.

**American National Standards Institute (ANSI):** A non-profit organization chartered to develop, maintain, and promulgate voluntary U.S. national standards in a number of areas, especially with regards to setting EDI standards. ANSI is the U.S. representative to the International Standards Organization (ISO).

**American Society for Quality (ASQ):** Founded in 1946, a not-for-profit educational organization consisting of 144,000 members who are interested in quality improvement.

**American Society for Testing and Materials (ASTM):** Not-for-profit organization that provides a forum for the development and publication of voluntary consensus standards for materials, products, systems and services.

**American Society for Training and Development (ASTD):** A membership organization providing materials, education and support related to workplace learning and performance.

**American Society of Transportation & Logistics:** A professional organization in the field of logistics.

**American Standard Code for Information Interchange (ASCII):** ASCII format - simple text based data with no formatting. The standard code for information exchange among data processing systems. Uses a coded character set consisting of 7-bit coded characters (8 bits including parity check).

**American Trucking Association, Inc.:** A motor carrier industry association that is made up of Sub conferences representing various sectors of the motor carrier industry.

**American Waterway Operators:** A domestic water carrier industry association representing barge operators on the inland waterways.

**AMS:** *See Automated Manifest System*

**Amtrak:** The National Railroad Passenger Corporation, a federally created corporation that operates most of the United States' intercity passenger rail service.

**Animated GIF:** A file containing a series of GIF (Graphics Interchange Format) images that are displayed in rapid sequence by some Web browsers, giving an animated effect. *Also see: GIF*

**ANSI:** *See American National Standards Institute*

**ANSI ASC X12:** American National Standards Institute Accredited Standards Committee X12. The committee of ANSI that is charted with setting EDI standards.

**ANSI Standard:** A published transaction set approved by ANSI. The standards are reviewed every six months.

**Anticipated Delay Report:** A report, normally issued by both manufacturing and purchasing to the material planning function, regarding jobs or purchase orders that will not be completed on time and explaining why the jobs or purchases are delayed and when they will be completed. This report is an essential ingredient of the closed-loop

MRP system. It is normally a handwritten report. *Synonym: delay report*

**Anticipation Inventories:** Additional inventory above basic pipeline stock to cover projected trends of increasing sales, planned sales promotion programs, seasonal fluctuations, plant shutdowns, and vacations.

**Anti-Dumping Duty:** An additional import duty imposed in instances where imported goods are priced at less than the normal price charged in the exporter's domestic market and cause material injury to domestic industry in the importing country.

**Any-Quantity Rate (AQ):** The same rate applies to any size shipment tendered to a carrier; no discount rate is available for large shipments.

**A/P:** *See Accounts Payable*

**Applicability Statement 2 (AS2):** A specification for Electronic Data Interchange between businesses using the Internet's Web page protocol, the Hypertext Transfer Protocol (HTTP). The specification is an extension of the earlier version, Applicability Statement 1 (AS1). Both specifications were created by EDI over the Internet (EDIINT), a working group of the Internet Engineering Task Force (IETF) that develops secure and reliable business communications standards.

**Application Programming Interface (API):** A language and message format used by an application program to communicate with the operating system or some other control program such as a database management system (DBMS) or communications protocol. APIs are implemented by writing function calls in the program, which provide the linkage to the required subroutine for execution. Thus, an API implies that some program module is available in a device to perform the operation or that it must be linked into the existing program to perform the tasks.

**Application Service Provider (ASP):** A company that offers access over the Internet to application (examples of applications include word processors, database programs, Web browsers, development tools, communication programs) and related services that would otherwise have to be located in their own computers. Sometimes referred to as "apps-on-tap", ASP services are expected to become an important alternative, especially for smaller companies with low budgets for information technology. The purpose is to try to reduce a company's burden by installing, managing, and maintaining software.

**Application-to-Application:** The direct interchange of data between computers, without re-keying.

**Appraisal Costs:** Those costs associated with the formal evaluation and audit of quality in the firm. Typical costs include inspection, quality audits, testing, calibration, and checking time.

**Approved Vendor List (AVL):** List of the suppliers approved for doing business. The AVL is usually created by procurement or sourcing and engineering personnel using a variety of criteria such as technology, functional fit of the product, financial stability, and past performance of the supplier.

**API:** *See Application Programming Interface*

**APS:** *See Advanced Planning and Scheduling*

**AQ:** *See Any quantity rate*

**AQL:** *See Acceptable Quality Level*

**A/R:** *See Accounts Receivable*

**ASP:** *See Application Service Provider*

**Army Corps of Engineers**: A federal agency responsible for the construction and maintenance or waterways.

**Arrival Notice:** A notice from the delivering carrier to the Notify Party indicating the shipment's arrival date at a specific location (normally the destination).

**Arrow diagram:** A planning tool to diagram a sequence of events or activities (nodes) and the interconnectivity of such nodes. It is used for scheduling and especially for determining the critical path through nodes.

**Artificial Intelligence:** Understanding and computerizing the human thought process.

**ASC:** *See Accredited Standards Committee of ANSI*

**ASC X12:** Accredited Standards Committee X12. A committee of ANSI chartered in 1979 to develop uniform standards for the electronic interchange of business documents.

**ASCII:** *See American Standard Code for Information Interchange*

**ASN:** *See Advanced Shipping Notice.*

**ASP:** *See Application Service Provider*

**ASQ:** *See American Society for Quality*

**AS/RS:** *See Automated Storage and Retrieval System*

**Association of American Railroads:** A railroad industry association that represents the larger U.S. railroads.

**ASTM:** *See American Society for Testing and Materials*

**ASTD:** *See American Society for Training and Development*

**AS2:** *See Applicability Statement 2*

**Assemble-to-order:** A production environment where a good or service can be assembled after receipt of a customer's order. The key components (bulk, semi-finished, intermediate, subassembly, fabricated, purchased, packing, and so on) used in the assembly or finishing process are planned and usually stocked in anticipation of a customer order. Receipt of an order initiates assembly of the customized product. This strategy is useful where a large number of end products (based on the selection of options and accessories) can be assembled from common components. *Synonym: Finish to Order. Also see: Make to Order, Make to Stock*

**Assembly:** A group of subassemblies and/or parts that are put together and that constitute a major subdivision for the final product. An assembly may be an end item or a component of a higher level assembly.

**Assembly Line:** An assembly process in which equipment and work centers are laid out to follow the sequence in which raw materials and parts are assembled.

**Assignment:** A distribution of costs using causal relationships. Because cost causal relationships are viewed as more relevant for management decision-making, assignment of costs is generally preferable to allocation techniques. *Syn: Tracing. Contrast with Allocation*

**Assumed Receipt:** The principle of assuming that the contents of a shipment are the same as those presented on a shipping or delivery note. Shipping and receiving personnel do not check the delivery quantity. This practice is used in conjunction with bar codes and an EDI-delivered ASN to eliminate invoices and facilitate rapid receiving.

**Atemporal:** independent of, or unaffected by time

**Atemporality:** The theory that time is not a fundamental physical reality as matter, energy, and physical space are. Time exists only when we measure it; time is an "observer effect." *See Observer Effect*

**ATP:** *See Available to Promise*

**ATS:** *See Available to Sell*

**Attachment:** An accessory that has to be physically attached to the product.

**Attributes:** A label used to provide additional classification or information about a resource, activity, or cost object. Used for focusing attention and may be subjective. Examples are a characteristic, a score or grade of product or activity, or groupings of these items, and performance measures.

**Audit:** The inspection and examination of a process or quality system to ensure compliance to requirements. An audit can apply to an entire organization or may be specific to a function, process or production step.

**Audit Trail:** Manual or computerized tracing of the transactions affecting the contents or origin of a record.

**Auditing:** Determining the correct transportation charges due the carrier: auditing involves checking the accuracy of the freight bill for errors, correct rate, and weight.

**Auditability:** A characteristic of modern information systems, gauged by the ease with which data can be substantiated by trading it to source documents and the extent to which auditors can rely on pre-verified and monitored control processes.

**Augmented reality** (AR) is a term for a live direct or indirect view of a physical real-world environment whose elements are *augmented* by virtual computer-generated imagery. It is related to a more general concept called mediated reality in which a view of reality is modified (possibly even diminished rather than augmented) by a computer. As a result, the technology functions by enhancing one's current perception of reality.

**Authentication:** 1) The process of verifying the eligibility of a device, originator, or individual to access specific categories of information or to enter specific areas of a facility. This process involves matching machine-readable code with a predetermined list of authorized end users. 2) A practice of establishing the validity of a transmission, message, device, or originator, which was designed to provide protection against fraudulent transmissions.

**Authentication Key:** A short string of characters used to authenticate transactions between trading partners.

**Autodiscrimination:** The functionality of a bar code reader to recognize the bar code symbology being scanned thus allowing a reader to read several different symbologies consecutively.

**AutoID:** Referring to an automated identification system. This includes technology such as bar coding and radio frequency tagging (RFID).

**Automated Broker Interface (ABI):** The U.S. Customs program to automate the flow of customs related information among customs brokers, importers, and carriers.

**Automated Call Distribution (ACD):** A feature of large call center or "Customer Interaction Center" telephone switches that routes calls by rules such as next available employee, skill-set etc.

**Automated Clearinghouse (ACH):** A nationwide electronic payments system, which more than 15,000 financial institutions use, on behalf of 100,000 corporations and millions of consumer in the U.S. The funds transfer system of choice among businesses that make electronic payments to vendors, it is economical and can carry remittance information in standardized, computer processable data formats.

**Automated Commercial Environment (ACE):** Update of outmoded Automated Commercial System (ACS). It is intended to provide automated information system to enable the collection, processing and analysis of commercial import and export data, allowing for moving goods through the ports faster and at lower cost, as well as detection of terrorist threats.

**Automated Guided Vehicle System (AGVS):** A transportation network that automatically routes one or more material handling devices, such as carts or pallet trucks, and positions them at predetermined destinations without operator intervention.

**Automated Manifest System (AMS):** A multi-modular cargo inventory control and release notification system through which carriers submit their electronic cargo declaration 24 hours before loading. *See 24-hour Rule*

**Automated Storage/Retrieval System (AS/RS):** A high-density rack inventory storage system with un-manned vehicles automatically loading and unloading products to/from the racks.

**Automatic Relief:** A set of inventory bookkeeping methods that automatically adjusts computerized inventory records based on a production transaction. Examples of automatic relief methods are back flushing, direct-deduct, pre-deduct, and post-deduct processing.

**Automatic Rescheduling:** Rescheduling done by the computer to automatically change due dates on scheduled receipts when it detects that due dates and need dates are out of phase. *Ant: manual rescheduling*

**Available Inventory:** The on-hand inventory balance minus allocations, reservations, backorders, and (usually) quantities held for quality problems. Often called "beginning available balance". *Synonyms: Beginning Available Balance, Net Inventory*

**Available to Promise (ATP):** The uncommitted portion of a company's inventory and planned production maintained in the master schedule to support customer-order promising. The ATP quantity is the uncommitted inventory balance in the first period and is normally calculated for each period in which an MPS receipt is scheduled. In the first period, ATP includes on-hand inventory less customer orders that are due and overdue. Three methods of calculation are used: discrete ATP, cumulative ATP with look ahead, and cumulative ATP without look ahead.

**Available to Sell (ATS):** Total quantity of goods committed to the pipeline for a ship to or selling location. This includes the current inventory at a location and any open purchase orders.

**Average Annual Production Materials Related A/P (Accounts Payable):** The value of direct materials acquired in that year for which payment has not yet been made. Production-related materials are those items classified as material purchases and included in the Cost of Goods Sold (COGS) as raw material purchases. Calculate using the 5-Point Annual Average.

**Average Cost per Unit:** The estimated total cost, including allocated overhead, to produce a batch of goods divided by the total number of units produced.

**Average Inventory:** The average inventory level over a period of time. Implicit in this definition is a "sampling period" which is the amount of time between inventory measurements. For example, daily inventory levels over a two-week period of time, hourly inventory levels over one day, etc. The average inventory for the same total period of time can fluctuate widely depending upon the sampling period used.

**Average Payment Period (for materials):** The average time from receipt of production-related materials and payment for those materials. Production-related materials are those items classified as material purchases and included in the Cost of Goods Sold (COGS) as raw material purchases. (An element of Cash-to-Cash Cycle Time).

**Calculation:** [Five point annual average production-related material accounts payable] / [Annual production-related material receipts/365]

**AVL:** *See Approved Vendor List*

**Avoidable Cost:** A cost associated with an activity that would not be incurred if the activity was not performed (e.g., telephone cost associated with vendor support).

**AWB:** *See Air Waybill*


# B

**B2B:** *See Business to Business*

**B2C:** *See Business to Consumer*

**Back Order**: Product ordered but out of stock and promised to ship when the product becomes available.

**Back Scheduling:** A technique for calculating operation start dates and due dates. The schedule is computed starting with the due date for the order and working backward to determine the required start date and/or due dates for each operation.

**Backflush:** A method of inventory bookkeeping where the book (computer) inventory of components is automatically reduced by the computer after completion of activity on the component's upper-level parent item based on what should have been used as specified on the bill of material and allocation records. This approach has the disadvantage of a built-in differential between the book record and what is physically in stock. Synonym: explode-to-deduct. *Also see: Pre-deduct Inventory Transaction Processing*

**Backhaul:** The process of a transportation vehicle returning from the original destination point to the point of origin. The 1980 Motor Carrier Act deregulated interstate commercial trucking and thereby allowed carriers to contract for the return trip. The backhaul can be with a full, partial, or empty load. An empty backhaul is called deadheading. *Also see: Deadhead*

**Backlog Customer:** Customer orders received but not yet shipped; also includes backorders and future orders.

**Backorder:** 1) The act of retaining a quantity to ship against an order when other order lines have already been shipped. Backorders are usually caused by stock shortages. 2) The quantity remaining to be shipped if an initial shipment(s) has been processed. Note: In some cases backorders are not allowed, this results in a lost sale when sufficient quantities are not available to completely ship and order or order line. *Also see: Balance to Ship*

**Backsourcing:** The process of recapturing and taking responsibility internally for processes that were previously outsourced to a contract manufacturer, fulfillment or other service provider. Backsourcing typically involves the cancellation or expiration of an outsourcing contract and can be nearly as complex as the original outsourcing process.

**Back Order:** Product ordered but out of stock and promised to ship when the product becomes available.

**Balance-of-Stores Record:** A double-entry record system that shows the balance of inventory items on hand and the balances of items on order and available for future orders. Where a reserve system of materials control is used, the balance of material on reserve is also shown.

**Balance of Trade:** The surplus or deficit which results from comparing a country's exports and imports of merchandise only.

**Balance to Ship (BTS):** Balance or remaining quantity of a promotion or order that has yet to ship. *Also see: Backorder*

**Balanced Scorecard:** A structured measurement system developed by David Norton and Robert Kaplan of the Harvard Business School. It is based on a mix of financial and non financial measures of business performance. A list of financial and operational measurements used to evaluate organizational or supply chain performance. The dimensions of the balanced scorecard might include customer perspective, business process perspective, financial perspective, and innovation and learning perspectives. It formally connects overall objectives, strategies, and measurements. Each dimension has goals and measurements. *Also see: Scorecard*

**BAM:** *See Business Activity Monitoring*

**Bar Code:** A symbol consisting of a series of printed bars representing values. A system of optical character reading, scanning, and tracking of units by reading a series of printed bars for translation into a numeric or alphanumeric identification code. A popular example is the UPC code used on retail packaging.

**Bar code scanner:** A device to read bar codes and communicate data to computer systems.

**Barge:** The cargo-carrying vehicle used primarily by inland water carriers. The basic barges have open tops, but there are covered barges for both dry and liquid cargoes.

**Barrier to Entry:** Factors that prevent companies from entering into a particular market, such as high initial investment in equipment.

**Base Demand:** The percentage of a company's demand that is derived from continuing contracts and/or existing customers. Because this demand is well known and recurring, it becomes the basis of management's plans. *Synonym: Baseload Demand*

**Base Index:** *See Base Series*

**Base Inventory Level:** The inventory level made up of aggregate lot-size inventory plus the aggregate safety stock inventory. It does not take into account the anticipation inventory that will result from the production plan. The base inventory level should be known before the production plan is made. *Also see: Aggregate Inventory.*

**Base Series:** A standard succession of values of demand-over-time data used in forecasting seasonal items. This series of factors is usually based on the relative level of demand during the corresponding period of previous years. The average value of the base series over a seasonal cycle will be 1.0. A figure higher than 1.0 indicates that the demand for that period is more than the average; a figure less than 1.0 indicates less than the average. For forecasting purposes, the base series is superimposed upon the average demand and trend in demand for the item in question. *Synonym: Base Index. Also see: Seasonality*

**Base Stock System:** A method of inventory control that includes as special cases most of the systems in practice. In this system, when an order is received for any item, it is used as a picking ticket, and duplicate copies, called replenishment orders, are sent back to all stages of production to initiate replenishment of stocks. Positive or negative orders (called base stock orders) are also used from time to time to adjust the level of the base stock of each item. In actual practice, replenishment orders are usually accumulated when they are issued and are released at regular intervals.

**Baseload Demand:** *See Base Demand*

**Basic Producer:** A manufacturer that uses natural resources to produce materials for other manufacturing. A typical example is a steel company that processes iron ore and produces steel ingots; others are those making wood pulp, glass, and rubber.

**Basing-Point Pricing:** A pricing system that includes a transportation cost from a particular city or town in a zone or region even though the shipment does not originate at the basing point.

**Batch Control Totals:** The result of grouping transactions at the input stage and establishing control totals over them to ensure proper processing. These control totals can be based on document counts, record counts, quantity totals, dollar totals, or hash (mixed data, such as customer AR numbers) totals.

**Batch Number:** A sequence number associated with a specific batch or production run of products and used for tracking purposes. *Synonym: Lot Number*

**Batch Picking:** A method of picking orders in which order requirements are aggregated by product across orders to reduce movement to and from product locations. The aggregated quantities of each product are then transported to a common area where the individual orders are constructed. *Also See: Discrete Order Picking, Order Picking, Zone Picking*

**Batch Processing:** A computer term which refers to the processing of computer information after it has been accumulated in one group, or batch. This is the opposite of "real-time" processing where transactions are processed in their entirety as they occur.

**Baud:** A computer term describing the rate of transmission over a channel or circuit. The baud rate is equal to the number of pulses that can be transmitted in one second, often the same as the number of bits per second. Common rates are now 1200, 2400, 4800, 9600 bits and 19.2 and 56 kilobytes (Kbs) for "dial-up" circuits, and may be much higher for broadband circuits.

**BCP:** *See Business Continuity Plan*

**Beginning Available Balance:** *See Available Inventory*

**Benchmarking:** The process of comparing performance against the practices of other leading companies for the purpose of improving performance. Companies also benchmark internally by tracking and comparing current performance with past performance. Benchmarking seeks to improve any given business process by exploiting "best practices" rather than merely measuring the best performance. Best practices are the cause of best performance. Studying best practices provides the greatest opportunity for gaining a strategic, operational, and financial advantage.

**Benefit-cost ratio:** An analytical tool used in public planning; a ratio of total measurable benefits divided by the initial capital cost.

**Bespoke:** An individual or custom-made product or service. Traditionally applied to custom-tailored clothing, the term has been extended to information technology, especially for custom-designed software as an alternative to commercial (COTS) software.

**Best-in-Class:** An organization, usually within a specific industry, recognized for excellence in a specific process area.

**Best Practice:** A specific process or group of processes which have been recognized as the best method for conducting an action. Best Practices may vary by industry or geography depending on the environment being used. Best practices methodology may be applied with respect to resources, activities, cost object, or processes.

**Beta Release:** A pre-released version of a product that is sent to customers for evaluation and feedback.

**Big-box retailer:** (also **supercenter**, **superstore**, or **megastore**) is a physically large retail establishment, usually part of a chain. The term sometimes also refers, by extension, to the company that operates the store. Examples include large department stores such as Wal-Mart and Target.

**Bilateral Contract:** An agreement wherein each party makes a promise to the other party.

**Bill of Activities:** A listing of activities required by a product, service, process output or other cost object. Bill of activity attributes could include volume and or cost of each activity in the listing.

**Bill of Lading (BOL):** A transportation document that is the contract of carriage containing the terms and conditions between the shipper and carrier.

**Bill of Lading, Through:** A bill of lading to cover goods from point of origin to final destination when interchange or transfer from one carrier to another is necessary to complete the journey.

**Bill of Material (BOM):** A structured list of all the materials or parts and quantities needed to produce a particular finished product, assembly, subassembly, or manufactured part, whether purchased or not.

**Bill of Material Accuracy:** Conformity of a list of specified items to administrative specifications, with all quantities correct.

**Bill of Resources:** A listing of resources required by an activity. Resource attributes could include cost and volumes.

**Bin:** 1) A storage device designed to hold small discrete parts. 2) A shelving unit with physical dividers separating the storage locations.

**Binary:** A computer term referring to a system of numerical notation that assumes only two possible states or values, zero (0) and one (1). Computer systems use a binary technique where an individual bit or "Binary Digit" of data can be "on" or "off" (1 or 0). Multiple bits are combined into a "Byte" which represents a character or number.

**Bisynchronous:** A computer term referring to a communication protocol whereby messages are sent as blocks of characters. The blocks of data are checked for completeness and accuracy by the receiving computer.

**Bitmap Image (BMP):** The standard image format on Windows-compatible computers. Bitmap images can be saved for Windows or OS/2 systems and support 24-bit color.

**Blanket Order:** *See Blanket Purchase Order*

**Blanket Purchase Order:** A long-term commitment to a supplier for material against which shortterm releases will be generated to satisfy requirements. Often blanket orders cover only one item with predetermined delivery dates. *Synonym: Blanket Order, Standing Order*

**Blanket Release:** The authorization to ship and/or produce against a blanket agreement or contract.

**Blanket Rate:** A rate that does not increase according to the distance the commodity is shipped.

**Bleeding Edge:** An unproven process or technology so far ahead of its time that it may create a competitive disadvantage.

**Block Diagram:** A diagram that shows the operation, interrelationships and interdependencies of components in a system. Boxes, or blocks (hence the name), represent the components; connecting lines between the blocks represent interfaces. There are two types of block diagrams: a functional block diagram, which shows a system's subsystems and lower level products and their interrelationships and which interfaces with other systems; and a reliability block diagram, which is similar to the functional block diagram except that it is modified to emphasize those aspects influencing reliability.

**Blocking Bug:** A defect that prevents further or more detailed analysis or verification of a functional area or feature, or any issue that would prevent the product from shipping.

**Blow Through:** An MRP process which uses a "phantom bill of material" and permits MRP logic to drive requirements straight through the phantom item to its components. The MRP system usually retains its ability to net against any occasional inventories of the item. *Also see: Phantom Bill of Material*

**Body of Knowledge (BOK):** The prescribed aggregation of knowledge in a particular area an individual is expected to have mastered to be considered or certified as a practitioner.

**BOL:** *See Bill of Lading*

**BOK:** *See Body of Knowledge*

**BOM:** *See Bill of Materials*

**Book Inventory:** An accounting definition of inventory units or value obtained from perpetual inventory records rather than by actual count.

**Bookings:** The sum of the value of all orders received (but not necessarily shipped), net of all discounts, coupons, allowances, and rebates.

**Bundle:** A group of products that are shipped together as an unassembled unit.

**Bonded Warehouse:** Warehouse approved by the Treasury Department and under bond/guarantee for observance of revenue laws. Used for storing goods until duty is paid or goods are released in some other proper manner.

**Bottleneck:** A constraint, obstacle or planned control that limits throughput or the utilization of capacity.

**Bottom-up Replanning:** In MRP, the process of using pegging data to solve material availability or other problems. This process is accomplished by the planner (not the computer system), who evaluates the effects of possible solutions. Potential solutions include compressing lead time, cutting order quantity, substituting material, and changing the master schedule.

**Box-Jenkins Model:** A forecasting method based on regression and moving average models. The model is based not on regression of independent variables, but on past observations of the item to be forecast at varying time lags and on previous error values from forecasting. *See also: Forecast*

**Boxcar:** An enclosed rail car typically 40 to 50 feet long; used for packaged freight and some bulk commodities.

**BMP:** *See Bitmap Imagine*

**BPM:** *See Business Performance Measurement*

**BPO:** *See Business Process Outsourcing*

**BPR:** *See Business Process Reengineering*

**Bracing:** Securing a shipment inside a carrier's vehicle to prevent damage.

**Bracketed Recall:** Recall from customers of suspect lot numbers plus a specified number of lots produced before and after the suspect ones.

**Branding:** The use of a name, term, symbol, or design, or a combination of these, to identify a product.

**Breadman:** A specific application of Kanban, used in coordinating vendor replenishment activities. In making bread or other route type deliveries, the deliveryman typically arrives at the customer's location and fills a designated container or storage location with product. The size of the order is not specified on an ongoing basis, nor does the customer even specify requirements for each individual delivery. Instead, the supplier assumes the responsibility for quantifying the need against a prearranged set of rules and delivers the requisite quantity.

**Break-Bulk:** The separation of a single consolidated bulk load into smaller individual shipments for delivery to the ultimate consignees. This is preceded by a consolidation of orders at the time of shipment, where many individual orders which are destined for a specific geographic area are grouped into one shipment in order to reduce cost.

**Break-Even Chart:** A graphical tool showing the total variable cost and fixed cost curve along with the total revenue curve. The point of intersection is defined as the break-even point, i.e., the point at which total revenues exactly equal total costs. *Also see: Total Cost Curve*

**Break-Even Point:** The level of production or the volume of sales at which operations are neither profitable nor unprofitable. The break-even point is the intersection of the total revenue and total cost curves. *Also see: Total Cost Curve*

**BRIC:** In economics, **BRIC** (typically rendered as "the **BRICs**" or "the **BRIC** countries" or known as the "Big Four") is a grouping acronym that refers to the countries of Brazil, Russia, India, and China that are deemed to all be at a similar stage of newly advanced economic development.

**Bricks and Mortar:** The act of selling through a physical location. The flip side of clicks and mortar, where selling is conducted via the Internet. An informal term for representing the old economy versus new economy or the Industrial economy versus information economy.

**Broadband:** A high-speed, high-capacity transmission channel. Broadband channels are carried on radio wave, coaxial or fiber-optic cables that have a wider bandwidth than conventional tele-phone lines, giving them the ability to carry video, voice, and data simultaneously.

**Broken Case:** An open case. The term is often used interchangeably with "repack" or "less-than-fullcase" to name the area in which materi-als are picked in that form.

**Broker:** An intermediary between the shipper and the carrier. The broker arranges transportation for shippers and represents carriers.

**Brokered Systems:** Independent computer systems, owned by inde-pendent organizations or entities, linked in a manner to allow one sys-tem to retrieve information from another. For example, a customer's computer system is able to retrieve order status from a supplier's computer.

**Browser:** A utility that allows an internet user to look through col-lections of things. For example, Netscape Navigator and Microsoft Explorer allow you to view contents on the World Wide Web.

**BTS:** *See Balance to Ship*

**Bulletin Board:** An electronic forum that hosts posted messages and articles related to a common subject.

**Bucketed System:** An MRP, DRP, or other time-phased system in which all time-phased data are accumulated into time periods, or buck-ets. If the period of accumulation is one week, then the system is said to have weekly buckets.

**Bucketless System:** An MRP, DRP, or other time-phased system in which all time-phased data are processed, stored, and usually displayed using dated records rather than defined time periods, or buckets.

**Buffer:** 1) A quantity of materials awaiting further processing. It can refer to raw materials, semi finished stores or hold points, or a work backlog that is purposely maintained behind a work center. 2) In the theory of constraints, buffers can be time or material and support throughput and/or due date performance. Buffers can be maintained at the constraint, convergent points (with a constraint part), divergent points, and shipping points.

**Buffer Management:** In the theory of constraints, a process in which all expediting in a shop is driven by what is scheduled to be in the buffers (constraint, shipping, and assembly buffers). By expediting this material into the buffers, the system helps avoid idleness at the constraint and missed customer due dates. In addition, the causes of items missing from the buffer are identified, and the frequency of occurrence is used to prioritize improvement activities.

**Buffer Stock:** *See Safety Stock*

**Bulk Area:** A storage area for large items which at a minimum are most efficiently handled by the pallet load.

**Bulk storage:** The process of housing or storing materials and packages in larger quantities, generally using the original packaging or shipping containers or boxes.

**Bulk packing:** The process or act of placing numbers of small cartons or boxes into a larger single box to aid in the movement of product and to prevent damage or pilferage to the smaller cartons or boxes.

**Bullwhip Effect:** An extreme change in the supply position upstream in a supply chain generated by a small change in demand downstream in the supply chain. Inventory can quickly move from being backordered to being excess. This is caused by the serial nature of communicating orders up the chain with the inherent transportation delays of moving product down the chain. The bullwhip effect can be eliminated by synchronizing the supply chain.

**Bundle:** A group of products that are shipped together as an unassembled unit.

**Bundling:** An occurrence where two or more products are combined into one transaction for a single price.

**Burn Rate:** The rate of consumption of cash in a business. Burn rate is used to determine cash requirements on an on-going basis. A burn-rate of $50,000 would mean the company spends $50,000 a month above any incoming cash flow to sustain its business. Entrepreneurial companies will calculate their burn-rate in order to understand how much time they have before they need to raise more money, or show a positive cash flow.

**Business Activity Monitoring (BAM):** A term which refers to capturing operational data in real-time or close to it, making it possible for an enterprise to react more quickly to events. This is typically done through software and includes features to provide alerts / notifications when specific events occur. *See also: Supply Chain Event Management*

**Business Application:** Any computer program, set of programs, or package of programs created to solve a particular business problem or function.

**Business Continuity Plan (BCP):** A contingency plan for sustained operations during periods of high risk, such as during labor unrest or natural disaster. CSCMP provides suggestions for helping companies do continuity planning in their Securing the Supply Chain Research. A copy of the research is available on the CSCMP website.

**Business Logistics:** The systematic and coordinated set of activities required to provide the physical movement and storage of goods (raw materials, parts, finished goods) from vendor/supply services through company facilities to the customer (market) and the associated activities—packaging, order processing, etc.—in an efficient manner necessary to enable the organization to contribute to the explicit goals of the company.

**Business Plan:** 1) A statement of long-range strategy and revenue, cost, and profit objectives usually accompanied by budgets, a projected balance sheet, and a cash flow (source and application of funds) statement. A business plan is usually stated in terms of dollars and grouped by product family. The business plan is then translated into synchronized tactical functional plans through the production planning process (or the sales and operations planning process). Although frequently stated in different terms (dollars versus units), these tactical plans should agree with each other and with the business plan. See: long-term planning, strategic plan. 2) A document consisting of the business details (organization, strategy, and financing tactics) prepared by an entrepreneur to plan for a new business.

**Business Performance Measurement (BPM):** A technique which uses a system of goals and metrics to monitor performance. Analysis of these measurements can help businesses in periodically setting business goals, and then providing feedback to managers on progress towards those goals. A specific measure can be compared to itself over time, compared with a preset target or evaluated along with other measures.

**Business Process Outsourcing (BPO):** The practice of outsourcing non-core internal functions to third parties. Functions typically outsourced include logistics, accounts payable, accounts receivable, payroll and human resources. Other areas can include IT development or complete management of the IT functions of the enterprise.

**Business Process Reengineering (BPR):** The fundamental rethinking and oftentimes, radical redesign of business processes to achieve dramatic organizational improvements.

**Business-to-Business (B2B):** As opposed to business-to-consumer (B2C). Many companies are now focusing on this strategy, and their sites are aimed at businesses (think wholesale) and only other businesses can access or buy products on the site. Internet analysts predict this will be the biggest sector on the Web.

**Business-to-Consumer (B2C):** The hundreds of e-commerce Web sites that sell goods directly to consumers are considered B2C. This distinction is important when comparing Websites that are B2B as the entire business model, strategy, execution, and fulfillment is different.

**Business Unit:** A division or segment of an organization generally treated as a separate profit-and loss center.

**Buyer Behavior:** The way individuals or organizations behave in a purchasing situation. The customer-oriented concept finds out the wants, needs, and desires of customers and adapts resources of the organization to deliver need-satisfying goods and services.

**Byte:** A computer term used to define a string of 7 or 8 bits, or binary digits. The length of the string determines the amount of data that can be represented. The 8-bit byte can represent numerous special characters, 26 uppercase and lowercase alphabetic characters, and 10 numeric digits, totaling 256 possible combinations.

# C

**Cabotage:** A federal law that requires coastal and inter-coastal traffic to be carried in U.S.-built and – registered ships.

**CAE:** *See Computer Aided Engineering*

**Cage:** (1) A secure enclosed area for storing highly valuable items, (2) a pallet-sized platform with sides that can be secured to the tines of a forklift and in which a person may ride to inventory items stored will above the warehouse floor.

**Caged:** Referring to the practice of placing high-value or sensitive products in a fenced off area within a warehouse.

**Calendar Days:** The conversion of working days to calendar days is based on the number of regularly scheduled workdays per week in your manufacturing calendar.

**Call Center:** A facility housing personnel who respond to customer phone queries. These personnel may provide customer service or technical support. Call centers may be in-house or outsourced.

**Can-order Point:** An ordering system used when multiple items are ordered from one vendor. The can-order point is a point higher than the original order point. When any one of the items triggers an order by reaching the must-order point, all items below their can-order point are also ordered. The can-order point is set by considering the additional holding cost that would be incurred should the item be ordered early.

**Cantilever rack:** Racking system that allows for storage of very long items.

**Capable to Promise (CTP):** A technique used to determine if product can be assembled and shipped by a specific date. Component availability throughout the supply chain, as well as available materials, is checked to determine if delivery of a particular product can be made. This process may involve multiple manufacturing or distribution sites. Capable-to-promise is used to determine when a new or unscheduled customer order can be delivered. Capable-to-promise employs a finite-scheduling model of the manufacturing system to determine when an item can be delivered. It includes any constraints that might restrict the production, such as availability of resources, lead times for raw materials or purchased parts, and requirements for lower-level components or subassemblies. The resulting delivery date takes into consideration production capacity, the current manufacturing environment, and future order commitments. The objective is to reduce the time spent by production planners in expediting orders and adjusting plans because of inaccurate delivery-date promises.

**Capability Maturity Model (CMM):** A framework that describes the key elements of an effective software process. It's an evolutionary improvement path from an immature process to a mature, disciplined process. The CMM covers practices for planning, engineering and managing software development and maintenance. When followed, these key practices improve the ability of organizations to meet goals for cost, schedule, functionality and product quality.

**Capacity:** The physical facilities, personnel and process available to meet the product or service needs of customers. Capacity generally refers to the maximum output or producing ability of a machine, a person, a process, a factory, a product, or a service. *Also see: Capacity Management*

**Capacity Management:** The concept that capacity should be understood, defined, and measured for each level in the organization to include market segments, products, processes, activities, and resources. In each of these applications, capacity is defined in a hierarchy of idle, non-productive, and productive views.

**Capacity Planning:** Assuring that needed resources (e.g., manufacturing capacity, distribution center capacity, transportation vehicles, etc.) will be available at the right time and place to meet logistics and supply chain needs.

**CAPEX:** A term used to describe the monetary requirements (*cap*ital *ex*penditure) of an initial investment in new machines or equipment.

**Capital:** The resources, or money, available for investing in assets that produce output.

**Carbon Footprint:** the total set of greenhouse gases (GHG) emissions caused by an organization, event or product. For simplicity of reporting, it is often expressed in terms of the amount of carbon dioxide, or its equivalent of other GHGs, emitted.

**Car Supply Charge:** A railroad charge for a shipper's exclusive use of special equipment.

**Cargo:** A product shipped in an aircraft, railroad car, ship, barge, or truck.

**Carload Lot:** A shipment that qualifies for a reduced freight rate because it is greater than a specified minimum weight. Since carload rates usually include minimum rates per unit of volume, the higher LCL (less than carload) rate may be less expensive for a heavy but relatively small shipment.

**Carmack Amendment:** An Interstate Commerce Act amendment that delineates the liability of common carriers and the bill of lading provision.

**Carousel:** Carousel: Automated equipment generally used for picking of small, high-volume parts.

**Carrier:** A firm which transports goods or people via land, sea or air.

**Cartel:** A group of companies that agree to cooperate, rather than compete, in producing a product or service, thus limiting or regulating competition.

**Case Code:** The UPC number for a case of product. The UPC case code is different from the UPC item code. This is sometimes referred to as the "Shipping Container Symbol" or ITF-14 code.

**Cash-to-Cash Cycle Time:** The time it takes for cash to flow back into a company after it has been spent for raw materials. *Synonym: Cash Conversion Cycle*

***Calculation:*** *Total Inventory Days of Supply + Days of Sales Outstanding - Average Payment Period for Material in days*

**Cash Conversion Cycle:** 1) In retailing, the length of time between the sale of products and the cash payments for a company's resources. 2) In manufacturing, the length of time from the purchase of raw materials to the collection of accounts receivable from customers for the sale of products or services. *Also see: Cash-to-Cash Cycle Time*

**Catalog Channel:** A call center or order processing facility that receives orders directly from the customer based on defined catalog offerings and ships directly to the customer.

**Categorical Plan:** A method of selecting and evaluating suppliers that considers input from many departments and functions within the buyer's organization and systematically categorizes that input. Engineering, production, quality assurance, and other functional areas evaluate all suppliers for critical factors within their scope of responsibility. For example, engineering would develop a category evaluating suppliers' design flexibility. Rankings are developed across categories, and performance ratings are obtained and supplier selections are made. *Also see: Weighted-Point Plan*

**Category Management:** The management of product categories as strategic business units. The practice empowers a category manager with full responsibility for the assortment decisions, inventory levels, shelf-space allocation, promotions and buying. With this authority and responsibility, the category manager is able to judge more accurately the consumer buying patterns, product sales and market trends of that category.

**Cause and Effect Diagram:** In quality management, a structured process used to organize ideas into logical groupings. Used in brainstorming and problem solving exercises. *Also known as Ishikawa or fish bone diagram.*

**Causal Forecast:** In forecasting, a type of forecasting that uses cause-and-effect associations to predict and explain relationships between the independent and dependent variables. An example of a causal model is an econometric model used to explain the demand for housing starts based on consumer base, interest rates, personal incomes, and land availability.

**CBP:** *See Customs and Border Protection, U.S.*

**CBT:** *See Computer-Based Training*

**Cell:** A manufacturing or service unit consisting of a number of workstations, and the materials transport mechanisms and storage buffers that interconnect them.

**Cellular Manufacturing:** A manufacturing approach in which equipment and workstations are arranged to facilitate small-lot, continuous-flow production. In a manufacturing "cell," all operations necessary to produce a component or subassembly are performed in close proximity, thus allowing for quick feedback between operators when quality problems and other issues arise. Workers in a manufacturing cell typically are cross-trained and, therefore, able to perform multiple tasks as needed.

**Center-of-Gravity Approach:** A supply chain planning methodology for locating distribution centers at approximately the location representing the minimum transportation costs between the plants, the distribution centers, and the markets.

**Centralized Authority:** Management authority to make decisions is restricted to few managers.

**Centralized Dispatching:** The organization of the dispatching function into one central location. This structure often involves the use of data collection devices for communication between the centralized dispatching function, which usually reports to the production control department, and the shop manufacturing departments.

**Centralized Inventory Control:** Inventory decision making (for all SKUs) exercised from one office or department for an entire company.

**Certificate of Analysis (COA):** A certification of conformance to quality standards or specifications for products or materials. It may include a list or reference of analysis results and process information. It is often required for transfer of the custody/ownership/title of materials.

**Certificate of Compliance:** A supplier's certification that the supplies or services in question meet specified-requirements.

**Certificate of origin:** An international business document that certifies the country of origin of the shipment.

**Certificate of Public Convenience and Necessity:** The grant of operating authority that is given to common carriers. A carrier must prove that a public need exists and that the carrier is fit, willing, and able to provide the needed service. The certificate may specify the commodities to be hauled, the area to be served, and the routes to be used.

**Certified Supplier:** A status awarded to a supplier who consistently meets predetermined quality, cost, delivery, financial, and count objectives. Incoming inspection may not be required.

**Certificated Carrier:** A for-hire air carrier that is subject to economic regulation and requires an operating certification to provide service.

**CFD:** *See Continuous Flow Distribution*

**CGMP:** *See Current Good Manufacturing Practice*

**Chain of Customers:** The sequence of customers who in turn consume the output of each other, forming a chain. For example, individuals are customers of a department store, which in turn is the customer of a producer, who is the customer of a material supplier.

**Chain Reaction:** A chain of events described by W. Edwards Deming: improve quality, decrease costs, improve productivity, increase market with better quality and lower price, stay in business, provide jobs and provide more jobs.

**Challenge and Response:** A method of user authentication. The user enters an ID and password and, in return, is issued a challenge by the system. The system compares the user's response to the challenge to a computed response. If the responses match, the user is allowed access to the system. The system issues a different challenge each time. In effect, it requires a new password for each logon.

**Champion:** A business leader or senior manager who ensures that resources are available for training and projects, and who is involved in project tollgate reviews; also an executive who supports and addresses Six Sigma organizational issues.

**Change agent:** An individual from within or outside an organization who facilitates change within the organization. May or may not be the initiator of the change effort.

**Change Management:** The business process that coordinates and monitors all changes to the business processes and applications operated by the business as well as to their internal equipment, resources, operating systems, and procedures. The change management discipline is carried out in a way that minimizes the risk of problems that will affect the operating environment and service delivery to the users.

**Change Order:** A formal notification that a purchase order or shop order must be modified in some way. This change can result from a revised quantity, date, or specification by the customer; an engineering change; a change in inventory requirement date; etc.

**Changeover:** Process of making necessary adjustments to change or switchover the type of products produced on a manufacturing line. Changeovers usually lead to downtime and for the most part companies try to minimize changeover time to help reduce costs.

**Channel:** 1) A method whereby a business dispenses its product, such as a retail or distribution channel, call center or web based electronic storefront. 2) A push technology that allows users to subscribe to a website to browse offline, automatically display updated pages on their screen savers, and download or receive notifications when pages in the website are modified. Channels are available only in browsers that support channel definitions, such as Microsoft Internet Explorer version 4.0 and above.

**Channel Conflict:** This occurs when various sales channels within a company's supply chain compete with each other for the same business. An example is where a retail channel is in competition with a web based channel set up by the company.

**Channel Partners:** Members of a supply chain (i.e. suppliers, manufacturers, distributors, retailers, etc.) who work in conjunction with one another to manufacture, distribute, and sell a specific product.

**Channels of Distribution:** Any series of firms or individuals that participates in the flow of goods and services from the raw material supplier and producer to the final user or consumer. *Also see: Distribution Channel*

**Charging Area:** A warehouse area where a company maintains battery chargers and extra batteries to support a fleet of electrically powered materials handling equipment. The company must maintain this area in accordance with government safety regulations.

**Chock:** A wedge, usually made of hard rubber or steel, that is firmly placed under the wheel of a trailer, truck, or boxcar to stop it from rolling.

**CI:** *See Continuous Improvement*

**CIF:** *See Cost, Insurance, Freight*

**City driver:** A motor carrier driver who drives a local route as opposed to a long-distance, intercity route.

**Civil Aeronautics Board:** A federal regulatory agency that implemented economic regulatory controls over air carriers.

**CL:** Carload rail service requiring shipper to meet minimum weight.

**Claim:** A charge made against a carrier for loss, damage, delay, or overcharge.

**Class I Carrier:** A classification of regulated carriers based upon annual operating revenues—motor carriers of property: > or = $5 million; railroads: > or =$50 million; motor carriers of passengers: > or =$3 million.

**Class II Carrier:** A classification of regulated carriers based upon annual operating revenues—motor carriers of property: $1-$5 million; railroads: $10-$50 million; motor carriers of passengers: < or = $3 million.

**Class III Carrier:** A classification of regulated carriers based upon annual operating revenues—motor carriers of property: < or = $1 million; railroads: < or = $10 million.

**Classification:** An alphabetical listing \of commodities, the class or rating into which the commodity is placed, and the minimum weight necessary for the rate discount; used in the class rate structure.

**Classification yard:** A railroad terminal area where rail cars are grouped together to form train units.

**Class Rate:** A rate constructed from a classification and a uniform distance system. A class rate is available for any product between any two points.

**Clearinghouse:** A conventional or limited purpose entity generally restricted to providing specialized services, such as clearing funds or settling accounts.

**Click-and-Mortar:** With reference to a traditional brick-and-mortar company that has expanded its presence online. Many brick-and-mortar stores are now trying to establish an online presence but often have a difficult time doing so for many reasons. Click-and-mortar is "the successful combination of online and real world experience."

**Clipboard:** A temporary storage area on a computer for cut or copied items.

**CLCA:** *See Closed-loop corrective action*

**CLM:** *See Council of Supply Chain Management Professionals*

**Closed-Loop Corrective Action (CLCA):** A sophisticated engineering system designed to document, verify and diagnose failures, recommend and initiate corrective action, provide follow-up and maintain comprehensive statistical records.

**Closed-Loop MRP:** A system built around material requirements planning that includes the additional planning processes of production planning (sales and operations planning), master production scheduling, and capacity requirements planning. Once this planning phase is complete and the plans have been accepted as realistic and attainable, the execution processes come into play. These processes include the manufacturing control processes of input-output (capacity) measurement, detailed scheduling and dispatching, as well as anticipated delay reports from both the plant and suppliers, supplier scheduling, and so on. The term closed loop implies not only that each of these processes is included in the overall system, but also that feedback is provided by the execution processes so that the planning can be kept valid at all times.

**CMI:** *See Co-Managed Inventory*

**CMM:** *See Capability Maturity Model*

**COA:** *See Certificate of Analysis*

**Coastal carriers**: Water carriers that provide service along coasts serving ports on the Atlantic or Pacific oceans or on the Gulf of Mexico

**Co-destiny:** The evolution of a supply chain from intra-organizational management to inter-organizational management.

**Co-Packer:** A contract co-packer produces goods and/or services for other companies, usually under the other company's label or name. Co-Packers are more frequently seen in CPG and Foods.

**Co-Managed Inventory (CMI):** A form of continuous replenishment in which the manufacturer is responsible for replenishment of standard merchandise, while the retailer manages the replenishment of promotional merchandise.

**Code:** A numeric, or alphanumeric, representation of text for exchanging commonly used information. For example: commodity codes, carrier codes,

**Codifying:** The process of detailing a new standard.

**COGS:** *See Cost of Goods Sold*

**Collaboration:** Joint work and communication among people and systems – including business partners, suppliers, and customers – to achieve a common business goal.

**Collaborative Planning, Forecasting and Replenishment (CPFR):** 1) A collaboration process whereby supply chain trading partners can jointly plan key supply chain activities from production and delivery of raw materials to production and delivery of final products to end customers. Collaboration encompasses business planning, sales forecasting, and all operations required to replenish raw materials and finished goods. 2) A process philosophy for facilitating collaborative communications. CPFR is considered a standard, endorsed by the Voluntary Inter-industry Commerce Standards.

**Collect Freight:** Freight payable to the carrier at the port of discharge or ultimate destination. The consignee does not pay the freight charge if the cargo does not arrive at the destination.

**Combined Lead Time:** *See Cumulative Lead Time*

**Commercial Invoice:** A document created by the seller. It is an official document which is used to indicate, among other things, the name and address of the buyer and seller, the product(s) being shipped, and their value for customs, insurance, or other purposes.

**Commercial Off-the-Shelf (COTS):** A computer software industry term which describes software which is offered for sale by commercial developers. This includes products from vendors such as SAP, Oracle, Microsoft, etc. and all of the smaller vendors.

**Commercial Zone:** The area surrounding a city or town to which rates quoted for the city or town also apply; the area is defined by the ICC.

**Committee of American Steamship Lines:** An industry association representing subsidized U.S. Flag steamship firms.

**Committed Capability:** The portion of the production capability that is currently in use, or is scheduled for use.

**Commodities clause:** A clause that prohibits railroads from hauling commodities that they produced, mined, owned, or had an interest in.

**Commodity:** An item that is traded in commerce. The term usually implies an undifferentiated product competing primarily on price and availability.

**Commodity Buying:** Grouping like parts or materials under one buyer's control for the procurement of all requirements to support production.

**Commodity Code:** A code describing a commodity or a group of commodities pertaining to goods classification. This code can be carrier tariff or regulating in nature.

**Commodity Procurement Strategy:** The purchasing plan for a family of items. This would include the plan to manage the supplier base and solve problems.

**Commodity rate:** A rate for a specific commodity and its origin-destination.

**Common Carrier:** Transportation available to the public that does not provide special treatment to any one party and is regulated as to the rates charged, the liability assumed, and the service provided. A common carrier must obtain a certificate of public convenience and necessity from the Federal Trade Commission for interstate traffic.

**Common Carrier Duties:** Common carriers are required to serve, deliver, charge reasonable rates, and not discriminate.

**Common Cost:** A cost that cannot be directly assignable to particular segments of the business but that is incurred for the business as a whole.

**Commuter:** An exempt for-hire air carrier that publishes a time schedule on specific routes; a special type of air taxi.

**Communication Protocol:** The method by which two computers coordinate their communications. BISYNC and MNP are two examples.

**Company Culture:** A system of values, beliefs, and behaviors inherent in a company. To optimize business performance, top management must define and create the necessary culture.

**Comparative Advantage:** A principle based on the assumption that an area will specialize in the production of goods for which it has the greatest advantage or least comparative disadvantage.

**Competitive Advantage:** Value created by a company for its customers that clearly distinguishes it from the competition, and provides its customers a reason to remain loyal.

**Competitive Benchmarking:** Benchmarking a product or service against competitors. *Also see: Benchmarking*

**Competitive Bid:** A price/service offering by a supplier that must compete with offerings from other suppliers.

**Complete & On-Time Delivery (COTD):** A measure of customer service. All items on any given order must be delivered on time for the order to be considered as complete and on time.

**Complete Manufacture to Ship Time:** Average time from when a unit is declared shippable by manufacturing until the unit actually ships to a customer.

**Compliance:** Meaning that products, services, processes and/or documents comply with requirements.

**Compliance Checking:** The function of EDI processing software that ensures that all transmissions contain the mandatory information demanded by the EDI standard. Compares information sent by an EDI user against EDI standards and reports exceptions. Does not ensure that documents are complete and fully accurate, but does reject transmissions with missing data elements or syntax errors.

**Compliance Monitoring:** A check done by the VAN/third party network or the translation software to ensure the data being exchanged is in the correct format for the standard being used.

**Compliance Program:** A method by which two or more EDI trading partners periodically report conformity to agreed upon standards of control and audit. Management produces statements of compliance, which briefly note any exceptions, as well as corrective action planned or taken, in accordance with operating rules. Auditors produce an independent and objective statement of opinion on management statements.

**Component:** Material that will contribute to a finished product but is not the finished product itself. Examples would include tires for an automobile, power supply for a personal computer, or a zipper for a ski parka. Note that what is a component to the manufacturer may be considered the finished product of their supplier.

**Computer-Aided Design (CAD)**—Computer-based systems for product design that may incorporate analytical and "what if" capabilities to optimize product designs. Many CAD systems capture geometric and other product characteristics for engineering-data-management systems, producibility and cost analysis, and performance analysis. In many cases, CAD-generated data.

**Computer Aided Engineering (CAE):** The use of computers to model design options to stimulate their performance.

**Computer-Aided Manufacturing (CAM):** Computerized systems in which manufacturing instructions are downloaded to automated equipment or to operator workstations.

**Computer-Aided Process Planning (CAPP):** Software-based systems that aid manufacturing engineers in creating a process plan to manufacture a product who's geometric, electronic, and other characteristics have been captured in a CAD database. CAPP systems address such manufacturing criteria as target costs, target lead times, anticipated production volumes, availability of

**Computer-Based Training (CBT):** Training that is delivered via computer workstation and includes all training and testing materials.

**Computer-Integrated Manufacturing (CIM):** A variety of approaches in which computer systems communicate or interoperate over a local-area network. Typically, CIM systems link management functions with engineering, manufacturing, and support operations. In the factory, CIM systems may control the sequencing of production operations, control operation of automated equipment and conveyor systems, transmit manufacturing instructions, capture data at various stages of the manufacturing or assembly process, facilitate tracking and analysis of test results and operating parameters, or a combination of these.

**Computerized Maintenance Management Systems (CMMS):** Software-based systems that analyze operating conditions of production equipment – vibration, oil analysis, heat, etc. – and equipment-failure data, and apply that data to the scheduling of maintenance and repair inventory orders and routine maintenance functions. A CMMS prevents unscheduled machine downtime and optimizes a plant's ability to process product at optimum volumes and quality levels.

**Computerized Process Simulation:** Use of computer simulation to facilitate sequencing of production operations, analysis of production flows, and layout of manufacturing facilities.

**Computerized SPC:** *See Statistical process control*

**Concurrent Engineering:** A cross-functional, team-based approach in which the product and the manufacturing process are designed and configured within the same time frame, rather than sequentially. Ease and cost of manufacturability, as well as customer needs, quality issues, and product-life-cycle costs are taken into account earlier in the development cycle. Fully configured concurrent engineering teams include representation from marketing, design engineering, manufacturing engineering, and purchasing, as well as supplier—and even customer—companies.

**Configuration:** The arrangement of components as specified to produce an assembly.

**Configure/Package-to-Order:** A process where the trigger to begin manufacture, final assembly or packaging of a product is an actual customer order or release, rather than a market forecast. In order to be considered a Configure-to-Order environment, less than 20% of the value-added takes place after the receipt of the order or release, and virtually all necessary design and process documentation is available at time of order receipt.

**Confirmation:** With regards to EDI, a formal notice (by message or code) from a electronic mailbox system or EDI server indicating that a message sent to a trading partner has reached its intended mailbox or been retrieved by the addressee.

**Confirming Order:** A purchase order issued to a supplier, listing the goods or services and terms of an order placed orally or otherwise before the usual purchase document.

**Conformance:** An affirmative indication or judgment that a product or service has met the requirements of a relevant specification, contract, or regulation. *Synonym: Compliance*

**Conrail:** The Consolidated Rail Corporation established by the Regional Reorganization Act of 1973 to operate the bankrupt Penn Central Railroad and other bankrupt railroads in the Northeast; funding was provided by the 4-R Act of 1976.

**Consensus:** A state in which all the members of a group support an action or decision, even if some of them don't fully agree with it.

**Consignee:** The party to whom goods are shipped and delivered. The receiver of a freight shipment.

**Consignment:** 1) A shipment that is handled by a common carrier. 2) The process of a supplier placing goods at a customer location without receiving payment until after the goods are used or sold. *Also see: Consignment Inventory*

**Consignment Inventory:** 1) Goods or product that are paid for when they are sold by the reseller, not at the time they are shipped to the reseller. 2) Goods or products which are owned by the vendor until they are sold to the consumer.

**Consignor:** The party who originates a shipment of goods (shipper). The sender of a freight shipment, usually the seller.

**Consolidation:** Combining two or more shipments in order to realize lower transportation rates. Inbound consolidation from vendors is called make-bulk consolidation; outbound consolidation to customers is called break-bulk consolidation.

**Consolidator:** An enterprise that provides services to group shipments, orders, and/or goods to facilitate movement.

**Consortium:** A group of companies that work together to jointly produce a product, service, or project.

**Constraint:** A bottleneck, obstacle or planned control that limits throughput or the utilization of capacity.

**Consul:** A government official residing in a foreign country, charged with representing the interests of his or her country and its nationals.

**Consular Declaration:** A formal statement made to the consul of a country describing merchandise to be shipped to that consul's country. Approval must be obtained prior to shipment.

**Consular Documents:** Special forms signed by the consul of a country to which cargo is destined.

**Consular Invoice:** A document, required by some foreign countries, describing a shipment of goods and showing information such as the consignor, consignee, and value of the shipment. Certified by a consular official of the foreign country, it is used by the country's custom.

**Consumer-Centric Database:** Database with information about a retailer's individual consumers, used primarily for marketing and promotion.

**Consumer Packaged Goods (CPG):** Consumable goods such as food and beverages, footwear and apparel, tobacco, and cleaning products. In general, CPGs are things that get used up and have to be replaced frequently, in contrast to items that people usually keep for a long time, such as cars and furniture.

**Consuming the Forecast:** The process of reducing the forecast by customer orders or other types of actual demands as they are received. The adjustments yield the value of the remaining forecast for each period.

**Consumption Entry:** An official Customs form used for declaration of reported goods, also showing the total duty due on such transaction.

**Contactless:** Refers to the practice of using RFID, Smart Card or other forms of Near Field Communications technology to gather data electronically without the need to actually make contact physically with the item.

**Container:** 1) A "box," typically 10 to 40 feet long, which is primarily used for ocean freight shipments. For travel to and from ports, containers are loaded onto truck chassis or on railroad flatcars. 2) The packaging, such as a carton, case, box, bucket, drum, bin, bottle, bundle, or bag, that an item is packed and shipped in.

**Container Security Initiative (CSI):** U.S. Customs program to prevent global containerized cargo from being exploited by terrorists. Designed to enhance security of sea cargo container.

**Containerization:** A shipment method in which commodities are placed in containers, and after initial loading, the commodities per se are not re-handled in shipment until they are unloaded at the destination.

**Contingency Planning:** Preparing to deal with calamities (e.g., floods) and non-calamitous situations (e.g., strikes) before they occur

**Continuous Flow Distribution (CFD):** The streamlined pull of products in response to customer requirements while minimizing the total costs of distribution.

**Continuous-Flow, Fixed-Path Equipment**: Materials handling devices that include conveyors and drag lines.

**Continuous Improvement (CI):** A structured measurement driven process that continually reviews and improves performance.

**Continuous Process Improvement (CPI):** A never-ending effort to expose and eliminate root causes of problems; small-step improvement as opposed to big-step improvement. *Synonym: Continuous Improvement. Also see: Kaizen*

**Continuous Replenishment:** Continuous Replenishment is the practice of partnering between distribution channel members that changes the traditional replenishment process from distributor generated purchase orders, based on economic order quantities, to the replenishment of products based on actual and forecasted product demand.

**Continuous Replenishment Planning (CRP):** A program that triggers the manufacturing and movement of product through the supply chain when the identical product is purchased by an end user.

**Contract:** An agreement between two or more competent persons or companies to perform or not to perform specific acts or services or to deliver merchandise. A contract may be oral or written. A purchase order, when accepted by a supplier, becomes a contract. Acceptance may be in writing or by performance, unless the purchase order requires acceptance in writing.

**Contract Administration:** Managing all aspects of a contract to guarantee that the contractor fulfills his obligations.

**Contract Carrier:** A carrier that does not serve the general public, but provides transportation for hire for one or a limited number of shippers under a specific contract.

**Contribution:** The difference between sales price and variable costs. Contribution is used to cover fixed costs and profits.

**Contribution Margin:** An amount equal to the difference between sales revenue and variable costs.

**Controlled Access:** Referring to an area within a warehouse or yard that is fenced and gated. These areas are typically used to store high-value items and may be monitored by security cameras

**Conveyor:** A materials handling device that moves freight from one area to another in a warehouse. Roller conveyors make sue of gravity, whereas belt conveyors use motors.

**Cookie:** A computer term. A piece of information from your computer that references what the user has clicked on, or references information that is stored in a text file on the user's hard drive (such as a username). Another way to describe cookies is to say they are tiny files containing information about individual computers that can be used by advertisers to track online interests and tastes. Cookies are also used in the process of purchasing items on the Web. It is because of the cookie that the "shopping cart" technology works. By saving in a text file, the name, and other important information about an item a user "clicks" on as they move through a shopping Website, a user can later go to an order form, and see all the items they selected, ready for quick and easy processing.

**Cooperative Associations:** Groups of firms or individuals having common interests: agricultural cooperative associations may haul up to 25% of their total interstate tonnage in nonfarm, non-member goods in movements incidental and necessary to their primary business.

**Co-opetition:** A combination of cooperation and competition that offers the counter intuitive possibility for rivals to benefit from each other's seemingly competitive activities. In short, there are circumstances where having more players to cut the pie means bigger pieces of pie for everyone. An example would be found in the group buying setting where its use refers to the activity of multiple, normally competitive buying group members leveraging each other's buying power to gain reduced pricing.

**Coordinated Transportation:** Two or more carriers of different modes transporting a shipment.

**Copacetic:** Very satisfactory or acceptable; fine; excellent

**Co-product:** The term co-product is used to describe multiple items that are produced simultaneously during a production run. Co-products are often used to increase yields in cutting operations such as die cutting or sawing when it is found that scrap can be reduced by combining multiple-sized products in a single production run. Co-products are also used to reduce the frequency of machine setups required in these same types of operations. Co-products, also known as byproducts, are also common in process manufacturing such as in chemical plants. Although the concept of co-products is fairly simple, the programming logic required to provide for planning and processing of co-products is very complicated.

**Core Competency:** Bundles of skills or knowledge sets that enable a firm to provide the greatest level of value to its customers in a way that is difficult for competitors to emulate and that provides for future growth. Core competencies are embodied in the skills of the workers and in the organization. They are developed through -collective -learning, communication, and commitment to work across levels and functions in the organization and with the customers and suppliers. For example, a core competency could be the capability of a firm to coordinate and harmonize diverse production skills and multiple technologies. To illustrate, advanced casting processes for making steel require the integration of machine design with sophisticated sensors to track temperature and speed, and the sensors require mathematical modeling of heat transfer. For rapid and effective development of such a process, materials scientists must work closely with machine designers, software engineers, process specialists, and operating personnel. Core competencies are not directly related to the product or market.

**Core Process:** That unique capability that is central to a company's competitive strategy.

**Cost Accounting:** The branch of accounting that is concerned with recording and reporting business operating costs. It includes the reporting of costs by departments, activities, and products.

**Cost Allocation:** In accounting, the assignment of costs that cannot be directly related to production activities via more measurable means, e.g., assigning corporate expenses to different products via direct labor costs or hours.

**Cost Center:** In accounting, a sub-unit in an organization that is responsible for costs.

**Cost Driver:** In accounting, any situation or event that causes a change in the consumption of a resource, or influences quality or cycle time. An activity may have multiple cost drivers. Cost drivers do not necessarily need to be quantified; however, they strongly influence the selection and magnitude of resource drivers and activity drivers.

**Cost Driver Analysis:** In cost accounting, the examination, quantification, and explanation of the effects of cost drivers. The results are often used for continuous improvement programs to reduce through-put times, improve quality, and reduce cost.

**Cost Element:** In cost accounting, the lowest level component of a resource, activity, or cost object.

**Cost, Insurance, Freight (CIF):** A freight term indicating that the seller is responsible for cost, the marine insurance, and the freight charges on an ocean shipment of goods.

**Cost Management:** The management and control of activities and drivers to calculate accurate product and service costs, improve business processes, eliminate waste, influence cost drivers, and plan operations. The resulting information will have utility in setting and evaluating an organization's strategies.

**Cost of Capital:** The cost to borrow or invest capital.

**Cost of Goods Sold (COGS):** The amount of direct materials, direct labor, and allocated overhead associated with products sold during a given period of time, determined in accordance with Generally Accepted Accounting Principles (GAAP)

**Cost of lost sales:** The forgone profit associated with a stock out.

**Cost Trade-off:** The interrelationship among system variables indicates that a change in one variable has cost impact upon other variables. A cost reduction in one variable may be at the expense of increased cost for other variables, and vice versa.

**Cost Variance:** In cost accounting, the difference between what has been budgeted for an activity and what it actually costs.

**COTD:** *See Complete & On-Time Delivery*

**COTS:** *See Commercial Off-the-Shelf*

**Courier Service:** A fast, door-to-door service for high-valued goods and documents; firms usually limit service to shipments of 50 pounds or less.

**Council of Logistics Management (CLM):** *See Council of Supply Chain Management Professionals.*

**Council of Supply Chain Management Professionals (CSCMP):** The CSCMP is a not-for-profit professional business organization consisting of individuals throughout the world who have interests and/or responsibilities in logistics and supply chain management, and the related functions that make up these professions. Its purpose is to enhance the development of the logistics and supply chain management professions by providing these individuals with educational opportunities and relevant information through a variety of programs, services, and activities.

**CPFR:** *See Collaborative Planning Forecasting and Replenishment*

**CPG:** *See Consumer Packaged Goods*

**CPI:** *See Continuous Process Improvement*

**Credit Level:** The amount of purchasing credit a customer has available. Usually defined by the internal credit department and reduced by any existing unpaid bills or open orders.

**Critical Differentiators:** This is what makes an idea, product, service or business model unique.

**Critical value analysis:** A modified ABC analysis in which a subjective value of criticalness is assigned to each item in the inventory.

**Cross Docking:** A distribution system in which merchandise received at the warehouse or distribution center is not put away, but instead is readied for shipment to retail stores. Cross docking requires close synchronization of all inbound and outbound shipment movements. By eliminating the put-away, storage and selection operations, it can significantly reduce distribution costs.

**Cross Functional:** A term used to describe a process or an activity that crosses the boundary between functions. A cross functional team consists of individuals from more than one organizational unit or function.

**Cross Functional "Process" Metric:** A number resulting from an equation, showing the output of a process that spans departments. These types of measures are also known as a process measures because they span across the breadth of a process, regardless for functional/departmental segregation within the process. Example: Perfect Order Index

**Cross Sell:** The practice of attempting to sell additional products to a customer during a sales call. For example, when the CSR presents a camera case and accessories to a customer that is ordering a camera

**Cross-Shipment:** Material flow activity where materials are shipped to customers from a secondary shipping point rather than from a preferred shipping point.

**Cross-Subsidy:** In cost accounting, the inequitable assignment of costs to cost objects, which leads to over costing or under costing them relative to the amount of activities and resources actually consumed. This may result in poor management decisions that are inconsistent with the economic goals of the organization.

**Crowdsourcing** is the act of outsourcing tasks, traditionally performed by an employee or contractor, to a large group of people or community (a crowd), through an open call.

**CRP:** *See Continuous Replenishment Program*

**Critical Success Factor (CSF):** Those activities and/or processes that must be completed and/or controlled to enable a company to reach its goals.

**CRM:** *See Customer Relationship Management*

**CSCMP:** *See Council of Supply Chain Management Professionals*

**CSF:** *See Critical Success Factor*

**CSI:** *See Container Security Initiative*

**CSR:** *See Customer Service Representative*

**CTP:** *See Capacity to Promise*

**C-TPAT:** *See Customs-Trade Partnership against Terrorism*

**Cube:** The volume of the shipment or package (the product of the length x width x depth).

**Cubage:** Cubic volume of space being used or available for shipping or storage.

**Cube Utilization:** In warehousing, a measurement of the utilization of the total storage capacity of a vehicle or warehouse.

**Cubic Space:** In warehousing, a measurement of space available or required in transportation and warehousing.

**Cumulative Available-to-Promise:** A calculation based on the available-to-promise (ATP) figure in the master schedule. Two methods of computing the cumulative available-to-promise are used, with and without look ahead calculation. The cumulative with look ahead ATP equals the ATP from the previous period plus the MPS of the period minus the backlog of the period minus the sum of the differences between the backlogs and MPSs of all future periods until, but not to include, the period where point production exceeds the backlogs. The cumulative without look ahead procedure equals the ATP in the previous period plus the MPS, minus the backlog in the period being considered. *Also see: Available-to-Promise*

**Cumulative Lead Time:** The total time required to source components, build and ship a product.

**Cumulative Source/Make Cycle Time:** The cumulative internal and external lead time to manufacture shippable product, assuming that there is no inventory on-hand, no materials or parts on order, and no prior forecasts existing with suppliers. (An element of Total Supply Chain Response Time)

**Currency Adjustment Factor (CAF):** An added charge assessed by water carriers for currency value changes.

**Current Good Manufacturing Practices (CGMP):** Regulations enforced by the U.S. Food and Drug Administration for food and chemical manufacturers and packagers.

**Customer:** 1) In distribution, the Trading Partner or reseller, i.e. Wal-Mart, Safeway, or CVS. 2) In Direct-to-Consumer, the end customer or user.

**Customer Acquisition or Retention:** The rate by which new customers are acquired, or existing customers are retained. A key selling point to potential marquis partners. *Also see: Marquis Partner*

**Customer Driven:** The end user, or customer, motivates what is produced or how it is delivered.

**Customer Facing:** Those personnel whose jobs entail actual contact with the customer.

**Customer Interaction Center:** *See Call Center*

**Customer Order:** An order from a customer for a particular product or a number of products. It is often referred to as an actual demand to distinguish it from a forecasted demand.

**Customer/Order Fulfillment Process:** A series of customers' interactions with an organization through the order filling process, including product/service design, production and delivery, and order status reporting.

**Customer Profitability:** The practice of placing a value on the profit generated by business done with a particular customer.

**Customer Receipt of Order to Installation Complete:** Average lead-time from receipt of goods at the customer to the time when installation (if applicable) is complete, including the following supplements: time to get product up and running, and product acceptance by customer. (An element of Order Fulfillment Lead Time)

Note: Determined separately for Make-to-Order, Configure/Package-to-Order, Engineer-to-Order, and Make-to-Stock products.

**Customer Relationship Management (CRM):** This refers to information systems that help sales and marketing functions, as opposed to the ERP (Enterprise Resource Planning), which is for back-end integration.

**Customer Segmentation:** Dividing customers into groups based on specific criteria, such as products purchased, customer geographic location, etc.

**Customer Service:** Activities between the buyer and seller that enhance or facilitate the sale or use of the seller's products or services.

**Customer Service Ratio:** *See Percent of Fill*

**Customer Service Representative (CSR):** The individual who provides customer support via telephone in a call center environment.

**Customer Signature/Authorization to Order Receipt:** Average lead-time from when a customer authorizes an order to the time that that order is received and order entry can commence. (An element of Order Fulfillment Lead Time)

Note: Determined separately for Make-to-Order, Configure/Package-to-Order, Engineer-to-Order, and Make-to-Stock products.

**Customer-Supplier Partnership:** A long-term relationship between a buyer and a supplier characterized by teamwork and mutual confidence. The supplier is considered an extension of the buyer's organization. The partnership is based on several commitments. The buyer provides long-term contracts and uses fewer suppliers. The supplier implements quality assurance processes so that incoming inspection can be minimized. The supplier also helps the buyer reduce costs and improve product and process designs.

**Customization:** Creating a product from existing components into an individual order. Synonym: Build to Order.

**Customs and Border Protection, U.S. (CBP):** Formed during the creation of the Department of Homeland Security in 2003, CBP consists primarily of the customs inspection function formerly performed by the U.S. Customs Service as part of the Department of Treasury, the immigration inspection function formerly performed by the Immigration and Naturalization Service (INS), and the Border Patrol, formerly part of the Department of Justice.

**Customs House Broker:** A business firm that oversees the movement of international shipments through customs and ensures that the documentation accompanying a shipment is complete and accurate.

**Customs-Trade Partnership against Terrorism (C-TPAT):** A joint government/business initiative to build cooperative relationships that strengthen overall supply chain and border security. The voluntary program is designed to share information that will protect against terrorists' compromising the supply chain.

**CWT:** *See Hundredweight*

**Cycle Counting:** An inventory accuracy audit technique where inventory is counted on a cyclic schedule rather than once a year. A cycle inventory count is usually taken on a regular, defined basis (often more frequently for high-value or fast-moving items and less frequently for low-value or slow moving items). Most effective cycle counting systems require the counting of a certain number of items every workday with each item counted at a prescribed frequency. The key purpose of cycle counting is to identify items in error, thus triggering research, identification, and elimination of the cause of the errors.

**Cycle Inventory:** An inventory system where counts are performed continuously, often eliminating the need for an annual overall inventory. It is usually set up so that A items are counted regularly (i.e., every month), B items are counted semi-regularly (every quarter or six months), and C items are counted perhaps only once a year.

**Cycle Time:** The amount of time it takes to complete a business process.

**Cycle Time to Process Excess Product Returns for Resale:** The total time to process goods returned as Excess by customer or distribution centers, in preparation for resale. This cycle time includes the time a Return Product Authorization (RPA) is created to the time the RPA is approved, from Product Available for Pick-up to Product Received and from Product Receipt to Product Available for use.

**Cycle Time to Process Obsolete and End-of-Life Product Returns for Disposal:** The total time to process goods returned as Obsolete & End of Life to actual Disposal. This cycle time includes the time a Return Product Authorization (RPA) is created to the time the RPA is approved, from Product Available for Pick-up to Product Received and from Product Receipt to Product Disposal/Recycle.

**Cycle Time to Repair or Refurbish Returns for Use:** The total time to process goods returned for repair or refurbishing. This cycle time includes the time a Return Product Authorization (RPA) is created to the time the RPA is approved, from Product Available for Pick-up to Product Received, from Product Receipt to Product Repair/Refurbish begin, and from Product Repair/Refurbish begin to Product Available for use.

**Cyclical Demand:** A situation where demand patterns for a product run in cycles driven by seasonality or other predictable factors.

# D

**Dangerous Goods:** Articles or substances capable of posing significant health, safety, or environmental risk, and that ordinarily require special attention including packaging and labeling when stored or transported. *Also referred to as Hazardous Goods or Hazardous Materials (HazMat).*

**Dashboard:** A performance measurement tool used to capture a summary of the Key Performance Indicators (KPIs)/metrics of a company. Metrics dashboards/scorecards should be easy to read and usually have "red, yellow, green" indicators to flag when the company is not meeting its metrics targets. Ideally, a dashboard/scorecard should be cross-functional in nature and include both financial and non-financial measures. In addition, scorecards should be reviewed regularly – at least on a monthly basis and weekly in key functions such as manufacturing and distribution where activities are critical to the success of a company. The dashboard/scorecards philosophy can also be applied to external supply chain partners such as suppliers to ensure that supplier's objectives and practices align. *Synonym: Scorecard*

**Data Communications:** The electronic transmission of data, usually in computer readable form, using a variety of transmission vehicles and paths.

**Data Dictionary:** Lists the data elements for which standards exist. The Joint Electronic Document Interchange (JEDI) committee developed a data dictionary that is employed by many EDI users.

**Data Interchange Standards Association (DISA):** The secretariat, which provides clerical and administrative support to the ASC X12 Committee.

**Data Mining:** The process of studying data to search for previously unknown relationships. This knowledge is then applied to achieving specific business goals.

**Data Warehouse:** A repository of data that has been specially prepared to support decision-making applications. *Synonym: Decision-Support Data*

**Database:** Data stored in computer-readable form, usually indexed or sorted in a logical order by which users can find a particular item of data they need.

**Date Code:** A label on products with the date of production. In food industries, it is often an integral part of the lot number.

**Days of Supply:** Measure of quantity of inventory-on-hand, in relation to number of days for which usage which will be covered. For example, if a component is consumed in manufacturing at the rate of 100 per day, and there are 1,585 units available on-hand, this represents 15.85 days supply.

**Days Sales Outstanding (DSO):** Measurement of the average collection period (time from invoicing to cash receipt).
*Calculation:*[5 Point Annual Gross Accounts Receivables] / [Total Annual Sales / 365]

**DBR:** See *Drum-Buffer-Rope*

**DC:** See *Distribution Center*

**DD:** *See Direct Debit*

**DDSN:** *See Demand-Driven Supply Network*

**Dead Freight:** Charge payable on space booked on a ship but not utilized by the charterer or the shipper. It is imposed at full freight rates, less loading and handling charges.

**Dead on Arrival (DOA):** A term used to describe products which are not functional when delivered. Synonym: Defective.

**Deadhead:** The return of an empty transportation container to its point of origin. See: backhauling.

**Deadweight:** The total lifting capacity of a ship expressed in tons of 2240 lbs. It is the difference between the displacement light (without cargo, passengers, fuel, etc.) and the displacement loaded.

**Decentralized Authority:** A situation in which management decision-making authority is given to managers at many levels in the organizational hierarchy.

**Decision Support System (DSS):** Software that speeds access and simplifies data analysis, queries, etc. within a database management system.

**Declaration of Dangerous Goods:** To comply with the U.S. regulations, exporters are required to provide special notices to inland and ocean transport companies when goods are hazardous.

**Declared Value:** The value of the goods, declared by the shipper on a bill of lading, for the purpose of determining a freight rate or the limit of the carrier's liability. Also used by customs as the basis for calculation of duties, etc.

**Decomposition:** A method of forecasting where time series data are separated into up to three components: trend, seasonal, and cyclical; where trend includes the general horizontal upward or downward movement over time; seasonal includes a recurring demand pattern such as day of the week, weekly, monthly, or quarterly; and cyclical includes any repeating, non-seasonal pattern. A fourth component is random, that is, data with no pattern. The new forecast is made by projecting the patterns individually determined and then combining them.

**Dedicated Contract Carriage:** A third-party service that dedicates equipment (vehicles) and drivers to a single customer for its exclusive use on a contractual basis.

**Defective goods inventory (DGI):** Those items that have been returned, have been delivered damaged and have a freight claim outstanding, or have been damaged in some way during warehouse handling.

**Delimiters:** 1) ASCII, characters which are used to separate data elements within a data stream. 2) EDI, two levels of separators and a terminator that are integrals part of a transferred data stream. Delimiters are specified in the interchange header. From highest to lowest level, the separators and terminator are segment terminator, data element separator, and component element separator (used only in EDIFACT).

**Delivery-Duty-Paid:** Supplier/manufacturer arrangement in which suppliers are responsible for the transport of the goods they have produced, which is being sent to a manufacturer. This responsibility includes tasks such as ensuring products get through Customs.

**Delivery Appointment:** The time agreed upon between two enterprises for goods or transportation equipment to arrive at a selected location. Typically used to help plan warehouse and receiving / inspection operations and to manage backup of carriers at loading docks.

**Delivery Performance to Commit Date:** The percentage of orders that are fulfilled on or before the internal Commit date, used as a measure of internal scheduling systems effectiveness. Delivery measurements are based on the date a complete order is shipped or the ship-to date of a complete order. A complete order has all items on the order delivered in the quantities requested. An order must be complete to be considered fulfilled. Multiple line items on a single order with different planned delivery dates constitute multiple orders, and multiple planned delivery dates on a single line item also constitute multiple orders.

*Calculation:*[Total number of orders delivered in full and on time to the scheduled commit date] / [Total number of orders delivered]

**Delivery Performance to Request Date:** The percentage of orders that are fulfilled on or before the customer's requested date used as a measure of responsiveness to market demand. Delivery measurements are based on the date a complete order is shipped or the ship-to date of a complete order. A complete order has all items on the order delivered in the quantities requested. An order must be complete to be considered fulfilled. Multiple line items on a single order with different planned delivery dates constitute multiple orders, and multiple planned delivery dates on a single line item also constitute multiple orders.

*Calculation:*[Total number of orders delivered in full and on time to the customer's request date] / [Total number of orders delivered]

**Delphi Method:** A qualitative forecasting technique where the opinions of experts are combined in a series of iterations. The results of each iteration are used to develop the next, so that convergence of the experts' opinions is obtained.

**Delta Nu Alpha**: A professional association of transportation and traffic practitioners.

**Demand Chain:** Another name for the supply chain, with emphasis on customer or end-user demand pulling materials and product through the chain.

**Demand Chain Management:** Same as supply chain management, but with emphasis on consumer pull versus supplier push.

**Demand-Driven Supply Network (DDSN):** A system of technologies and processes that sense and react to real-time demand across a network of customers, suppliers and employees. In other words, a consumer purchase triggers real-time information movement throughout the supply network, which then initiates movement of product through the network.

**Demand Management:** The proactive compilation of requirements information regarding demand (i.e., customers, sales, marketing, finance) and the firm's capabilities from the supply side (i.e., supply, operations and logistics management); the development of a consensus regarding the ability to match the requirements and capabilities; and the agreement upon a synthesized plan that can most effectively meet the customer requirements within the constraints imposed by supply chain capabilities.

**Demand Planning:** The process of identifying, aggregating, and prioritizing, all sources of demand for the integrated supply chain of a product or service at the appropriate level, horizon and interval. The sales forecast is comprised of the following concepts:

1. The *sales forecasting level* is the focal point in the corporate hierarchy where the forecast is needed at the most generic level, i.e. Corporate forecast, Divisional forecast, Product Line forecast, SKU, SKU by Location.

2. The *sales forecasting time horizon* generally coincides with the time frame of the plan for which it was developed, i.e. Annual, 1-5 years, 1- 6 months, Daily, Weekly, Monthly.

3. The *sales forecasting time interval* generally coincides with how often the plan is updated, i.e. Daily, Weekly, Monthly, and Quarterly.

**Demand Planning Systems:** The systems that assist in the process of identifying, aggregating, and prioritizing, all sources of demand for the integrated supply chain of a product or service at the appropriate level, horizon and interval.

**Demand Pull:** The triggering of material movement to a work center only when that work center is ready to begin the next job. It in effect eliminates the queue from in front of a work center, but it can cause a queue at the end of a previous work center.

**Demand-Side Analysis:** Techniques such as market research, surveys, focus groups, and Performance / cost modeling used to identify emerging technologies.

**Demand Signal:** A signal from a consumer, customer or using operation that triggers the issue of product or raw material. The demand signal is most efficiently an electronic data transmission, but could be a physical document, kanban or telephone call.

**Demand Supply Balancing:** The process of identifying and measuring the gaps and imbalances between demand and resources in order to determine how to best resolve the variances through marketing, pricing, packaging, warehousing, outsource plans or some other action that will optimize service, flexibility, costs, assets (or other supply chain inconsistencies) in an iterative and collaborative environment.

**Demand Time Fence (DTF):** 1) That point in time inside of which the forecast is no longer included in total demand and projected available inventory calculations; inside this point, only customer orders are considered. Beyond this point, total demand is a combination of actual orders and forecasts, depending on the forecast consumption technique chosen. 2) In some contexts, the demand time fence may correspond to that point in the future inside which changes to the master schedule must be approved by an authority higher than the master scheduler. Note, however, that customer orders may still be promised inside the demand time fence without higher authority approval if there are quantities available-to-promise (ATP). Beyond the demand time fence, the master scheduler may change the MPS within the limits of established rescheduling rules, without the approval of higher authority. See: planning time fence, time fence.

**De-Manufacturing:** Refers to the process of going in and taking back assets and harvesting the components and parts. After the components are tested, they may be sold into the secondary market or may be upgraded to "as new" and used in production again.

**Deming Circle:** The concept of a continuously rotating wheel of plan-do-check-action (PDCA) used to show the need for interaction among market research, design, production, and sales to improve quality. *Also see: Plan-Do-Check-Action*

**Demographic Segmentation:** In marketing, dividing potential markets by characteristics of potential customers, such as age, sex, income, and education.

**Demurrage:** The carrier charges and fees applied when rail freight cars and ships are retained beyond a specified loading or unloading time. *Also see: Detention, Express*

**Denied Party List (DPL):** A list of organizations that are unauthorized to submit a bid for an activity or to receive a specific product. For example, some countries have bans for certain products such as weapons or sensitive technology.

**Density:** A physical characteristic of a commodity measuring its mass per unit volume or pounds per cubic foot; an important factor in rate making, since density affects the utilization of a carrier's vehicle.

**Density Rate:** A rate based upon the density and shipment weight.

**Deregulation:** Revisions or complete elimination of economic regulations controlling transportation. The Motor Carrier Act of 1980 and the Staggers Act of 1980 revised the economic controls over motor carriers and railroads, and the Airline Deregulation Act of 1978 eliminated economic controls over air carriers.

**Derived Demand:** Demand for component products that arises from the demand for final design products. For example, the demand for steel is derived from the demand for automobiles.

**Design For Manufacture / Assembly (DFMA):** A product design methodology that provides a quantitative evaluation of product designs.

**Design of Experiments (DoE):** A branch of applied statistics dealing with planning, conducting, analyzing, and interpreting controlled tests to evaluate the factors that control the value of a parameter or group of parameters.

**Destination-Enhanced Consolidation:** Ganging of smaller shipments to cut cost, often as directed by a system or via pooling with a third party.

**Detention:** The carrier charges and fees applied when rail freight cars and ships are retained beyond a specified loading or unloading time. *Also see: Demurrage, Express*

**Deterministic Models:** Models where no uncertainty is included, e.g., inventory models without safety stock considerations.

**DFMA:** *See Design for Manufacture/ Assembly*

**DFZ:** *See Duty Free Zone*

**DGI:** *See Defective Goods Inventory*

**Dial Up:** Access a network by dialing a phone number or initiating a computer to dial the number. The dial-up line connects to the network access point via a node or a PAD.

**Differential**: A discount offered by a carrier that faces a service time disadvantage over a route.

**Digital Signature:** Electronically generated, digitized (as opposed to graphically created) authorization that is uniquely linkable and traceable to an empowered officer.

**Direct Channel:** Your own sales force sells to the customer. Your entity may ship to the customer, or a third party may handle shipment, but in either case your entity owns the sales contract and retains rights to the receivable from the customer. Your end customer may be a retail outlet. The movement to the customer may be direct from the factory, or the product may move through a distribution network owned by your company. Order information in this channel may be transmitted by electronic means.

**Direct Cost:** A cost that can be directly traced to a cost object since a direct or repeatable cause-andeffect relationship exists. A direct cost uses a direct assignment or cost causal relationship to transfer costs. *Also see: Indirect Cost, Tracing*

**Direct Debit (DD):** A method of ACH collection used where the debtor gives authorization to debit his or her account upon the receipt of an entry issued by a creditor. *See also automated clearinghouse*

**Direct Product Profitability (DPP):** Calculation of the net profit contribution attributable to a specific product or product line.

**Direct Production Material:** Material that is used in the manufacturing/content of a product (example: Purchased parts, solder, SMT glues, adhesives, mechanical parts etc. Bill-of-Materials parts, etc.)

**Direct Retail Locations:** A retail location that purchases products directly from your organization or responding entity.

**Direct Store Delivery (DSD):** Process of shipping direct from a manufacturer's plant or distribution center to the customer's retail store, thus bypassing the customer's distribution center. Also called Direct-to-Store Delivery

**Direct Transmission:** A transmission whereby data is exchanged directly between sender and receiver computers, without an intervening third-party service. *Also called a point-to-point transmission*

**Direct-to-Consumer (DTC):** fulfillment services that send products to your home, or office

**Direct-to-Store (DTS) Delivery:** Same as Direct Store Delivery.

**Directed tasks:** Tasks that can be completed based upon detailed information provided by the computer system. An order picking task where the computer details the specific item, location, and quantity to pick is an example of a directed task. If the computer could not specify the location and quantity forcing the worker to choose locations or change quantities, it would not be a directed task. Directed tasks set up the opportunity for confirmation transactions.

**DISA:** *See Data Interchange Standards Association.*

**Disaster Recovery Planning:** Contingency planning specifically related to recovering hardware and software (e.g. data centers, application software, operations, personnel, telecommunications) in information system outages.

**Discontinuous Demand:** A demand pattern that is characterized by large demands interrupted by periods with no demand, as opposed to a continuous or steady (e.g., daily) demand. Synonym: Lumpy Demand.

**Discrete Available-to-Promise:** A calculation based on the available-to-promise figure in the master schedule. For the first period, the ATP is the sum of the beginning inventory plus the MPS quantity minus backlog for all periods until the item is master scheduled again. For all other periods, if a quantity has been scheduled for that time period then the ATP is this quantity minus all customer commitments for this and other periods, until another quantity is scheduled in the MPS. For those periods where the quantity scheduled is zero, the ATP is zero (even if deliveries have been promised). The promised customer commitments are accumulated and shown in the period where the item was most recently scheduled. *Also see: Available-to-Promise*

**Discrete Manufacturing:** Discrete manufacturing processes create products by assembling unconnected distinct parts as in the production of distinct items such as automobiles, appliances, or computers.

**Discrete Order Picking:** A method of picking orders in which the items on one order are picked before the next order is picked. *Also see: Batch Picking, Order Picking, Zone Picking*

**Discrete Order Quantity:** An order quantity that represents an integer number of periods of demand. Most MRP systems employ discrete order quantities. *Also see: Fixed-period Requirements, Least Total Cost, Least Unit Cost, Lot-for-Lot, Part Period Balancing, Period Order Quantity, Wagner-Whitin Algorithm*

**Disintermediation:** When the traditional sales channels are disassembled and the middleman gets cut out of the deal. Such as where the manufacturer ships direct to a retailer, bypassing the distributor.

**Dispatching**: The carrier activities involved with controlling equipment; involves arranging for fuel, drivers, crews, equipment, and terminal space.

**Distributed Inventory:** Inventory that is geographically dispersed. For example, where a company maintains inventory in multiple distribution centers to provide a higher level of customer service.

**Distribution:** Outbound logistics, from the end of the production line to the end user. 1) The activities associated with the movement of material, usually finished goods or service parts, from the manufacturer to the customer. These activities encompass the functions of transportation, warehousing, inventory control, material handling, order administration, site and location analysis, industrial packaging, data processing, and the communications network necessary for effective management. It includes all activities related to physical distribution, as well as the return of goods to the manufacturer. In many cases, this movement is made through one or more levels of field warehouses. *Synonym: Physical Distribution.* 2) The systematic division of a whole into discrete parts having distinctive characteristics.

**Distribution Center (DC):** The warehouse facility which holds inventory from manufacturing pending distribution to the appropriate stores.

**Distribution Channel:** One or more companies or individuals who participate in the flow of goods and services from the manufacturer to the final user or consumer.

**Distribution Channel Management:** The organizational and pipeline strategy for getting products to customers. Direct channels involve company sales forces, facilities, and/or direct shipments to customers. Indirect channels involve the use of wholesalers, distributors, and/or other parties to supply the products to customers. Many companies use both strategies, depending on markets and effectiveness.

**Distribution On Demand (DOD):** The order fulfillment state a distribution operation achieves when it can respond, closest to real time, to changes in demand while shipping 100 percent customer compliant orders at the least cost.

**Distribution Planning:** The planning activities associated with transportation, warehousing, inventory levels, materials handling, order administration, site and location planning, industrial packaging, data processing, and communications networks to support distribution.

**Distribution Requirements Planning (DRP):** A system of determining demands for inventory at distribution centers and consolidating demand information in reverse as input to the production and materials system.

**Distribution Resource Planning (DRP II):** The extension of distribution requirements planning into the planning of the key resources contained in a distribution system: warehouse space, workforce, money, trucks, freight cars, etc.

**Distribution Warehouse:** A warehouse that stores finished goods and from which customer orders are assembled.

**Distributor:** A business that does not manufacture its own products, but purchases and resells these products. Such a business usually maintains a finished goods inventory. *Synonym: Wholesaler*

**Diversion:** The practice of selling goods to a competitor that the vendor assumes would be used to service that Customer's store. Example; Grocery Store Chain A buys orange juice from Minute Maid. Grocery Store Chain A, because of their sales volume or because of promotion, can buy product for $12.50 per case. Grocery Store Chain B, because of a lower sales volume, buys the same orange juice for $14.50 per case. Grocery Store Chain A and Grocery Store Chain B get together and make a deal. Grocery Store Chain A resells that product to Grocery Store Chain B for $13.50 per case. Grocery Store Chain A makes $1.00 per case and Grocery Store Chain B gets product for $1.00 less per case than it can buy from Minute Maid.

**Dock-to-Stock:** A program by which specific quality and packaging requirements are met before the product is released. Pre-qualified product is shipped directly into the customer's inventory. Dock-tostock eliminates the costly handling of components, specifically in receiving and inspection and enables product to move directly into production.

**Document:** In EDI, a form, such as an invoice or a purchase order, that trading partners have agreed to exchange and that the EDI software handles within its compliance-checking logic.

**DOA:** *See Dead on Arrival*

**Dock Receipt:** A receipt that indicates an export shipment has been delivered to a steamship company by a domestic carrier.

**Documentation:** The papers attached or pertaining to goods requiring transportation and/or transfer of ownership. These may include the packing list, hazardous materials declarations, export / customs documents, etc.

**DOD:** *See Distribution on Demand*

**DOE:** *See Design of Experiments*

**Domain:** A computer term for the following: 1) Highest subdivision of the Internet, for the most part by country (except in the U.S., where it's by type of organization, such as educational, commercial, and government). Usually the last part of a host name; for example, the domain part of ibm.com is .com, which represents the domain of commercial sites in the U.S. 2) In corporate data networks, a group of client computers controlled by a server system.

**Domestic Trunk Line Carrier:** An air carrier classification for carriers that operate between major population centers. These carriers are now classified as major carriers.

**Dormant route:** A route over which a carrier failed to provide service 5 days a week for 13 weeks out of a 26-week period.

**Double Bottoms:** A motor carrier operation involving two trailers being pulled by one tractor.

**Double Order Point System:** A distribution inventory management system that has two order points. The smallest equals the original order point, which covers demand during replenishment lead time. The second order point is the sum of the first order point plus normal usage during manufacturing lead time. It enables warehouses to forewarn manufacturing of future replenishment orders.

**Double-pallet jack:** A mechanized device for transporting two standard pallets simultaneously.

**Double Stack:** Two containers, one on top of the other, loaded on a railroad flatcar; an intermodal service.

**Download:** To merge temporary files containing a day's or week's worth of information with the main data base in order to update it.

**Downstream:** Referring to the demand side of the supply chain. One or more companies or individuals who participate in the flow of goods and services moving from the manufacturer to the final user or consumer. Opposite of Upstream.

**DPC:** *See Dynamic Process Control*

**DPL:** *See Denied Party List*

**DPP:** *See Direct product profitability*

**Drayage:** Transportation of materials and freight on a local basis, but intermodal freight carriage may also be referred to as drayage.

**Driving Time Regulations:** Rules administered by the U.S. Department of Transportation that limit the maximum time a driver may drive in interstate commerce; both daily and weekly maximums are prescribed.

**Drop:** A situation in which an equipment operator deposits a trailer or boxcar at a facility at which it is to be loaded or unloaded.

**Drop Ship:** To take the title of the product but not actually handle, stock, or deliver it, e.g., to have one supplier ship directly to another or to have a supplier ship directly to the buyer's customer.

**DRP:** *See Disaster Recovery Planning*

**DRP:** *See Distribution Requirements Planning*

**DRPII:** *See Distribution Resources Planning*

**Drum-Buffer-Rope (DBR):** In the theory of constraints, the generalized process used to manage resources to maximize throughput. The drum is the rate or pace of production set by the system's constraint. The buffers establish the protection against uncertainty so that the system can maximize throughput. The rope is a communication process from the constraint to the gating operation that checks or limits material released into the system to support the constraint. *Also see: Finite Scheduling*

**DSD:** *See Direct Store Delivery*

**DSO:** *See Days Sales Outstanding*

**DSS:** *See Decision Support System*

**DTC:** *See Direct to Consumer*

**DTF:** *See Demand Time Fence*

**DTS:** *See Direct Store Delivery*

**Dual Operation:** A motor carrier that has both common and contract carrier operating authority.

**Dual Rate System:** An international water carrier pricing system where a shipper signing an exclusive use agreement with the conference pays a lower rate (10% to %15) than non-signing shippers for an identical shipment.

**Dumping:** Selling goods below costs in selected markets.

**Dunnage:** The packing material used to protect a product from damage during transport.

**DUNS Number:** A unique nine-digit number assigned by Dun and Bradstreet to identify a company. DUNS stands for Data Universal Numbering System.

**DUNS:** Data Universal Numbering System.

**Durable Goods:** Generally, any goods whose continuous serviceability is likely to exceed three years (e.g., trucks, furniture).

**Duty Free Zone (DFZ):** An area where goods or cargo can be stored without paying import customs duties while awaiting manufacturing or future transport.

**Dynamic Lot Sizing:** Any lot-sizing technique that creates an order quantity subject to continuous Re-computation. *See: Least total cost, Least unit cost, Part period balancing, Period order quantity, Wagner-Whitin algorithm*

**Dynamic Process Control (DPC):** Continuous monitoring of process performance and adjustment of control parameters to optimize process output.

# E

**EAI:** *See Enterprise Application Integration*

**EAN.UCC:** European Article Numbering/ Uniform Code Council (now the European office of GS1). The EAN.UCC System provides identification standards to uniquely identify trade items, logistics units, locations, assets, and service relations worldwide. The identification standards define the construction of globally-unique and unambiguous numbers.

**Early Supplier Involvement (ESI):** The process of involving suppliers early in the product design activity and drawing on their expertise, insights, and knowledge to generate better designs in less time and designs that are easier to manufacture with high quality.

**Earnings Before Interest and Taxes (EBIT):** A measure of a company's earning power from ongoing operations, equal to earnings (revenues minus cost of sales, operating expenses, and taxes) before deduction of interest payments and income taxes. *Also called operating profit*

**EBIT:** *See Earnings Before Interest and Taxes*

**EC:** *See Electronic Commerce*

**ECO:** *See Engineering Change Order*

**E-Commerce:** *See Electronic Commerce*

**Economic Order Quantity (EOQ):** An inventory model that determines how much to order by determining the amount that will meet customer service levels while minimizing total ordering and holding costs.

**Economic Value Added (EVA):** A measurement of shareholder value as a company's operating profits after tax, less an appropriate charge for the capital used in creating the profits.

**Economy of Scale:** A phenomenon whereby larger volumes of production reduce unit cost by distributing fixed costs over a larger quantity.

**ECR:** *See Efficient Consumer Response*

**EDI:** *See Electronic Data Interchange*

**EDIA:** *See Electronic Data Interchange Association*

**EDIFACT:** Electronic Data Interchange for Administration, Commerce, and Transport. The United Nations EDI standard.

**EDI Standards:** Criteria that define the data content and format requirements for specific business transactions (e.g. purchase orders). Using standard formats allows companies to exchange transactions with multiple trading partners easily. *Also see: American National Standards Institute, GS1 Group*

**EDI Transmission:** A functional group of one or more EDI transactions that are sent to the same location, in the same transmission, and are identified by a functional group header and trailer.

**EduPunk:** Avoiding mainstream teaching tools like Powerpoint and Blackboard, edupunks bring the rebellious attitude and DIY ethos of '70s bands like the Clash to the classroom.

**Efficient Consumer Response (ECR):** A demand driven replenishment system designed to link all parties in the logistics channel to create a massive flow-through distribution network. Replenishment is based upon consumer demand and point of sale information.

**EFT:** *See Electronic Funds Transfer*

**EH&S:** *See Environmental Health and Safety*

**EI:** *See Emotional Intelligence*

**EIN:** *See Exporter Identification Number*

**Electronic Commerce (EC):** Also written as e-commerce. Conducting business electronically via traditional EDI technologies, or online via the Internet. In the traditional sense of selling goods, it is possible to do this electronically because of certain software programs that run the main functions of an e-commerce website, such as product display, online ordering, and inventory management. The definition of e-commerce includes business activity that is business-to-business (B2B), business-to consumer (B2C).

**Electronic Data Interchange (EDI):** Intercompany, computer-to-computer transmission of business information in a standard format. For EDI purists, "computer-to-computer" means direct transmission from the originating application program to the receiving, or processing, application program. An EDI transmission consists only of business data, not any accompanying verbiage or free-form messages. Purists might also contend that a standard format is one that is approved by a national or international standards organization, as opposed to formats developed by industry groups or companies.

**Electronic Data Interchange Association:** A national body that propagates and controls the use of EDI in a given country. All EDIAs are nonprofit organizations dedicated to encouraging EDI growth. The EDIA in the United States was formerly TDCC and administered the development of standards in transportation and other industries.

**Electronic Funds Transfer (EFT):** A computerized system that processes financial transactions and information about these transactions or performs the exchange of value. Sending payment instructions across a computer network, or the company-to-company, company-to-bank, or bank-to bank electronic exchange of value.

**Electronic Mail (E-Mail):** The computer-to-computer exchange of messages. E-mail is usually unstructured (free-form) rather than in a structured format. X.400 has become the standard for email exchange.

**Electronic Product Code (EPC or ePC):** An electronically coded tag that is intended as an improvement to the UPC bar code system. The EPC is a 96-bit tag which contains a number called the Global Trade Identification Number (GTIN). Unlike a UPC number, which only provides information specific to a group of products, the GTIN gives each product its own specific identifying number, giving greater accuracy in tracking. EPC standards are managed by the Global Standards organization known as GS1.

**Electronic Signature:** A form of authentication that provides identification and validation of a transaction by means of an authorization code identifying the individual or organization.

**Elkins Act:** An amendment to the IC Act that prohibits giving rebates.

**E-mail:** *See Electronic Mail*

**Embargo:** A prohibition upon exports or imports, either with specific products or specific countries.

**Emotional Intelligence:** describes the ability, capacity, skill or, in the case of the trait EI model, a self-perceived ability to identify, assess, and control the emotions of one's self, of others, and of groups.

**Empirical:** Pertaining to a statement or formula based upon experience or observation rather than on deduction or theory.

**Empowerment:** A condition whereby employees have the authority to make decisions and take action in their work areas without prior approval. For example, an operator can stop a production process if he or she detects a problem, or a customer service representative can send out a replacement product if a customer calls with a problem.

**Encryption:** The transformation of readable text into coded text for security purposes.

**End item:** A product sold as a completed item or repair part; any item subject to a customer order or sales forecast. Synonym: Finished Goods Inventory.

**End-of-Life:** Planning and execution at the end of the life of a product. The challenge is making just the right amount to avoid A) ending up with excess, which have to be sold at great discounts or scrapped or B) ending up with shortages before the next generation is available.

**End-of-Life Inventory:** Inventory on hand that will satisfy future demand for products that are no longer in production at your entity.

**Engineering Change:** A revision to a drawing or design released by engineering to modify or correct a part. The request for the change can be from a customer or from production, quality control, another department, or a supplier. *Synonym: Engineering Change Order*

**Engineering Change Order (ECO):** A documented and approved revision to a product or process specification.

**Engineer-to-Order:** A process in which the manufacturing organization must first prepare (engineer) significant product or process documentation before manufacture may begin.

**Enroute:** A term used for goods in transit or on the way to a destination.

**Enterprise Application Integration (EAI):** A computer term for the tools and techniques used in linking ERP and other enterprise systems together. Linking systems is key for e-business. Gartner say 'firms implementing enterprise applications spend at least 30% on point-to-point interfaces'.

**Enterprise-Wide ABM:** A management information system that uses activity-based information to facilitate decision making across an organization.

**Enterprise Resource Planning (ERP) System:** A class of software for planning and managing "enterprise-wide" the resources needed to take customer orders, ship them, account for them and replenish all needed goods according to customer orders and forecasts. Often includes electronic commerce with suppliers. Examples of ERP systems are the application suites from SAP, Oracle, PeopleSoft and others.

**Enveloping:** An EDI management software function that groups all documents of the same type, or functional group, and bound for the same destination into an electronic envelope. Enveloping is useful where there are multiple documents such as orders or invoices issued to a single trading partner that need to be sent as a packet.

**Environmental Health and Safety (EH&S):** The category of processes, procedures and regulations related to addressing the needs of maintaining environmental quality standards for health and safety. Includes the RoHS (Restriction of Hazardous Substances) and WEEE (Waste Electrical and Electronic) standards.

**Environmentally Sensitive Engineering:** Designing features in a product and its packaging that improve recycling, etc. It can include elimination of compounds that are hazardous to the environment.

**E&O:** *See Excess and Obsolescence*

**EOL:** *See End-of-Life*

**EOQ:** *See Economic Order Quantity*

**EPC or ePC:** *See: Electronic Product Code*

**EPS:** A computer term. Encapsulated Postscript. An extension of the PostScript graphics file format developed by Adobe Systems. EPS lets PostScript graphics files be incorporated into other documents.

**Equipment:** The rolling stock carriers use to facilitate the transportation services that they provide, including containers, trucks, chassis, vessels, and airplanes, among others.

**Equipment I.D.:** An identifier assigned by the carrier to a piece of equipment. *See also Container ID*

**Equipment Positioning:** The process of placing equipment at a selected location.

**Ergonomic:** The science of creating workspaces and products which are human friendly to use.

**ERP:** *See Enterprise Resources Planning System*

**ERS:** *See Evaluated Receipts Settlement*

**ESI:** *See Early Supplier Involvement*

**ETA:** The Estimated Time of Arrival

**ETD:** The Estimated Time of Departure

**Ethernet:** A computer term for the most commonly used type of local area network (LAN) communication protocol using coaxial or twisted pair wiring.

**Ethical Standards:** A set of guidelines for proper conduct by business professionals.

**European Article Number (EAN):** A defined numbering mechanism used in Europe to uniquely identify every retail product and packaging option. The EAN is similar in concept and design to the UPC code and is usually what the barcode represents on goods. *Also see: Uniform Product Code*

**EVA:** *See Economic Value Added*

**Evaluated Receipts Settlement (ERS):** A process for authorizing payment for goods based on actual receipts with purchase order data, when price has already been negotiated. The basic premise behind ERS is that all of the information in the invoice is already transmitted in the shipping documentation. Therefore, the invoice is eliminated and the shipping documentation is used to pay the vendor.

**Exception-Based Processing:** A computer term for applications that automatically highlight particular events or results which fall outside pre-determined parameters. This saves considerable effort by automatically finding problems and alerting the right persons. An example would be where a shorted item on a purchase order receipt would automatically notify a purchasing agent for follow-up.

**Exception Message:** *See Action Message*

**Exception Rate:** A deviation from the class rate; changes (exceptions) made to the classification.

**Excess and Obsolescence (E&O):** The accounting value assigned to the cost associated with inventory that is disposed of as being excess or obsolete.

**Exclusive Patronage Agreements:** A shipper agrees to use only member liner firms of a conference in return for a 10% to 15% rate reduction.

**Exclusive Use:** Carrier vehicles that are assigned to a specific shipper for its exclusive use.

**Executive Dashboard:** A series of cross-functional metrics that span the performance of the entire company and indicate the overall health of the company. Usually an Executive Dashboard includes the top KPIs for the company – and when possible is limited to the 'vital few' that fit on a one page summary.

**Exempt Carrier:** A for-hire carrier that is free from economic regulation. Trucks hauling certain commodities are exempt from Interstate Commerce Commission economic regulation. By far the largest portion of exempt carriers transports agricultural commodities or seafood.

**Expediting:** 1) Moving shipments through regular channels at an accelerated rate. 2) To take extraordinary action because of an increase in relative priority. *Synonym: Stock-chase*

**Expert System:** A computer program that mimics a human expert.

**Explode-to-Deduct:** *See Back-flush*

**Exponential Smoothing Forecast:** In forecasting, a type of weighted moving average forecasting technique in which past observations are geometrically discounted according to their age. The heaviest weight is assigned to the most recent data. The smoothing is termed exponential because data points are weighted in accordance with an exponential function of their age. The technique makes use of a smoothing constant to apply to the difference between the most recent forecast and the critical sales data, thus avoiding the necessity of carrying historical sales data. The approach can be used for data that exhibit no trend or seasonal patterns. Higher order exponential smoothing models can be used for data with either (or both) trend and seasonality

**Export:** 1) In logistics, the movement of products from one country to another. For example, significant volumes of cut flowers are exported from The Netherlands to other countries of the world. 2) A computer term referring to the transfer of information from a source (system or database) to a target.

**Export Broker:** An enterprise that brings together buyer and seller for a fee, then eventually withdraws from the transaction.

**Export Compliance:** Complying with rules for exporting products, including packaging, labeling, and documentation.

**Export Declaration:** A document required by the Department of commerce that provides information as to the nature, value, etc., of export activity.

**Export License:** A document secured from a government authorizing an exporter to export a specific quantity of a controlled commodity to a certain country. An export license is often required if a government has placed embargoes or other restrictions upon exports.

**Export sales contract:** The initial document in any international transaction; it details the specifics of the sales agreement between the buyer and seller.

**Exporter Identification Number (EIN):** A number required for the exporter on the Shipper's Export Declaration. A corporation may use their Federal Employer Identification Number as issued by the IRS; individuals can use their Social Security Numbers.

**Exports:** A term used to describe products produced in one country and sold in another. *Also see: Export*

**Express**: 1) Carrier payment to its customers when ships, rail cars, or trailers are unloaded or loaded in less than the time allowed by contract and returned to the carrier for use. See: demurrage, detention. 2) The use of priority package delivery to achieve overnight or second-day delivery.

**Extended Enterprise:** The notion that supply chain partners form a larger entity which works together as though it were a single unit.

**Extensible Markup Language (XML):** A computer term for a language that facilitates direct communication among computers on the Internet. Unlike the older hypertext markup language (HTML), which provides data tags giving instructions to a web browser about how to display information, XML tags give instructions to a browser or to application software which help to define the specifics about the category of information.

**External Factory:** A situation where suppliers are viewed as an extension of the firm's manufacturing capabilities and capacities. The same practices and concerns that are commonly applied to the management of the firm's manufacturing system should also be applied to the management of the external factory.

**Extranet:** A computer term describing a private network (or a secured link on the public internet) that links separate organizations and that uses the same software and protocols as the Internet. Used for improving supply chain management. For example, extranets are used to provide access to a supply chain partner's internal inventory data which is not available to unrelated parties. *Antonym: Intranet*

**Extrinsic Forecast:** In forecasting, a forecast based on a correlated leading indicator, such as estimating furniture sales based on housing starts. Extrinsic forecasts tend to be more useful for large aggregations, such as total company sales, than for individual product sales. *Ant: intrinsic forecast method*

**EXW:** *See Ex Works*

**Ex Works (EXW):** An international trade term (Incoterms, International Chamber of Commerce) requiring the seller to deliver goods at his or her own place of business. All other transportation costs and risks are assumed by the buyer.

# F

**FA:** *See Functional Acknowledgment*

**Fabricator:** A manufacturer that turns the product of a raw materials supplier into a larger variety of products. A fabricator may turn steel rods into nuts, bolts, and twist drills, or may turn paper into bags and boxes.

**Facilities:** The physical plant, distribution centers, service centers, and related equipment.

**Factory Gate Pricing:** Like DSD in reverse, factory gate pricing (FGP) is a supply chain initiative that has been gaining popularity among retailers in England. With FGP, retailers buy goods at the suppliers' "gate" and take care of getting it to their stores or distribution centers, either with their own trucks or those of their contracted carriers.

**Failure Modes Effects Analysis (FMEA):** A pro-active method of predicting faults and failures so that preventive action can be taken.

**Fair Return:** A level of profit that enables a carrier to realize a rate of return on investment or property value that the regulatory agencies deem acceptable for that level of risk.

**Fair-share Quantity Logic:** In inventory management, the process of equitably allocating available stock among field distribution centers. Fair-share quantity logic is normally used when stock available from a central inventory location is less than the cumulative requirements of the field stocking locations. The use of fair-share quantity logic involves procedures that "push" stock out to the field, instead of allowing the field to "pull" in what is needed. The objective is to maximize customer service from the limited available inventory.

**Fair value:** The value of the carrier's property; the basis of calculation has included original cost minus depreciation, replacement cost, and market value.

**FAK:** *See Freight all kinds*

**Faraday Bag:** are made of translucent metalized plastic film which shields against electrostatic fields and charges by creating a Faraday cage. The metalized layer attracts electrostatic charges which disperse harmlessly around the exterior or drain to ground when in contact with a conductive work surface. Can block cell, GPS, and RFID data as well. Also know as Faraday Cage.

**FAS:** *See Final Assembly Schedule*

**FAS:** *See Free Alongside Ship*

**FAST:** *See Fast and Secure Trade*

**FAS:** *See Free Alongside Ship*

**Fast and Secure Trade (FAST):** U.S. Customs program that allows importers on the U.S./Canada border to obtain expedited release for qualifying commercial shipments.

**Fast Moving Consumer Goods (FMCG):** Fast Moving Consumer Goods are packaged commercial products that are consumed through use. They include pre-packaged food and drinks, alcohol, health and beauty items, tobacco products, paper products, household cleansers and chemicals, animal care items, anything that we need, can buy right off the shelf, and use up through daily living.

**FCL:** *See Full Container Load*

**Feature:** A distinctive characteristic of a good or service. The characteristic is provided by an option, accessory, or attachment. For example, in ordering a new car, the customer must specify an engine type and size (option), but need not necessarily select an air conditioner (attachment).

**Federal Aviation Administration:** The federal agency charged with administering federal safety regulations governing air transportation.

**Federal Maritime Commission:** A regulatory agency that controls services, practices, and agreements of international water common carriers and noncontiguous domestic water carriers.

**Feeder Railroad Development Program:** A Federal program which allows any financially responsible person (except Class I and Class II carriers) with ICC approval to acquire a rail line having a density of less than 3 million gross ton-miles per year, in order to avert the line being abandoned.

**FEU:** *See Forty-foot Equivalent Unit*

**FG:** *See Finished Goods Inventory*

**FGI:** *See Finished Goods Inventory*

**Field Finished Goods:** Inventory which is kept at locations outside the four walls of the manufacturing plant (i.e., distribution center or warehouse).

**Field Service:** *See After-Sale Service*

**Field Service Parts:** Parts inventory kept at locations outside the four walls of the manufacturing plant (i.e., distribution center or warehouse).

**Field warehouse:** A warehouse on the property of the owner of the goods that stores goods that are under the custody of a bona fide public warehouse manager. The public warehouse receipt is used as collateral for a loan.

**FIFO:** *See First In, First Out*

**File Transfer Protocol (FTP):** The Internet service that transfers files from one computer to another, over standard phone lines.

**Filed rate doctrine:** The legal rate the common carrier may charge; is the rate published in the carrier's tariff on file with the ICC.

**Fill Rate:** The percentage of order items that the picking operation actually fills within a given period of time.

**Fill Rates by Order:** Whether orders are received and released consistently, or released from a blanket purchase order, this metric measures the percentage of ship-from-stock orders shipped within 24 hours of order "release". Make-to-Stock schedules attempt to time the availability of finished goods to match forecasted customer orders or releases. Orders that were not shipped within 24 hours due to consolidation but were available for shipment within 24 hours are reported separately. In calculating elapsed time for order fill rates, the interval begins at ship release and ends when material is consigned for shipment.

***Calculation:***[Number of orders filled from stock shipped within 24 hours of order release] / [Total number of stock orders]

**Final Assembly:** The highest level assembled product, as it is shipped to customers. This terminology is typically used when products consist of many possible features and options that may only be combined when an actual order is received. *Also see: End Item, Assemble to Order*

**Final Assembly Schedule (FAS):** A schedule of end items to finish the product for specific customers' orders in a make-to-order or assemble-to-order environment. It is also referred to as the finishing schedule because it may involve operations other than just the final assembly; also, it may not involve assembly, but simply final mixing, cutting, packaging, etc. The FAS is prepared after receipt of a customer order as constrained by the availability of material and capacity, and it schedules the operations required to complete the product from the level where it is stocked (or master scheduled) to the end-item level.

**Finance Lease:** An equipment-leasing arrangement that provides the lessee with a means of financing for the leased equipment; a common method for leasing motor carrier trailers.

**Financial Responsibility:** Motor carriers are required to have body injury and property damage (not cargo) insurance or not less than $500,000 per incident per vehicle; higher financial responsibility limits apply for motor carriers transporting oil or hazardous materials.

**Finished Goods Inventory (FG or FGI):** Products completely manufactured, packaged, stored, and ready for distribution. *Also see: End Item*

**Finite Forward Scheduling:** An equipment scheduling technique that builds a schedule by proceeding sequentially from the initial period to the final period while observing capacity limits. A Gantt chart may be used with this technique. *Also see: Finite Scheduling*

**Finite Scheduling:** A scheduling methodology where work is loaded into work centers such that no work center capacity requirement exceeds the capacity available for that work center. See: drumbuffer-rope, finite forward scheduling.

**Firewall:** A computer term for a method of protecting the files and programs on one network from users on another network. A firewall blocks unwanted access to a protected network while giving the protected network access to networks outside of the firewall. A company will typically install a firewall to give users access to the Internet while protecting their internal information.

**Firm Planned Order:** A planned order which has been committed to production. *Also see: Planned Order*

**First In, First Out (FIFO):** Warehouse term meaning first items stored are the first used. In accounting this term is associated with the valuing of inventory such that the latest purchases are reflected in book inventory. *Also see: Book Inventory*

**First Mover Advantage:** Market innovator, putting the company in the leadership position.

**First Pass Yield:** The ratio of usable, specification conforming output from a process to its input, achieved without rework or reprocessing.

**Fixed Costs:** Costs, which do not fluctuate with business volume in the short run. Fixed costs include items such as depreciation on buildings and fixtures.

**Fixed Interval Inventory Model:** A setup wherein each time an order is placed for an item, the same (fixed) quantity is ordered.

**Fixed Interval Order System:** *See Fixed Reorder Cycle Inventory Model*

**Fixed Order Quantity:** A lot-sizing technique in MRP or inventory management that will always cause planned or actual orders to be generated for a predetermined fixed quantity, or multiples thereof if net requirements for the period exceed the fixed order quantity.

**Fixed Order Quantity System:** *See Fixed Reorder Cycle Inventory Model*

**Fixed Overhead:** Traditionally, all manufacturing costs, other than direct labor and direct materials, that continue even if products are not produced. Although fixed overhead is necessary to produce the product, it cannot be directly traced to the final product. *Also see: Indirect Cost*

**Fixed-Period Requirements:** A lot-sizing technique that sets the order quantity to the demand for a given number of periods. *Also see: Discrete Order Quantity*

**Fixed Quantity Inventory Model:** A setup wherein a company orders the same (fixed) quantity each time it places an order for an item.

**Fixed Reorder Cycle Inventory Model:** A form of independent demand management model in which an order is placed every "n" time units. The order quantity is variable and essentially replaces the items consumed during the current time period. Let "M" be the maximum inventory desired at any time, and let x be the quantity on hand at the time the order is placed. Then, in the simplest model, the order quantity will be $M - x$. The quantity M must be large enough to cover the maximum expected demand during the lead time plus a review interval. The order quantity model becomes more complicated whenever the replenishment lead time exceeds the review interval, because outstanding orders then have to be factored into the equation. These reorder systems are sometimes called fixed interval order systems, order level systems, or periodic review systems. *Synonyms: Fixed-Interval Order System, Fixed-Order Quantity System, Order Level System, Periodic Review System, Time-Based Order System. Also see: Fixed Reorder Quantity Inventory Model, Hybrid Inventory System, Independent Demand Item Management Models, Optional Replenishment Model*

**Fixed Reorder Quantity Inventory Model:** A form of independent demand item management model in which an order for a fixed quantity is placed whenever stock on hand plus on order reaches a predetermined reorder level. The fixed order quantity may be determined by the economic order quantity, by a fixed order quantity (such as a carton or a truckload), or by another model yielding a fixed result. The reorder point may be deterministic or stochastic, and in either instance is large enough to cover the maximum expected demand during the replenishment lead time. Fixed reorder quantity models assume the existence of some form of a perpetual inventory record or some form of physical tracking, e.g., a two-bin system that is able to determine when the reorder point is reached. *Synonym: Fixed Order Quantity System, Lot Size System, Order Point-Order Quantity System, Quantity Based Order System. Also see: Fixed Reorder Cycle Inventory Model, Hybrid Inventory System, Independent Demand Item Management Models, Optional Replenishment Model, Order Point – Order Management System*

**Fixed-Location Storage:** A method of storage in which a relatively permanent location is assigned for the storage of each item in a storeroom or warehouse. Although more space is needed to store parts than in a random-location storage system, fixed locations become familiar, and therefore a locator file may not be needed. *Also see: Random-Location Storage*

**Flag of Convenience:** A ship owner registers a ship in a nation that offers conveniences in the areas of taxes, manning, and safety requirements; Liberia and Panama are two nations known for flags of convenience.

**Flat:** A loadable platform having no superstructure whatever but having the same length and width as the base of a container and equipped with top and bottom corner fittings. This is an alternative term used for certain types of specific purpose containers - namely platform containers and platform-based containers with incomplete structures

**Flatbed:** A flatbed is a type of truck trailer that consists of a floor and no enclosure. A flatbed may be used with "sideboards" or "tie downs" which keep loose cargo from falling off.

**Flatcar:** A rail car without sides; used for hauling machinery.

**Flat File:** A computer term which refers to any file having fixed-record length, or in EDI, the file produced by EDI translation software to serve as input to the interface. Usually includes the same fields as the original file, but each field is expanded to its maximum length. Does not have delimiters.

**Flexibility:** Ability to respond quickly and efficiently to changing customer and consumer demands.

**Flexible-Path Equipment:** Materials handling devices that include hand trucks and forklifts.

**Flexible Specialization:** a strategy based on multi-use equipment, skilled workers and innovative senior management to accommodate the continuous change that occurs in the marketplace.

**Float:** The time required for documents, payments, etc. to get from one trading partner to another.

**Floor-Ready Merchandise (FRM):** Goods shipped by suppliers to retailers with all necessary tags, prices, security devices, etc. already attached, so goods can be cross docked rapidly through retail DCs, or received directly at stores.

**Flow Center:** A flexible, scalable facility that enables quick movement of goods in varying supply chain scenarios.

**Flow Rack:** Storage rack that utilizes shelves (metal) that are equipped with rollers or wheels. Such an arrangement allows product and materials to "flow" from the back of the rack to the front and therein making the product more accessible for small-quantity order-picking.

**Flow-Through Distribution:** A process in a distribution center in which products from multiple locations are brought in to the D.C. and are re-sorted by delivery destination and shipped in the same day. Also known as a "cross-dock" process in the transportation business. *See Cross Docking.*

**FMCG:** *See Fast Moving Consumer Goods*

**FMEA:** *See Failure Modes Effects Analysis*

**FMG:** Fast Moving Goods

**FOB:** *See Free on Board*

**FOB Destination:** Title passes at destination, and seller has total responsibility until shipment is delivered.

**FOB Origin:** Title passes at origin, and buyer has total responsibility over the goods while in shipment.

**For-Hire Carrier:** A carrier that provides transportation service to the public on a fee basis.

**Forecast:** An estimate of future demand. A forecast can be constructed using quantitative methods, qualitative methods, or a combination of methods, and it can be based on extrinsic (external) or intrinsic (internal) factors. Various forecasting techniques attempt to predict one or more of the four components of demand: cyclical, random, seasonal, and trend. *Also see: Box-Jenkins Model, Exponential Smoothing Forecast, Extrinsic Forecasting Method, Intrinsic Forecasting Method, Qualitative Forecasting Method, Quantitative Forecasting Method*

**Forecast Accuracy:** Measures how accurate your forecast is as a percent of actual units or dollars shipped, calculated as 1 minus the absolute value of the difference between forecasted demand and actual demand, as a percentage of actual demand.

**Calculation:** *[1-(|Sum of Variances|/Sum of Actual)]*

**Forecast Cycle:** Cycle time between forecast regenerations that reflect true changes in marketplace demand for shippable end products.

**Forecasting:** Predictions of how much of a product will be purchased by customers. Relies upon both quantitative and qualitative methods. *Also see: Forecast*

**Foreign Trade Zone (FTZ):** An area or zone set aside at or near a port or airport, under the control of the U.S. Customs Service, for holding goods duty-free pending customs clearance.

**Forklift truck:** A machine-powered device that is used to raise and lower freight and to move freight to different warehouse locations.

**Form utility:** The value created in a good by changing its form, through the production process.

**Four P's:** A set of marketing tools to direct the business offering to the customer. The four P's are product, price, place, and promotion.

**Fourier Series:** In forecasting, a form of analysis useful for forecasting. The model is based on fitting sine waves with increasing frequencies and phase angles to a time series.

**Four Wall Inventory:** The stock which is contained within a single facility or building.

**Fourth-Party Logistics (4PL):** Differs from third party logistics in the following ways; 1)4PL organization is often a separate entity established as a joint venture or long-term contract between a primary client and one or more partners; 2) 4PL organization acts as a single interface between the client and multiple logistics service providers; 3) All aspects (ideally) of the client's supply chain are managed by the 4PL organization; and, 4) It is possible for a major third-party logistics provider to form a 4PL organization within its existing structure. The term was registered by Accenture as a trademark in 1996 and defined as "A supply chain integrator that assembles and manages the resources, capabilities, and technology of its own organization with those of complementary service providers to deliver a comprehensive supply chain solution.", but is no longer registered *Also see: Lead Logistics Provider*

**Forty-foot Equivalent Unit (FEU):** A standard size intermodal container.

**Foxhole:** *See Silo*

**Free Alongside Ship (FAS):** A term of sale indicating the seller is liable for all changes and risks until the goods sold are delivered to the port on a dock that will be used by the vessel. Title passes to the buyer when the seller has secured a clean dock or ship's receipt of goods. The seller agrees to deliver the goods to the dock alongside the overseas vessel that is to carry the shipment. The seller pays the cost of getting the shipment to the dock; the buyer contracts the carrier, obtains documentation, and assumes all responsibility from that point forward.

**Free on Board (FOB):** Contractual terms between a buyer and a seller, that define where title transfer takes place.

**Free Time:** The period of time allowed for the removal or accumulation of cargo before charges become applicable.

**Freezing Inventory Balances:** In most cycle counting programs the term "freezing" refers to copying the current on-hand inventory balance into the cycle count file. This may also be referred to as taking a snapshot of the inventory balance. It rarely means that the inventory is actually frozen in a way that prevents transactions from occurring.

**Freight:** Goods being transported from one place to another.

**Freight-all-kinds (FAK):** An approach to rate making whereby the ante is based only upon the shipment weight and distance; widely used in TOFC service.

**Freight Bill:** The carrier's invoice for transportation charges applicable to a freight shipment.

**Freight Carriers:** Companies that haul freight, also called "for-hire" carriers. Methods of transportation include trucking, railroads, airlines, and sea borne shipping.

**Freight Charge:** The rate established for transporting freight.

**Freight Collect:** The freight and charges to be paid by the consignee.

**Freight Consolidation:** The grouping of shipments to obtain reduced costs or improved utilization of the transportation function. Consolidation can occur by market area grouping, grouping according to scheduled deliveries, or using third-party pooling services such as public warehouses and freight forwarders.

**Freight Forwarder:** An organization which provides logistics services as an intermediary between the shipper and the carrier, typically on international shipments. Freight forwarders provide the ability to respond quickly and efficiently to changing customer and consumer demands and international shipping (import/export) requirements.

**Freight Forwarders Institute:** The freight forwarder industry association.

**Freight Prepaid:** The freight and charges to be paid by the consignor.

**FRM:** *See Floor Ready Merchandise*

**Fronthaul:** The first leg of the truck trip that involves hauling a load or several loads to targeted destinations.

**Frozen Zone:** In forecasting, this is the period in which no changes can be made to scheduled work orders based on changes in demand. Use of a frozen zone provides stability in the manufacturing schedule.

**FTE:** *See Full Time Equivalents*

**FTL:** *See Full Truckload*

**FTP:** *See File Transfer Protocol*

**FTZ:** *See Free Trade Zone*

**FUBAR:** F...ed Up Beyond All Recognition

**Fulfillment:** The act of fulfilling a customer order. Fulfillment includes order management, picking, packaging, and shipping.

**Full Container load (FCL):** A term used when goods occupy a whole container.

**Full-Service Leasing:** An equipment-leasing arrangement that includes a variety of services to support leased equipment (i.e., motor carrier tractors).

**Full-Time Equivalents (FTE):** Frequently organizations make use of contract and temporary employees; please convert contract, part-time, and temporary employees to full-time equivalents. For example, two contract employees who worked for six months full-time and a half-time regular employee would constitute 1.5 full-time equivalents. 1 FTE = 2000 hours per year.

**Full Truckload (FTL):** A term which defines a shipment which occupies at least one complete truck trailer, or allows for no other shippers goods to be carried at the same time.

**Fully allocated cost:** The variable cost associated with a particular unit of output plus an allocation of common cost.

**Functional Acknowledgment (FA):** A specific EDI Transaction Set (997) sent by the recipient of an EDI message to confirm the receipt of data but with no indication as to the recipient application's response to the message. The FA will confirm that the message contained the correct number of lines, etc. via control summaries, but does not report on the validity of the data.

**Functional Group:** Part of the hierarchical structure of EDI transmissions, a Functional Group contains one or more related Transaction Sets preceded by a Functional Group header and followed by a Functional Group trailer

**Functional Metric:** A number resulting from an equation, showing the impact of one or more parts of a functional/department process. This is also known as a results measure as the metric measures the results of one aspect of the business. Example: Distribution Center Fill Rate.

**Functional Silo:** A view of an organization where each department or functional group is operated independent of other groups within the organization. Each group is referred to as a "Silo". This is the opposite of an integrated structure.

**Future Order:** An order entered for shipment at some future date. This may be related to new products which are not currently available for shipment, or scheduling of future needs by the customer.

# G

**Gain Sharing:** A method of incentive compensation where supply chain partners share collectively in savings from productivity improvements. The concept provides an incentive to both the buying and supplier organizations to focus on continually re-evaluating, re-energizing, and enhancing their business relationship. All aspects of value delivery are scrutinized, including specification design, order processing, inbound transportation, inventory management, obsolescence programs, material yield, forecasting and inventory planning, product performance and reverse logistics. The focus is on driving out limited value cost while protecting profit margins.

**Gateway:** The connection that permits messages to flow freely between two networks.

**Gathering lines:** Oil pipelines that bring oil from the oil well to storage areas.

**GATT:** *See General Agreement on Tariffs and Trade*

**GDSN:** *See Global Data Synchronization Network*

**General Agreement on Tariffs and Trade (GATT):** The General Agreement on Tariffs and Trade started as an international trade organization in 1947, and has been superseded by the World Trade Organization (WTO). GATT (the agreement) covers international trade in goods. An updated General Agreement is now the WTO agreement governing trade in goods. The 1986-1994 "Uruguay Round" of GATT member discussions gave birth to the WTO and also created new rules for dealing with trade in services, relevant aspects of intellectual property, dispute settlement, and trade policy reviews. GATT 1947: The official legal term for the old (pre-1994) version of the GATT. GATT 1994: The official legal term for new version of the General Agreement, incorporated into the WTO, and including GATT 1947.

**General Commodities Carrier:** A common motor carrier that has operating authority to transport general commodities, or all commodities not listed as special commodities.

**General-Merchandise Warehouse:** A warehouse that is used to store goods that are readily handled, are packaged, and do not req1ire a controlled environment.

**General Order (GO):** A customs term referring to a warehouse where merchandise not entered within five working days after the carrier's arrival is stored at the risk and expense of the importer.

**Geographic Information Systems (GIS):** GIS is a system of hardware and software used for storage, retrieval, mapping, and analysis of geographic data. Practitioners also regard the total GIS as including the operating personnel and the data that go into the system. Spatial features are stored in a coordinate system (latitude/longitude, state plane, UTM, etc.), which references a particular place on the earth. Descriptive attributes in tabular form are associated with spatial features. Spatial data and associated attributes in the same coordinate system can then be layered together for mapping and analysis. GIS can be used for scientific investigations, resource management, and development planning.

**GIF:** *See Graphics Interchange Format*

**Gitter Box:** A **skeleton** or **lattice box,** or just "gitter" is one made of a steel frame and of grid-design for product or parts used in the automotive and truck manufacturing process. Four feet enable the manipulation of the box by means of a forklift from all four sides.

**Global Data Synchronization Network (GDSN):** The GDSN is an Internet-based, interconnected network of interoperable data pools and a Global Registry, the GS1 Global Registry, that enables companies around the world to exchange standardized and synchronized supply chain data with their trading partners.

**Global Standards Management Process (GSMP):** The Global Standards Management Process (GSMP) is the Global Process established in January 2002 by EAN International and the Uniform Code Council, Inc. (UCC) for the development and maintenance of Global Standards and Global Implementation Guidelines that are part of the EAN.UCC system.

**Global Strategy:** A strategy that focuses on improving worldwide performance through the sales and marketing of common goods and services with minimum product variation by country. Its competitive advantage grows through selecting the best locations for operations in other countries.

**Global Trade Item Number (GTIN):** A unique number that comprises up to 14 digits and is used to identify an item (product or service) upon which there is a need to retrieve pre-defined information that may be priced, ordered or invoiced at any point in the supply chain. The definition covers raw materials through end user products and includes services, all of which have pre-defined characteristics. GTIN is the globally-unique EAN.UCC System identification number, or key, used for trade items (products and services). It's used for uniquely identifying trade items (products and services) sold, delivered, warehoused, and billed throughout the retail and commercial distribution channels. Unlike a UPC number, which only provides information specific to a group of products, the GTIN gives each product its own specific identifying number, giving greater accuracy in tracking. *See EPC*

**Global Positioning System (GPS):** A system which uses satellites to precisely locate an object on earth. Used by trucking companies to locate over-the-road equipment.

**Globalization:** The process of making something worldwide in scope or application.

**GO:** *See General Order*

**Going-Concern Value:** The value that a firm has as an entity, as opposed to the sum of the values of each of its parts taken separately; particularly important in determining what constitutes a reasonable railroad rate.

**Gondola:** A rail car with a flat platform and sides three to five feet high; used for top loading of items that are long and heavy.

**Good Manufacturing Practices (GMP) or 21 CFR, parts 808, 812, and 820:** Requirements governing the quality procedures of medical device manufacturers.

**Goods:** A term associated with more than one definition: 1) Common term indicating movable property, merchandise, or wares. 2) All materials which are used to satisfy demands. 3) Whole or part of the cargo received from the shipper, including any equipment supplied by the shipper.

**Goods Received Note (GRN):** Documentation raised by the recipient of materials or products.

**GMP:** *See Good manufacturing practices*

**GNP:** *See Gross National Product*

**GPS:** *See Global Positioning System*

**Grandfather Clause:** A provision that enabled motor carriers engaged in lawful trucking operations before the passage of the Motor Carrier Act of 1935 to secure common carrier authority without proving public convenience and necessity; a similar provision exists for other modes.

**Granger Laws:** State laws passed before 1870 in Midwestern states to control rail transportation.

**Graphics Interchange Format (GIF):** A graphical file format commonly used to display indexed color images on the World Wide Web. GIF is a compressed format, designed to minimize file transfer time over standard phone lines.

**Green Lane:** A concept that would give C-TPAT members that demonstrate the highest standard of secure practices additional benefits for exceeding the minimum requirements of the program. Green Lane benefits would include expedited movement of cargo, especially during an incident of national significance.

**GRI:** General rate increase

**Grid technique:** A quantitative technique to determine the least-cost center, given raw materials sources and markets, for locating a plant or warehouse.

**GRN:** *See Goods Received Note*

**GPS:** *See Global Positioning System*

**Groupthink:** A situation in which critical information is withheld from the team because individual members censor or restrain themselves, either because they believe their concerns are not worth discussing or because they are afraid of confrontation.

**Gross Inventory:** Value of inventory at standard cost before any reserves for excess and obsolete items are taken.

**Gross Margin:** The difference between total revenue and the cost of goods sold. *Syn: gross profit margin*

**Gross National Product (GNP):** A measure of a nation's output; the total value of all final goods and services produced during a period of time.

**Gross Weight**: The total weight of the vehicle and the payload of freight or passengers.

**GS1:** The new name of EAN International. The GS1 US is the new name of the Uniform Code Council, Inc® (UCC®) the GS1 Member Organization for the U.S. The association that administrates UCS, WINS, and VICS and provides UCS identification codes and UPCs. Also, a model set of legal rules governing commercial transmissions, such as sales, contracts, bank deposits and collections, commercial paper, and letters of credit. Individual states give legal power to the GS1 by adopting its articles of law.

**GSMP:** *See Global Standards Management Process*

**GTIN:** *See Global Trade Item Number*

**Guaranteed Loans:** Loans made to railroads that are cosigned and guaranteed by the federal government.


# H

**Handling Costs:** The cost involved in moving, transferring, preparing, and otherwise handling inventory.

**Hard copy:** Computer output printed on paper.

**Harmonized Code:** An international classification system that assigns identification numbers to specific products. The coding system ensures that all parties in international trade use a consistent classification for the purposes of documentation, statistical control, and duty assessment.

**Haulage:** The inland transport service which is offered by the carrier under the terms and conditions of the tariff and of the relative transport document.

**Hawaiian carrier:** A for-hire air carrier that operates within the state of Hawaii

**Hawthorne Effect:** From a study conducted at the Hawthorne Plant of Western Electric Company in 1927-1932 which found that the act of showing people that you are concerned usually results in better job performance. Studying and monitoring of activities are typically seen as being concerned and results in improved productivity.

**Hazardous Goods:** *See: Hazardous Material*

**Hazardous Material:** A substance or material, which the Department of Transportation has determined to be capable of posing a risk to health, safety, and property when stored or transported in commerce. *Also see: Material Safety Data Sheet*

**HazMat:** *See Hazardous Material*

**Hedge Inventory:** A form of inventory buildup to buffer against some event that may not happen. Hedge inventory planning involves speculation related to potential labor strikes, price increases, unsettled governments, and events that could severely impair a company's strategic initiatives. Risk and consequences are unusually high, and top management approval is often required.

**Heijunka:** In the Just-in-Time philosophy, an approach to level production throughout the supply chain to match the planned rate of end product sales.

**Hierarchy of Cost Assignability:** In cost accounting, an approach to group activity costs at the level of an organization where they are incurred, or can be directly related to. Examples are the level where individual units are identified (unit-level), where batches of units are organized or processed (batch-level), where a process is operated or supported (process-level), or where costs cannot be objectively assigned to lower level activities or processes (facility-level). This approach is used to better understand the nature of the costs, including the level in the organization at which they are incurred, the level to which they can be initially assigned (attached) and the degree to which they are assignable to other activity and/or cost object levels, i.e. activity or cost object cost, or sustaining costs.

**Highway Trust Fund:** Federal highway use tax revenues are paid into this fund, and the federal government's share of highway construction is paid from the fund.

**Highway Use Taxes:** Taxes assessed by federal and state governments against users of the highway (the fuel tax is an example). The use tax money is used to pay for the construction, maintenance, and policing of highways.

**Hi-low:** Usually refers to a forklift truck on which the operator must stand rather than sit.

**Home Page:** The starting point for a website. It is the page that is retrieved and displayed by default when a user visits the website. The default home-page name for a server depends on the server's configuration. On many web servers, it is index.html or default.htm. Some web servers support multiple home pages.

**Honeycombing:** 1. The practice of removing merchandise in pallet load quantities where the space is not exhausted in an orderly fashion. This results in inefficiencies due to the fact that the received merchandise may not be efficiently stored in the space which is created by the honeycombing. 2. The storing or withdrawal or supplies in a manner that results in vacant space that is not usable for storage of other items. 3. Creation of unoccupied space resulting from withdrawal of unit loads. This is one of the major hidden costs of warehousing.

**Hopper Cars:** Rail cars that permit top loading and bottom unloading of bulk commodities; some hopper cars have permanent tops with hatches to provide protection against the elements.

**Horizontal Play/Horizontal Hub:** This is a term for a function that cuts across many industries, usually defines a facility or organization that is providing a common service.

**Hoshin Planning:** Breakthrough planning. A Japanese strategic planning process in which a company develops up to four vision statements that indicate where the company should be in the next five years. Company goals and work plans are developed based on the vision statements. Periodic audits are then conducted to monitor progress.

**Hostler:** An individual employed to move trucks and trailers within a terminal or warehouse yard area.

**Household Goods Warehouse:** A warehouse that is used to store household goods.

**HR:** *See Human Resources*

**HTML:** *See HyperText Markup Language*

**HTTP:** *See HyperText Transport Protocol*

**Hub:** 1) A large retailer or manufacturer having many trading partners. 2) A reference for a transportation network as in "hub and spoke" which is common in the airline and trucking industry. For example, a hub airport serves as the focal point for the origin and termination of long-distance flights where flights from outlying areas are fed into the hub airport for connecting flights. 3) A common connection point for devices in a network. 4) A Web "hub" is one of the initial names for what is now known as a "portal". It came from the creative idea of producing a website, which would contain many different "portal spots" (small boxes that looked like ads, with links to different yet related content). This content, combined with Internet technology, made this idea a milestone in the development and appearance of websites, primarily due to the ability to display a lot of useful content and store one's preferred information on a secured server. The web term "hub" was replaced with portal.

**Hub Airport:** An airport that serves as the focal point for the origin and termination of long-distance flights; flights from outlying areas are fed into the hub airport for connecting flights.

**Human-Machine Interface:** Any point where data is communicated from a worker to a computer or from a computer to a worker. Data entry programs, inquire programs, reports, documents, LED displays, and voice commands are all examples of human-machine interfaces.

**Human Resources (HR):** The function broadly responsible for personnel policies and practices within an organization.

**Hundredweight (cwt):** A pricing unit used in transportation (equal to 100 pounds).

**Hybrid Inventory System:** An inventory system combining features of the fixed reorder quantity inventory model and the fixed reorder cycle inventory model. Features of the fixed reorder cycle inventory model and the fixed reorder quantity inventory model can be combined in many different ways. For example, in the order point-periodic review combination system, an order is placed if the inventory level drops below a specified level before the review date; if not, the order quantity is determined at the next review date. Another hybrid inventory system is the optional replenishment model. *Also see: Fixed Reorder Cycle Inventory Model, Fixed Reorder Quantity Inventory Model, Optional Replenishment Model*

**Hyperlink:** A computer term. Also referred to as "link". The text you find on a website which can be "clicked on" with a mouse which, in turn, will take you to another web page or a different area of the same web page. Hyperlinks are created or "coded" in HTML.

**Hyperlink:** Also known as link. The text you find on a website which can be "clicked on" with a mouse which, in turn, will take you to another web page or a different area of the same web page. Hyperlinks are created or "coded" in HTML.

**HyperText Markup Language (HTML):** The standard language for describing the contents and appearance of pages on the World Wide Web.

**HyperText Transport Protocol (HTTP):** The Internet protocol that allows World Wide Web browsers to retrieve information from servers.

# I

**IATA:** *See International Air Transport Association*

**ICAO:** *See International Civil Aeronautics Organization*

**ICC:** *See Interstate Commerce Commission*

**Idea Practitioners:** people who know how to get new ideas across and implemented.

**Igloos:** Pallets and containers used in air transportation; the igloo shape is designed to fit the internal wall contours of a narrow-body airplane.

**Image Processing:** allows a company to take electronic photographs of documents. The electronic photograph then can be stored in a computer and retrieved from computer storage to replicate the document on a printer. The thousands of bytes of data composing a single document are encoded in an optical disk. Many carriers now use image processing to provide proof-of-delivery documents to a shipper. The consignee signs an electronic pad that automatically digitizes a consignee's signature for downloading into a computer. A copy of that signature then can be produced to demonstrate that a delivery took place.

**IMB:** *See International Maritime Bureau*

**IMC:** *See Intermodal marketing company*

**IMO:** *See International Maritime Organization*

**Import:** Movement of products from one country into another. The import of automobiles from Germany to the U.S. is an example.

**Importation Point:** The location (port, airport or border crossing) where goods will be cleared for importation into a country.

**Import/Export License:** Official authorization issued by a government allowing the shipping or delivery of a product across national boundaries.

**Impressions:** With regard to online advertising, it is the number of times an ad banner is downloaded and presumably seen by users. Guaranteed impressions refer to the minimum number of times an ad banner will be seen by users.

**In Bond:** Goods are held or transported In-Bond under customs control either until import duties or other charges are paid, or to avoid paying the duties or charges until a later date.

**Inbound Logistics:** The movement of materials from suppliers and vendors into production processes or storage facilities.

**Incentive Rate:** A rate designed to induce the shipper to ship heavier volumes per shipment.

**INCOTERMS:** International terms of sale developed by the International Chamber of Commerce to define sellers' and buyers' responsibilities.

**Independent action:** A carrier that is a member of a rate bureau has the right to publish a rate that differs from the rate published by the rate bureau.

**Independent Demand Item Management Models:** Models for the management of items whose demand is not strongly influenced by other items managed by the same company. These models can be characterized as follows: (1) stochastic or deterministic, depending on the variability of demand and other factors; (2) fixed quantity, fixed cycle, or hybrid - (optional replenishment). *Also see: Fixed Reorder Cycle Inventory Model, Fixed Reorder Quantity Inventory Model, Optional Replenishment Model*

**Independent Trading Exchange (ITE):** Often used synonymously with B2B, e-marketplace or Virtual Commerce Network (VCN). ITE is a more precise term, connoting many-to-many transactions, whereas the others do not specify the transactions.

**Indirect Cost:** A resource or activity cost that cannot be directly traced to a final cost object since no direct or repeatable cause-and-effect relationship exists. An indirect cost uses an assignment or allocation to transfer cost. *Also see: Direct Cost, Support Costs*

**Indirect/Distributor Channel:** Your company sells and ships to the distributor. The distributor sells and ships to the end user. This may occur in multiple stages. Ultimately your products may pass through the Indirect/Distributor Channel and arrive at a retail outlet. Order information in this channel may be transmitted by electronic means. These means may include EDI, brokered systems, or linked electronic systems.

**Indirect Retail Locations:** A retail location that ultimately sells your product to consumers, but who purchases your products from an intermediary, like a distributor or wholesaler.

**Infinite Loading:** Calculation of the capacity required at work centers in the time periods required regardless of the capacity available to perform this work.

**Information Systems (IS):** Managing the flow of data in an organization in a systematic, structured way to assist in planning, implementing, and controlling.

**Inherent Advantage:** The cost and service benefits of one mode compared with other modes.

**Inland Bill of Lading:** The carriage contract used in transport from a shipping point overland to the exporter's international carrier location.

**Inland Carrier:** An enterprise that offers overland service to or from a point of import or export.

**Insourcing:** The opposite of outsourcing, that is, a serve performed in-house.

**Inspection Certificate:** A document certifying that merchandise (such as perishable goods) was in good condition immediately prior to shipment.

**Integrated Carrier:** A company that offers a blend of transportation services such as land, sea and air carriage, freight forwarding, and ground handling.

**Integrated Logistics:** A comprehensive, system-wide view of the entire supply chain as a single process, from raw materials supply through finished goods distribution. All functions that make up the supply chain are managed as a single entity, rather than managing individual functions separately.

**Integrated Services Digital Network (ISDN):** A computer term describing the networks and equipment for integrated broadband transmissions of data, voice, and image, from rates of 144 Kbps to 2 Mbps. ISDN allows integration of data, voice, and video over the same digital links.

**Integrated Tow Barge:** A series of barges that are connected together to operate as one unit.

**Intellectual Property (IP):** Property of an enterprise or individual which is typically maintained in a digital form. This may include software program code or digital documents, music, videos, etc.

**Interchange:** In EDI, the exchange of electronic information between companies. Also, the group of transaction sets transmitted from one sender to one receiver at one time. Delineated by interchange control segments.

**Intercoastal Carriers:** Water carriers that transport freight between East and West Coast ports, usually by way of the Panama Canal.

**Intercorporate Hauling:** A private carrier hauling the goods of a subsidiary and charging the subsidiary a fee: this is legal if the subsidiary is wholly owned (100%) or if the private carrier has common carrier authority.

**Interleaving:** The practice of assigning an employee multiple tasks which are performed concurrently.

**Interline:** Two or more motor carriers working together to haul the shipment to a destination. Carrier equipment may be interchanged from one carrier to the next, but usually the shipment is Re-handled without the equipment.

**Intermediately Positioned Warehouse:** A warehouse located between customers and manufacturing plants to provide increased customer service and reduced distribution cost.

**Intermittent-flow, fixed-path equipment:** Materials handling devices that include cranes, monorails, and stacker cranes.

**Intermodal Container Transfer Facility:** A facility where cargo is transferred from one mode of transportation to another, usually from ship or truck to rail.

**Intermodal Marketing Company (IMC):** An intermediary that sells intermodal services to shippers.

**Intermodal Transportation:** Transporting freight by using two or more transportation modes such as by truck and rail or truck and oceangoing vessel.

**Intermodal transport unit (ITU):** Container, swap body or semi-trailer/goods road motor vehicle suitable for intermodal transport.

**Internal Customer:** The recipient (person or department) of another person's or department's output (good, service, or information) within an organization. *Also see: Customer*

**Internal Labor and Overhead:** The portion of COGS that is typically reported as labor and overhead, less any costs already classified as "outsourced."

**Internal Water Carriers:** Water carriers that operate over internal, navigable rivers such as the Mississippi, Ohio, and Missouri.

**International Air Transport Association (IATA):** An international air carrier rate bureau for passenger and freight movements.

**International Civil Aeronautics Organization (ICAO):** An international agency that is responsible for air safety and for standardizing air traffic control, airport design, and safety features worldwide.

**International Maritime Bureau (IMB):** A special division of the International Chamber of Commerce.

**International Maritime Organization (IMO):** A United Nations-affiliated organization representing all maritime countries in matters affecting maritime transportation, including the movement of dangerous goods. The organization also is involved in deliberations on marine environmental pollution.

**International Ship and Port Facility Security Code (ISPS):** Adopted by the IMO and based on the U.S. MTSA, came into force on July 1, 2004. It is a comprehensive, mandatory security regime for international shipping and port facility operations agreed to by the members of the IMO. Ships must be certified by their flag states to ensure that mandated security measures have been implemented; port facilities must undergo security vulnerability assessments that form the basis of security plans approved by their government authorities.

**International Standards Organization (ISO):** An organization within the United Nations to which all national and other standard setting bodies (should) defer. Develops and monitors international standards, including OSI, EDIFACT, and X.400

**Internet:** A computer term which refers to an interconnected group of computer networks from all parts of the world, i.e. a network of networks. Accessed via a modem and an on-line service provider, it contains many information resources and acts as a giant electronic message routing system.

**Interstate Commerce:** The transportation of persons or property between states; in the course of the movement, the shipment cresses a state boundary line.

**Interstate Commerce Commission (ICC):** An independent regulatory agency that implements federal economic regulations controlling railroads, motor carriers, pipelines, domestic water carriers, domestic surface freight forwarders, and brokers.

**Interstate System:** The National System of Interstate and Defense Highways, 42,000 miles of four lane, limited-access roads connecting major population centers.

**In the weeds:** when someone or something, becomes overwhelmed and falls really behind.

**Intra-Manufacturing Re-plan Cycle:** Average elapsed time, in calendar days, between the time a regenerated forecast is accepted by the end-product manufacturing/assembly location, and the time that the revised plan is reflected in the Master Production Schedule of all the affected internal subassembly/ component producing plant(s). (An element of Total Supply Chain Response Time)

**Intrastate Commerce:** The transportation of persons or property between points within a state. A shipment between two points within a state may be interstate if the shipment had a prior or subsequent move outside of the state and the intent of the shipper was an interstate shipment at the time of shipment.

**In-transit Inventory:** Material moving between two or more locations, usually separated geographically; for example, finished goods being shipped from a plant to a distribution center. In-transit inventory is an easily overlooked component of total supply chain availability.

**Intrinsic Forecast Method:** In forecasting, a forecast based on internal factors, such as an average of past sales.

**Inventory:** Raw materials, work in process, finished goods and supplies required for creation of a company's goods and services; The number of units and/or value of the stock of goods held by a company.

**Inventory Accuracy:** When the on-hand quantity is equivalent to the perpetual balance (plus or minus the designated count tolerances). Often referred to as a percentage showing the variance between book inventory and actual count. This is a major performance metric for any organization which manages large inventories. Typical minimum and best practice averages would be 95% and 99%.

**Inventory Balance Location Accuracy:** When the on-hand quantity in the specified locations is equivalent to the perpetual balance (plus or minus the designated count tolerances).

**Inventory Carrying Cost:** One of the elements comprising a company's total supply-chain management costs. These costs consist of the following:

1. Opportunity Cost: The opportunity cost of holding inventory. This should be based on your company's own cost of capital standards using the following formula. Calculation: Cost of Capital x Average Net Value of Inventory

2. Shrinkage: The costs associated with breakage, pilferage, and deterioration of inventories. Usually pertains to the loss of material through handling damage, theft, or neglect.

3. Insurance and Taxes: The cost of insuring inventories and taxes associated with the holding of inventory.

4. Total Obsolescence for Raw Material, WIP, and Finished Goods Inventory: Inventory reserves taken due to obsolescence and scrap and includes products exceeding the shelf life, i.e. spoils and is no good for use in its original purpose (do not include reserves taken for Field Service Parts).

5. Channel Obsolescence: Aging allowances paid to channel partners, provisions for buy-back agreements, etc. Includes all material that goes obsolete while in a distribution channel. Usually, a distributor will demand a refund on material that goes bad (shelf life) or is no longer needed because of changing needs.

6. Field Service Parts Obsolescence: Reserves taken due to obsolescence and scrap. Field Service Parts are those inventory kept at

locations outside the four walls of the manufacturing plant i.e., distribution center or warehouse.

**Inventory Days of Supply (for RM, WIP, PFG, and FFG):** Total gross value of inventory for the category (raw materials, work in process, partially finished goods, or fully-finished goods) at standard cost before reserves for excess and obsolescence. It includes only inventory that is on the books and currently owned by the business entity. Future liabilities such as consignments from suppliers are not included.

*Calculation:*[*5 Point Annual Average Gross Inventory] / [Calendar Year Value of Transfers / 365]*

**Inventory Deployment:** A technique for strategically positioning inventory to meet customer service levels while minimizing inventory and storage levels. Excess inventory is replaced with information derived through monitoring supply, demand and inventory at rest as well as in motion.

**Inventory Management:** The process of ensuring the availability of products through inventory administration.

**Inventory Planning Systems:** The systems that help in strategically balancing the inventory policy and customer service levels throughout the supply chain. These systems calculate time-phased order quantities and safety stock, using selected inventory strategies. Some inventory planning systems conduct what-if analysis and that compares the current inventory policy with simulated inventory scenarios and improves the inventory ROI.

**Inventory Turns:** The cost of goods sold divided by the average level of inventory on hand. This ratio measures how many times a company's inventory has been sold during a period of time. Operationally, inventory turns are measured as total throughput divided by average level of inventory for a given period; How many times a year the average inventory for a firm changes over, or is sold.

**Inventory Turnover:** *See Inventory Turns*

**Inventory Velocity:** The speed with which inventory moves through a defined cycle (i.e., from receiving to shipping).

**Invoice:** A detailed statement showing goods sold and amounts for each. The invoice is prepared by the seller and acts as the document that the buyer will use to make payment.

**IP:** *See Intellectual Property*

**Irregular Route Carrier:** A motor carrier that is permitted to provide service utilizing any route.

**IS:** *See Information Systems*

**ISDN:** *See Integrated services digital network*

**ISO:** *See International Standards Organization*

**ISO 9000:** A series of quality assurance standards compiled by the Geneva, Switzerland-based International Standardization Organization. In the United States, ISO is represented by the American National Standards Institute based in Washington, D.C.

**ISO 14000 Series Standards:** A series of generic environmental management standards under development by the International Organization of Standardization, which provide structure and systems for managing environmental compliance with legislative and regulatory requirements and affect every aspect of a company's environmental operations.

**ISPS:** *See International Ship and Port Facility Security Code*

**IT:** Information Technology.

**ITL:** International Trade Logistics.

**ITE:** *See Independent Trading Exchange*

**ITU:** *See Intermodal Transport Unit*

**Item:** Any unique manufactured or purchased part, material, intermediate, subassembly, or product.

# J

**Java:** A computer term for a general-purpose programming language created by Sun Microsystems. Java can be used to create Java applets. A Java program is downloaded from the web server and interpreted by a program running on the computer running the Web browser.

**Java Applet:** A computer term for a short program written in Java that is attached to a web page and executed by the computer on which the Web browser is installed.

**Java Script:** A computer term for a cross-platform, World Wide Web scripting language developed by Netscape Communications. JavaScript code is inserted directly into an HTML page.

**Jidoka:** The concept of adding an element of human judgment to automated equipment. In doing this, the equipment becomes capable of discriminating against unacceptable quality, and the automated process becomes more reliable. This concept, also known as autonomation, was pioneered by Sakichi Toyoda at the turn of the twentieth century when he invented automatic looms that stopped instantly when any thread broke. This permitted one operator to oversee many machines with no risk of producing large amounts of defective cloth. The term has since been extended beyond its original meaning to include any means of stopping production to prevent scrap (for example the andon cord which allows assembly-plant workers to stop the line), even where this capability is not built-in to the production machine itself.

**JIT:** *See Just-In-Time*

**JIT II:** *See Just-In-Time II*

**JIT/QC:** Just-In-Time/Quality Control.

**Joint Cost:** A type of common cost where products are produced in fixed proportions, and the cost incurred to produce on product necessarily entails the production of another; the backhaul is an example.

**Joint Photographic Expert Group (JPEG):** A computer term which is an abbreviation for the Joint Photographic Expert Group. A graphical file format used to display high-resolution color images on the World Wide Web. JPEG images apply a user-specified compression scheme that can significantly reduce the large file size usually associated with photo-realistic color images. A higher level of compression results in lower image quality, whereas a lower level of compression results in higher image quality.

**Joint Rate**: A rate over a route that involves two or more carriers to transport the shipment.

**Joint Supplier Agreement (JSA):** Indicative of Stage 3 Sourcing Practices, the JSA includes terms & conditions, objectives, process flows, performance targets, flexibility, balancing and incentives.

**JPEG:** *See Joint Photographic Expert Group*

**JSA:** *See Joint Supplier Agreement*

**Just-in-Time (JIT):** An inventory control system that controls material flow into assembly and manufacturing plants by coordinating demand

and supply to the point where desired materials arrive just in time for use. An inventory reduction strategy that feeds production lines with products delivered "just in time". Developed by the auto industry, it refers to shipping goods in smaller, more frequent lots.

**Just-in-Time II (JIT II):** Vendor-managed operations taking place within a customer's facility. JIT II was popularized by the Bose Corporation. The supplier reps, called "in-plants," place orders to their own companies, relieving the customer's buyers from this task. Many also become involved at a deeper level, such as participating in new product development projects, manufacturing planning (concurrent planning).

# K

**Kanban:** Japanese word for "visible record", loosely translated means card, billboard or sign. Popularized by Toyota Corporation, it uses standard containers or lot sizes to deliver needed parts to assembly line "just in time" for use.

**Kaizen:** The Japanese term for improvement; continuing improvement involving everyone—managers and workers. In manufacturing, kaizen relates to finding and eliminating waste in machinery, labor, or production methods. *Also see: Continuous Process Improvement*

**Kaizen Blitz:** A rapid improvement of a limited process area, for example, a production cell. Part of the improvement team consists of workers in that area. The objectives are to use innovative thinking to eliminate non-value-added work and to immediately implement the changes within a week or less. Ownership of the improvement by the area work team and the development of the team's problem solving skills are additional benefits.

**KD:** *See Knock-Down*

**Keiretsu:** A form of cooperative relationship among companies in Japan where the companies largely remain legally and economically independent, even though they work closely in various ways such as sole sourcing and financial backing. A member of a keiretsu generally owns a limited amount of stock in other member companies. A keiretsu generally forms around a bank and a trading company but "distribution" (supply chain) keiretsus exist linking companies from raw material suppliers to retailers.

**Key Custodians:** The persons, assigned by the security administrators of trading partners, that send or receive a component of either the master key or exchange key used to encrypt data encryption keys. This control technique involves dual control, with split knowledge that requires two key custodians.

**Key Performance Indicator (KPI):** A measure which is of strategic importance to a company or department. For example, a supply chain flexibility metric is Supplier On-time Delivery Performance which indicates the percentage of orders that are fulfilled on or before the original requested date. *Also see: Scorecard*

**Kitting:** Light assembly of components or parts into defined units. Kitting reduces the need to maintain an inventory of pre-built completed products, but increases the time and labor consumed at shipment. *Also see: Postponement*

**Knock-Down (KD):** A flat, unformed cardboard box or tray. Knock-downs, also known as KDs, are constructed and glued in the recoup or packaging areas and used for repacked product. Many KDs are provided by the customer for their recouped products.

**KPI:** *See Key Performance Indicator*

# L

**Lading:** The cargo carried in a transportation vehicle.

**Laid-Down Cost:** The sum of the product and transportation costs. The laid-down cost is useful in comparing the total cost of a product shipped from different supply sources to a customer's point of use.

**LAN:** *See Local Area Network*

**Land Bridge:** The movement of containers by ship-rail-sip on Japan-to-Europe moves; ships move containers to the U.S. Pacific Coast, rails move containers to an East Coast port, and ships deliver containers to Europe.

**Land Grants:** Grants of land given to railroads during their developmental stage to build tracks.

**Landed Cost:** Cost of product plus relevant logistics costs such as transportation, warehousing, handling, etc. *Also called Total Landed Cost or Net Landed Costs*

**Lash Barges:** Covered barges that are loaded on board oceangoing ships for movement to foreign destinations.

**Last In, First Out (LIFO):** Accounting method of valuing inventory that assumes latest goods purchased are first goods used during accounting period.

**LCL:** *See Less-Than-Carload or Less-Than-Container load*

**LDI:** *See Logistics data interchange*

**Lead Logistics Partner (LLP):** An organization that organizes other 3rd party logistics partners for outsourcing of logistics functions. An LLP serves as the client's primary supply chain management provider, defining processes and managing the provision and integration of logistics services through its own organization and those of its subcontractors. *Also see: Fourth Party Logistics*

**Lead Time:** The total time that elapses between an order's placement and its receipt. It includes the time required for order transmittal, order processing, order preparation, and transit.

**Lead Time from Complete Manufacture to Customer Receipt:** Includes time from when an order is ready for shipment to customer receipt of order. Time from complete manufacture to customer receipt including the following elements: pick/pack time, prepare for shipment, total transit time (all components to consolidation point), consolidation, queue time, and additional transit time to customer receipt.

**Lead Time from Order Receipt to Complete Manufacture:** Includes times from order receipt to order entry complete, from order entry complete to start to build, and from start to build to ready for shipment. Time from order receipt to order entry complete includes the following elements: order revalidation, configuration check, credit check, and scheduling. Time from order entry complete to start to build includes the following elements: customer wait time and engineering and design time. Time from start to build to ready for shipment includes the following elements: release to manufacturing or distribution, order configuration verification, production scheduling, and build or configure time.

**Least Total Cost:** A dynamic lot-sizing technique that calculates the order quantity by comparing the setup (or ordering) costs and the carrying cost for various lot sizes and selects the lot size where these costs are most nearly equal. *Also see: Discrete Order Quantity, Dynamic Lot Sizing*

**Least Unit Cost:** A dynamic lot-sizing technique that adds ordering cost and inventory carrying cost for each trial lot size and divides by the number of units in the lot size, picking the lot size with the lowest unit cost. *Also see: Discrete Order Quantity, Dynamic Lot Sizing*

**LEED: Leadership in Energy & Environmental Design** is an internationally recognized green building certification system, providing third-party verification that a building or community was designed and built using strategies intended to improve performance in metrics such as energy savings, water efficiency, $CO_2$ emissions reduction, improved indoor environmental quality, and stewardship of resources and sensitivity to their impacts.

**Leg:** A portion of a complete trip which has an origin, destination, and carrier and is composed of all consecutive segments of a route booked through the same carrier. *Also called Bookable Leg*

**Less-Than-Carload (LCL):** Shipment that is less than a complete rail car load (lot shipment).

**Less-Than-Truckload (LTL) Carriers:** Trucking companies that consolidate and transport smaller (less than truckload) shipments of freight by utilizing a network of terminals and relay points.

**Lessee:** A person or firm to whom a lease is granted.

**Lessor:** A person or firm that grants a lease.

**Letter of credit (LOC):** An international business document that assures the seller that payment will be made by the bank issuing the letter of credit upon fulfillment of the sales agreement.

**Leverage:** Taking something small and exploding it. Can be financial or technological.

**License Plate:** A pallet tag; refers to a uniquely numbered bar code sticker placed on a pallet of product. Typically contains information about product on the pallet.

**Life Cycle Cost:** In cost accounting, a product's life cycle is the period that starts with the initial product conceptualization and ends with the withdrawal of the product from the marketplace and final disposition. A product life cycle is characterized by certain defined stages, including research, development, introduction, maturity, decline, and abandonment. Life cycle cost is the accumulated costs incurred by a product during these stages.

**Lighter:** A flat-bottomed boat designed for cross-harbor or inland waterway freight transfer. While the terms barge and lighter are used interchangeably, a barge usually refers to a vessel used for a long haul, while a lighter is used for a short haul.

**LIFO:** *See Last In, First Out*

**Lift truck:** Vehicles used to lift, move, stack, rack, or otherwise manipulate loads. Material handling people use a lot of terms to describe lift trucks, some terms describe specific types of vehicles, others are slang terms or trade names that people often mistakenly use to describe trucks. Terms include industrial truck, forklift, reach truck, motorized pallet trucks, turret trucks, counterbalanced forklift, walkie, rider, walkie rider, walkie stacker, straddle lift, side loader, order pickers, high lift, cherry picker, Jeep, Towmotor, Yale, Crown, Hyster, Raymond, Clark, Drexel.

**Line:** 1) A specific physical space for the manufacture of a product that in a flow shop layout is represented by a straight line. In actuality, this may be a series of pieces of equipment connected by piping or conveyor systems. 2) A type of manufacturing process used to produce a narrow range of standard items with identical or highly similar designs. Production volumes are high, production and material handling equipment is specialized, and all products typically pass through the same sequence of operations. *Also see: Assembly Line*

**Line Functions:** The decision-making areas associated with daily operations. Logistics line functions include traffic management, inventory control, order processing, warehousing, and packaging.

**Line-Haul Shipment:** A shipment that moves between cities and distances over 100 to 150 miles.

**Line Scrap:** Value of raw materials and work-in-process inventory scrapped as a result of improper processing or assembly, as a percentage of total value of production at standard cost.

**Liner Service:** International water carriers that ply fixed routes on published schedules.

**Link:** The transportation method used to connect the nodes (plants, warehouses) in a logistics system.

**Linked Distributed Systems:** Independent computer systems, owned by independent organizations, linked in a manner to allow direct updates to be made to one system by another. For example, a customer's computer system is linked to a supplier's system, and the customer can create orders or releases directly in the supplier's system.

**Little Inch:** A federally built pipeline constructed during World War II that connected Corpus Christi and Houston, Texas.

**Live:** A situation in which the equipment operator stays with the trailer or boxcar while it is being loaded or unloaded.

**LLP:** *See Lead Logistics Partner*

**Load Factor:** A measure of operating efficiency used by air carriers to determine the percentage of a plane's capacity that is utilized, or the number of passengers divided by the total number of seats.

**Load Tender (Pick-Up Request):** An offer of cargo for transport by a shipper. Load tender terminology is primarily used in the motor industry.

**Load Tendering:** The practice of providing a carrier with detailed information and negotiated pricing (the tender) prior to scheduling pickup. This practice can help assure contract compliance and facilitate automated payments (self billing).

**Loading allowance:** A reduced rate offered to shippers and/or consignees who load and/or unload LTL or AQ shipments.

**Loading Port:** The port where the cargo is loaded onto the exporting vessel. This port must be reported on the Shipper's Export Declaration, Schedule D and is used by U.S. companies to determine which tariff is used to freight rate the cargo for carriers with more than one tariff.

**LOC:** *See Letter of credit*

**Local Area Network (LAN):** A data communications network spanning a limited geographical area, usually a few miles at most, providing communications between computers and peripheral devices.

**Local Rate:** A rate published between two points served by one carrier.

**Local Service Carriers:** An air carrier classification of carriers that operate between areas of lesser and major population centers. These carriers feed passengers into the major cities to major hubs.

**Location Tag:** A bar coded sign that hangs above or on a warehouse location. The location number can be read from the tag or scanned with an RF gun.

**Locational Determinant:** The factors that determine the location of a facility. For industrial facilities, the determinants include logistics.

**Locative Logistics:** A scalable supply chain platform based on API/GIS applications, which supplies specific information about the physical presence, strategic importance, and economic impact of products or cargo in-transit. This is a situational assessment of a location, or locations in a supply chain.

**Locator System:** Locator systems are inventory-tracking systems that allow you to assign specific physical locations to your inventory to facilitate greater tracking and the ability to store product randomly. Location functionality in software can range from a simple text field attached to an item that notes a single location, to systems that allow multiple locations per item and track inventory quantities by location. Warehouse management systems (WMS) take locator systems to the next level by adding functionality to direct the movement between locations.

**Logbook:** A daily record of the hours an interstate driver spends driving, off, duty, sleeping in the berth, or on duty but not driving.

**Logistics:** The process of planning, implementing, and controlling procedures for the efficient and effective transportation and storage of goods including services, and related information from the point of origin to the point of consumption for the purpose of conforming to customer requirements. This definition includes inbound, outbound, internal, and external movements.

**Logistics Channel:** The network of supply chain participants engaged in storage, handling, transfer, transportation, and communications functions that contribute to the efficient flow of goods.

**Logistics Data Interchange (LDI):** A computerized system to electronically transmit logistics information.

**Logistics Management:** As defined by the Council of Supply Chain Management Professionals (CSCMP): "Logistics management is that part of supply chain management that plans, implements, and controls the efficient, effective forward and reverse flow and storage of goods, services, and related information between the point of origin and the point of consumption in order to meet customers' requirements. Logistics management activities typically include inbound and outbound transportation management, fleet management, warehousing, materials handling, order fulfillment, logistics network design, inventory management, supply/demand planning, and management of third party logistics services providers. To varying degrees, the logistics function also includes sourcing and procurement, production planning and scheduling, packaging and assembly, and customer service. It is involved in all levels of planning and execution—strategic, operational, and tactical. Logistics management is an integrating function which coordinates and optimizes all logistics activities, as well as integrates logistics activities with other functions, including marketing, sales, manufacturing, finance, and information technology."

**Long Tail:** The long tail is a frequency distribution pattern in which occurrences are most densely clustered close to the Y-axis and the distribution curve tapers along the X-axis. The long tail refers to the low-frequency population displayed in the right-hand portion of the graph, represented by a gradually sloping distribution curve that becomes asymptotic to the x-axis. In most applications, the number of events in the tail is greater than the number of events in the high frequency area, simply because the tail is long.

**Long Ton:** Equals 2,240 pounds.

**Lot Control:** A set of procedures (e.g., assigning unique batch numbers and tracking each batch) used to maintain lot integrity from raw materials, from the supplier through manufacturing to consumers.

**Lot-for-Lot:** A lot-sizing technique that generates planned orders in quantities equal to the net requirements in each period. *Also see: Discrete Order Quantity*

**Lot Number:** *See Batch Number*

**Lot Size:** The quantity of goods purchased or produced in anticipation of use or sale in the future.

**Lot Sized System:** *See Fixed Reorder Quantity Inventory Model*

**LTL:** *See Less-than-truckload Carriers*

**Lumping:** A term applied to a person who assists a motor carrier owner-operator in the loading and unloading of property: quite commonly used in the food industry.

**Lumpy Demand:** *See Discontinuous Demand*

# M

**M2M:** *See Machine-to-Machine interface*

**Machine Downtimes:** Time during which a machine cannot be utilized. Machine downtimes may occur during breakdowns, maintenance, changeovers, etc.

**Machine-to-Machine interface (M2M):** A term describing the process whereby machines are remotely monitored for status and problems reported and resolved automatically or maintenance scheduled by the monitoring systems.

**Macro Environment:** The environment external to a business including technological, economic, natural, and regulatory forces that marketing efforts cannot control.

**Mainframe:** A term sometimes generically used to refer to an organization's central computer system. Specifically the largest class of computer systems manufactured.

**Maintenance, Repair, and Operating supplies (MRO):** Items used in support of general operations and maintenance such as maintenance supplies, spare parts, and consumables used in the manufacturing process and supporting operations.

**Major Carrier:** A for-hire certificated air carrier that has annual operating revenues of $1 billion or more: the carrier usually operates between major population centers.

**Make-or-Buy Decision:** The act of deciding whether to produce an item internally or buy it from an outside supplier. Factors to consider in the decision include costs, capacity availability, proprietary and/or specialized knowledge, quality considerations, skill requirements, volume, and timing.

**Make-to-Order (Manufacture-to-order) (MTO):** A manufacturing process strategy where the trigger to begin manufacture of a product is an actual customer order or release, rather than a market forecast. For Make-to-Order products, more than 20% of the value-added takes place after the receipt of the order or release, and all necessary design and process documentation is available at time of order receipt.

**Make-to-Stock (Manufacture-to-stock) (MTS):** A manufacturing process strategy where finished product is continually held in plant or warehouse inventory to fulfill expected incoming orders or releases based on a forecast.

**Manifest:** A document which describes individual orders contained within a shipment.

**Manufacturer's Representative:** One who sells goods for several firms but does not take title to them.

**Manufacturing Calendar:** A calendar used in inventory and production planning functions that consecutively numbers only the working days so that the component and work order scheduling may be done based on the actual number of workdays available. Synonyms: M-Day Calendar, Planning Calendar, Production Calendar, Shop Calendar.

**Manufacturing Capital Asset Value:** The asset value of the "Manufacturing fixed assets" after allowance for depreciation. Examples of equipment are SMT placement machines, conveyors, Auto guided vehicles, robot cells, testers, X-ray solder machines, Burn-in chambers, Logic testers, Auto packing equipment, PLC station controllers, Scanning equipment, PWB magazines.

**Manufacturing Critical-Path Time (MCT):** The typical amount of calendar time from when a manufacturing order is created through the critical-path until the first, single piece of that order is delivered to the customer.

**Manufacture Cycle Time:** The average time between commencement and completion of a manufacturing process, as it applies to make-to-stock products.

*Calculation*: [Average # of units in WIP] / [Average daily output in units]

**Manufacturing Execution Systems (MES):** Programs and systems that participate in shop floor control, including programmed logic controllers and process control computers for direct and supervisory control of manufacturing equipment; process information systems that gather historical performance information, then generate reports; graphical displays; and alarms that inform operations personnel what is going on in the plant currently and a very short history into the past. Quality control information is also gathered and a laboratory information management system may be part of this configuration to tie process conditions to the quality data that are generated. Thereby, cause-and-effect relationships can be determined. The quality data at times affect the control parameters that are used to meet product specifications either dynamically or off line.

**Manufacturing Lead Time:** The total time required to manufacture an item, exclusive of lower level purchasing lead time. For make-to-order products, it is the length of time between the release of an order to the production process and shipment to the final customer. For make-to-stock products, it is the length of time between the release of an order to the production process and receipt into finished goods inventory. Included here are order preparation time, queue time, setup time, run time, move time, inspection time, and put-away time. *Synonyms: Manufacturing Cycle Time. Also see: Lead Time*

**Manufacturing Resource Planning (MRP II):** A method for the effective planning of all resources of a manufacturing company. Ideally, it addresses operational planning in units, financial planning in dollars, and has a simulation capability to answer what-if questions. It is made up of a variety of processes, each linked together: business planning, production planning (sales and operations planning), master production scheduling, material requirements planning, capacity requirements planning, and the execution support systems for capacity and material. Output from these systems is integrated with financial reports such as the business plan, purchase commitment report, shipping budget, and inventory projections in dollars. Manufacturing resource planning is a direct outgrowth and extension of closed-loop MRP.

**Mapping:** A computer term referring to diagramming data that is to be exchanged electronically, including how it is to be used and what business management systems need it. Preliminary step for developing an applications link. Performed by the functional manager responsible for a business management system.

**Marginal Cost:** The cost to produce one additional unit of output. The change in total variable cost resulting from a one-unit change in output.

**Marine Insurance:** Insurance to protect against cargo loss and damage when shipping by water transportation.

**Maritime Administration:** A federal agency that promotes the merchant marine, determines ocean ship routes and services, and awards maritime subsidies.

**Maritime Transportation Security Act (MTSA):** Law passed in 2002 to create a comprehensive national system of transportation security enhancements. The MTSA designated the U.S. Coast Guard as the lead federal agency for maritime homeland security and requires federal agencies, ports, and vessel owners to take numerous steps to upgrade security. The MTSA requires the Coast Guard to develop national and regional area maritime transportation security plans and requires seaports, waterfront terminals, and vessels to submit security and incident response plans to the Coast Guard for approval. The MTSA also requires the Coast Guard to conduct antiterrorism assessments of certain foreign ports.

**Market Demand:** In marketing, the total demand that would exist within a defined customer group in a given geographical area during a particular time period given a known marketing program.

**Market Dominance:** In transportation rating this refers to the absence of effective competition for railroads from other carriers and modes for the traffic to which the rate applies. The Staggers Act stated that market dominance does not exist if the rate is below the revenue-to-variable-cost ratio of 160% in 1981 and 170% in 1983

**Market Segment:** A group of potential customers sharing some measurable characteristics based on demographics, psychographics, lifestyle, geography, benefits, etc.

**Market Share:** The portion of the overall market demand for a specific product or service which is provided by any single provider.

**Market-Positioned Warehouse:** Warehouse positioned to replenish customer inventory assortments and to afford maximum inbound transport consolidation economies from inventory origin points with relatively short-haul local delivery.

**Marks and Numbers:** Identifying marks and numbers affixed to or placed on goods used to identify a shipment or parts of a shipment.

**Marquis Partners:** Key strategic relationships. This has emerged as perhaps the key competitive advantage and barrier to entry of e-marketplaces. Get the big players in the fold first, offering equity if necessary.

**Marshaller or Marshalling Agent:** This is a service unique to international trade and relates to an individual or firm that specializes in one or more of the activities preceding Main Carriage, such as consolidation, packing, marking, sorting of merchandise, inspection, storage, etc. References state that Marshaling Agent, Consolidation Agent and Freight Forwarder all have the same meaning.

**Mass Customization:** The creation of a high-volume product with large variety so that a customer may specify his or her exact model out of a large volume of possible end items while manufacturing cost is low because of the large volume. An example is a personal computer order in which the customer may specify processor speed, memory size, hard disk size and speed, removable storage device characteristics, and many other options when PCs are assembled on one line and at low cost.

**Master Pack:** A large box that is used to pack a number of smaller boxes or containers. Aids in protecting the smaller cartons or packages and reduces the number of cartons to be handled during the material handling process.

**Master Production Schedule (MPS):** The master level or top level schedule used to set the production plan in a manufacturing facility.

**Material Acquisition Costs:** One of the elements comprising a company's total supply-chain management costs. These costs consist of the following:

1. Materials (Commodity) Management and Planning: All costs associated with supplier sourcing, contract negotiation and qualification, and the preparation, placement, and tracking of a purchase order, including all costs related to buyer/planners.

2. Supplier Quality Engineering: The costs associated with the determination, development/certification, and monitoring of suppliers' capabilities to fully satisfy the applicable quality and regulatory requirements.

3. Inbound Freight and Duties: Freight costs associated with the movement of material from a vendor to the buyer and the associated administrative tasks. Duties are those fees and taxes levied by government for moving purchased material across international borders. Customs broker fees should also be considered in this category.

4. Receiving and Put Away: All costs associated with taking possession of material and storing it.

*Note that carrying costs are not a part of acquisition, and inspection is handled separately.*

5. Incoming Inspection: All costs associated with the inspection and testing of received materials to verify compliance with specifications.

6. Material Process and Component Engineering: Those tasks required to document and communicate component specifications, as well as reviews to improve the manufacturability of the purchased item.

7. Tooling: Those costs associated with the design, development, and depreciation of the tooling required to produce a purchased item. A tooling cost would be incurred by a company if they actually paid for equipment and/or maintenance for a contract manufacturer that makes their product. Sometimes, there isn't enough incentive for a contract manufacturer to upgrade plant equipment to a level of quality that a company requires, so the company will pay for the upgrades and maintenance to ensure high quality. May not be common in some industries such as the Chemicals.

**Material Index:** The ratio of the sum of the localized raw material weights to the weight of the finished product.

**Material Safety Data Sheet (MSDS):** A document that is part of the materials information system and accompanies the product. Prepared by the manufacturer, the MSDS provides information regarding the safety and chemical properties and (if necessary) the long-term storage, handling, and disposal of the product. Among other factors, the MSDS describes the hazardous components of a product; how to treat leaks, spills, and fires; and how to treat improper human contact with the product. *Also see: Hazardous Materials*

**Materials Handling:** The physical handling of products and materials between procurement and shipping.

**Materials Management:** Inbound logistics from suppliers through the production process. The movement and management of materials and products from procurement through production.

**Materials planning:** The materials management function that attempts to coordinate the supply of materials with the demand for materials.

**Materials Requirements Planning (MRP):** A decision-making methodology used to determine the timing and quantities of materials to purchase.

**Matrix Organizational Structure:** An organizational structure in which two (or more) channels of command, budget responsibility, and performance measurement exist simultaneously. For example, both product and functional forms of organization could be implemented simultaneously, that is, the product and functional managers have equal authority and employees report to both managers.

**MAX:** The lowest inventory quantity that is desired at a ship to location or selling location. This quantity will over-ride the forecast number if the forecast climbs above the MAX. Maximum stock

**Maximum Inventory:** The planned maximum allowable inventory for an item based on its planned lot size and target safety stock.

**Maximum Order Quantity:** An order quantity modifier applied after the lot size has been calculated, that limits the order quantity to a pre-established maximum. m-**Commerce:** Mobile commerce applications involve using a mobile phone to carry out financial transactions. This usually means making a payment for goods or transferring funds electronically. Transferring money between accounts and paying for purchases are electronic commerce applications. An emerging application, electronic commerce has been facilitated by developments in other areas in the mobile world, such as dual slot phones and other smarter terminals and more standardized protocols, which allow greater interactivity and therefore more sophisticate services.

**MCT:** *See Manufacturing critical-path time*

**M-Day Calendar:** *See Manufacturing Calendar*

**Mean:** The arithmetic average of a group of values. *Syn: arithmetic mean*

**Measure:** A number used to quantify a metric, showing the result of part of a process often resulting from a simple count. Example: Number of units shipped.

**Measurement Ton:** Equals 40 cubic feet; used in water transportation rate making.

**Median:** The middle value in a set of measured values when the items are arranged in order of magnitude. If there is no single middle value, the median is the mean of the two middle values.

**Merge In Transit:** The process of combining or "merging" shipments from multiple suppliers which are going directly to the buyer or to the store, bypassing the seller. Effectively a "drop shipment" from several vendors to one buyer, which is being combined at an intermediary point prior to delivery.

**Merger:** The combination of two or more carriers into one company for the ownership, management, and operation of the properties previously operated on a separate basis.

**MES:** *See Manufacturing Execution Systems*

**Message:** The EDIFACT term for a transaction set. A message is the collection of data, organized in segments, exchanged by trading partners engaged in EDI. Typically, a message is an electronic version of a document associated with a common business transaction, such as a purchase order or shipping notice. A message begins with a message header segment, which identifies the start of the message (e.g., the series of characters representing one purchase order). The message header segment also carries the message type code, which identifies the business transaction type. EDIFACT's message header segment is called UNH; in ANSI X12 protocol, the message header is called ST. A message ends with a message trailer segment, which signals the end of the message (e.g., the end of one purchase order). EDIFACT's message trailer is labeled UNT; the ANSI X12 message trailer is referred to as SE.

**Metadata:** is loosely defined as data about data. Metadata is a concept that applies mainly to electronically archived or presented data and is used to describe the **a)** definition, **b)** structure and **c)** administration of data files with all contents in context to ease the use of the captured and archived data for further use. *See Meta Tag*

**Meta Tag:** An optional HTML tag that is used to specify information about a web document. Some search engines use "spiders" to index web pages. These spiders read the information contained within a page's META tag. So in theory, an HTML or web page author has the ability to control how their site is indexed by search engines and how and when it will "come up" on a user's search. The META tag can also be used to specify an HTTP or URL address for the page to "jump" to after a certain amount of time. This is known as Client-Pull. What this means, is a web page author can control the amount of time a web page is up on the screen as well as where the browser will go next.

**Metrics:** Specific areas of measurement. A metric must be quantitative and must support benchmarking, and it must be based on broad, statistically valid data. Therefore, it must exist in a format for which published data exists within the enterprise or industry. *See Performance Measures*

**Micro-Land Bridge:** An intermodal movement in which the shipment is moved from a foreign country to the U.S. by water and then moved across the U.S. by railroad to an interior, nonport city, or vice versa for exports from a nonport city.

**Mileage Allowance:** An allowance based upon distance and given by railroads to shippers using private rail cars.

**Mileage Rate:** A rate based upon the number of miles the commodity is shipped.

**Milk Run:** A regular route for pickup of mixed loads from several suppliers. For example, instead of each of five suppliers sending a truckload per week to meet the weekly needs of the customer, one truck visits each of the suppliers on a daily basis before delivering to the customer's plant. Five truckloads per week are still shipped, but each truckload contains the daily requirement from each supplier. *Also see: Consolidation*

**Min – Max System:** A type of order point replenishment system where the "min" (minimum) is the order point, and the "max" (maximum) is the "order up to" inventory level. The order quantity is variable and is the result of the max minus the available and on-order inventory. An order is recommended when the sum of the available and on-order inventory is at or below the min.

**Mini-Land Bridge:** An intermodal movement in which the shipment is moved from a foreign country to the U.S. by water and then moved across the U.S. by railroad to a destination that is a port city, or vice versa for exports from a U.S. port city.

**Minimum Weight:** The shipment weight specified by the carrier's tariff as the minimum weight required to use the TL or CL rate; the rate discount volume.

**Misguided Capacity Plans:** Plans or forecasts for capacity utilization, which are based on inaccurate assumptions or input data.

**Mixed loads:** The movement of both regulated and exempt commodities in the same vehicle at the same time.

**Modal Split:** The relative use made of the modes of transportation; the statistics used include ton miles, passenger-miles, and revenue.

**Mode:** *See Transportation Mode*

**MOTE (as in reMOTE):** A wireless receiver/transmitter that is typically combined with a sensor of some type to create a remote sensor.

Motes are being used in ocean containers to look for evidence of tampering. They have huge application in food, pharma, and other "cold chain" industries to closely monitor temperature, humidity and other factor.

**Motor Carrier:** An enterprise that offers service via land motor carriage.

**Move Ticket:** A document used to move inventory within a facility. Warehouse management systems use move tickets to direct and track material movements. In a paperless environment the electronic version of a move ticket is often called a task or a trip.

**MPS:** *See Master Production Schedule*

**MRO:** *See Maintenance, Repair, and Operating Supplies*

**MRP:** *See Material Requirements Planning*

**MRP-II:** *See Manufacturing Resource Planning*

**MSDS:** *See Material Safety Data Sheet*

**MTO:** *See Make-to-Order*

**MTS:** *See Make-to-Stock*

**MTSA:** *See Maritime Transportation Security Act*

**Multi-Currency:** The ability to process orders using a variety of currencies for pricing and billing.

**Multinational Company:** A company that both produces and markets products in different countries.

**Multiple-Car Rate:** A railroad rate that is lower for shipping more than one carload rather than just one carload at a time.

**Multi-Skilled:** Pertaining to individuals who are certified to perform a variety of tasks.

# N

**NAFTA:** *See North American Free Trade Agreement*

**National Carrier:** A for-hire certificated air carrier that has annual operating revenues of $75 million to $1 billion; the carrier usually operates between major population centers and areas of lesser population.

**National Industrial Traffic League:** An association representing the interests of shippers and receivers in matters of transportation policy and regulation.

**Nationalization:** Public ownership, financing, and operation of a business entity.

**National Motor Bus Operators Organization:** An industry association representing common and charter bus firms; now known as the American Bus Association.

**National Motor Freight Classification (NMFC):** A tariff, which contains descriptions and classifications of commodities and rules for domestic movement by motor carriers in the U.S.

**National Railroad Corporation:** Also known as Amtrak, the corporation established by the Rail Passenger Service Act of 1970 to operate most of the United States' rail passenger service.

**National Stock Number (NSN):** The individual identification number assigned to an item to permit inventory management in the federal (U.S.) supply system.

**NDA:** See Non Disclosure Agreement

**Net Asset Turns:** The number of times you replenish your net assets in your annual sales cycle. A measure of how quickly assets are used to generate sales.

***Calculation:***Total Product Revenue / Total Net Assets

**Net Assets:** Total Net assets are calculated as Total Assets - Total Liabilities; where: The total assets are made up of fixed assets (plant, machinery and equipment) and current assets which is the total of stock, debtors and cash (also includes A/R, inventory, prepaid assets, deferred assets, intangibles and goodwill). The total liabilities are made up in much the same way of long-term liabilities and current liabilities (includes A/P, accrued expenses, deferred liabilities).

**Net Change MRP:** An approach in which the material requirements plan is continually retained in the computer. Whenever a change is needed in requirements, open order inventory status, or bill of material, a partial explosion and netting is made for only those parts affected by the change. Antonym: Regeneration MRP.

**Net Requirements:** In MRP, the net requirements for a part or an assembly are derived as a result of applying gross requirements and allocations against inventory on hand, scheduled receipts, and safety stock. Net requirements, lot-sized and offset for lead time, become planned orders.

**Net Weight:** The weight of the merchandise, unpacked, exclusive of any containers.

**New Product Introduction (NPI):** The process used to develop products that are new to the sales portfolio of a company.

**NII:** *See Non Intrusive Inspection Technology*

**NES:** *See Not Otherwise Specified/Not Elsewhere Specified*

**NMFC:** *See National Motor Freight Classification*

**Node:** A fixed point in a firm's logistics system where goods come to rest; includes plants, warehouses, supply sources, and markets.

**No Location (No Loc):** A received item for which the warehouse has no previously established storage slot.

**Noncertified Carrier:** A for-hire air carrier that is exempt from economic regulation.

**Nonconformity:** Failure to fulfill a specified requirement. *See: blemish, defect, imperfection*

**Non-Conveyable:** Materials which cannot be moved on a conveyor belt.

**Non-Disclosure-Agreement:** also known as a **confidentiality agreement, confidential disclosure agreement** (CDA), **proprietary information agreement** (PIA), or **secrecy agreement**, is a legal contract between at least two parties that outlines confidential material, knowledge, or information that the parties wish to share with one another for certain purposes, but wish to restrict access to by third parties. It is a contract through which the parties agree not to disclose information covered by the agreement. An NDA creates a confidential relationship between the parties to protect any type of confidential and proprietary information.

**Non-Durable goods:** Goods whose serviceability is generally limited to a period of less than three years (such as perishable goods and semi-durable goods).

**Non-Intrusive Inspection technology (NII):** Originally developed to address the threat of smugglers using increasingly sophisticated techniques to conceal narcotics deep in commercial cargo and conveyances, NII systems, in many cases, give Customs inspectors the capability to perform thorough examinations of cargo without having to resort to the costly, time consuming process of unloading cargo for manual searches, or intrusive examinations of conveyances by methods such as drilling and dismantling.

**Non-Vessel-Owning Common Carrier (NVOCC):** A firm that offers the same services as an ocean carrier, but which does not own or operate a vessel. NVOCCs usually act as consolidators, accepting small shipments (LCL) and consolidating them into full container loads. They also consolidate and disperse international containers that originate at or are bound for inland ports. They then act as a shipper, tendering the containers to ocean common carriers. They are required to file tariffs with the Federal Maritime Commission and are subject to the same laws and statutes that apply to primary common carriers.

**North American Free Trade Agreement (NAFTA):** A free trade agreement, implemented January 1, 1994, between Canada, the United States and Mexico. It includes measures for the elimination of tariffs and non-tariff barriers to trade, as well as many more specific provisions concerning the conduct of trade and investment that reduce the scope for government intervention in managing trade.

**NOS:** *See Not Otherwise Specified/Not Elsewhere Specified*

**Not Otherwise Specified/Not Elsewhere Specified (NOS/NES):** This term often appears in ocean or airfreight tariffs respectively. If no rate for the specific commodity shipped appears in the tariff, then a general class rate (for example: printed matter NES) will apply. Such rates usually are higher than rates for specific commodities.

**NPI:** *See New Product Introduction*

**NSN:** *See National Stock Number*

**NVOCC:** *See Non-vessel-owning common carrier*

# O

**Object Linking and Embedding (OLE):** An object system created by Microsoft. OLE lets an author invoke different editor components to create a compound document.

**Observer Effect:** The impact of observing a process while it is running, or the impact of observing a physical system.

**Obsolete Inventory:** Inventory for which there is no forecast demand expected. A condition of being out of date. A loss of value occasioned by new developments that place the older property at a competitive disadvantage.

**Ocean Bill of Lading:** The bill of lading issued by the ocean carrier to its customer.

**OEE:** *See Overall Equipment Effectiveness*

**OEM:** *See Original Equipment Manufacturer*

**Offer:** *See Tender*

**Offline:** A computer term which describes work done outside of the computer system or outside of a main process within the corporate system. In general usage this term describes any situation where equipment is not available for use, or individuals cannot be contacted.

**Offshore:** Utilizing an outsourcing service provider (manufacturer or business process) located in a country other than where the purchasing enterprise is located.

**Offshoring:** The practice of moving domestic operations such as manufacturing to another country.

**OLE:** *See Object Linking and Embedding*

**On-Demand:** Pertaining to work performed when demand is present. Typically used to describe products which are manufactured or assembled only when a customer order is placed.

**On-Hand Balance:** The quantity shown in the inventory records as being physically in stock. On order: The quantity of goods that has yet to arrive at a location or retail store. This includes all open purchase orders including, but not limited to, orders in transit, orders being picked, and orders being processed through customer service.

**On-Line Receiving:** A system in which computer terminals are available at each receiving bay and operators enter items into the system as they are unloaded.

**On Order:** The amount of goods that has yet to arrive at a location or retail store. This includes all open purchase orders including, but not limited to, orders in transit, orders being picked, and orders being processed through customer service.

**On Time In Full (OTIF):** Sales order delivery performance measure which can be expressed as a target, say, of achieving 98% of orders delivered in full, no part shipments, on the requested date.

**One Piece Flow:** Moving parts through a process in batches of one

**One-Way Networks:** The advantages generally live with either the seller or buyer, but not both. B2C websites are one-way networks.

**Online:** A computer term which describes activities performed using computer systems.

**Open-to-Buy:** A control technique used in aggregate inventory management in which authorizations to purchase are made without being committed to specific suppliers. These authorizations are often reviewed by management using such measures as commodity in dollars and by time period.

**Open-to-Receive:** Authorization to receive goods, such as a blanket release, firm purchase order item, or supplier schedule. Open-to-receive represents near-term impact on inventory, and is often monitored as a control technique in aggregate inventory management. The total of open-to-receive, other longer term purchase commitments and open-to-buy represents the material and services cash exposure of the company.

**Operational Performance Measurements:** 1) In traditional management, performance measurements related to machine, worker, or department efficiency or utilization. These performance measurements are usually poorly correlated with organizational performance. 2) In theory of constraints, performance measurements that link causally to organizational performance measurements. Throughput, inventory, and operating expense are examples. *Also see: Performance Measures*

**Operating ratio:** A measure of operation efficiency defined as: *(Operating expenses / Operating revenues) x 100*

**Optimization:** The process of making something as good or as effective as possible with given resources and constraints.

**Option:** A choice that must be made by the customer or company when customizing the end product. In many companies, the term option means a mandatory choice from a limited selection.

**Optional Replenishment Model:** A form of independent demand item management model in which a review of inventory on hand plus on order is made at fixed intervals. If the actual quantity is lower than some predetermined threshold, a reorder is placed for a quantity $M - x$, where M is the maximum allowable inventory and x is the current inventory quantity. The reorder point, R, may be deterministic or stochastic, and in either instance is large enough to cover the maximum expected demand during the review interval plus the replenishment lead time. The optional replenishment model is sometimes called a hybrid system because it combines certain aspects of the fixed reorder cycle inventory model and the fixed reorder quantity inventory model. *Also see: Fixed Reorder Cycle Inventory Model, Fixed Reorder Quantity Inventory Model, Hybrid Inventory System, Independent Demand Item Management Models*

**Order:** A type of request for goods or services such as a purchase order, sales order, work order, etc.

**Order Batching:** Practice of compiling and collecting orders before they are sent in to the manufacturer.

**Order Complete Manufacture to Customer Receipt of Order:** Average lead time from when an order is ready for shipment to customer receipt of order, including the following sub-elements: pick/pack time, preparation for shipment, total transit time for all components to consolidation point, consolidation, queue time, and additional transit time to customer receipt. (An element of Order Fulfillment Lead-Time). Note: Determined separately for Make-to-Order, Configure/Package-to-Order, Engineer-to-Order and Make-to-Stock products.

**Order Consolidation Profile:** The activities associated with filling a customer order by bringing together in one physical place all of the line items ordered by the customer. Some of these may come directly from the production line others may be picked from stock.

**Order Cycle:** The time and process involved from the placement of an order to the receipt of the shipment.

**Order Entry and Scheduling:** The process of receiving orders from the customer and entering them into a company's order processing system. Orders can be received through phone, fax, or electronic media. Activities may include "technically" examining orders to ensure an orderable configuration and provide accurate price, checking the customer's credit and accepting payment (optionally), identifying and reserving inventory (both on hand and scheduled), and committing and scheduling a delivery date.

**Order Entry Complete to Start Manufacture:** Average lead-time from completion of customer order to the time manufacturing begins, including the following sub-elements: order wait time, engineering and design time. (An element of Order Fulfillment Lead-Time). Note: Determined separately for Make-to-Order, Configure/Package-to-Order, and Engineer-to-Order products. Does not apply to Make-to-Stock products.

**Order Fulfillment Lead Times:** Average, consistently achieved lead-time from customer order origination to customer order receipt, for a particular manufacturing process strategy (Make-to-Stock, Make-to-Order, Configure/Package-to-Order, Engineer-to-Order). Excess lead-time created by orders placed in advance of typical lead times (Blanket Orders, Annual Contracts, Volume Purchase Agreements, etc.), is excluded. (An element of Total Supply Chain Response Time)

**Order Interval:** The time period between the placement of orders.

**Order Level System:** *See Fixed Reorder Cycle Inventory Model*

**Order Management:** The planning, directing, monitoring, and controlling of the processes related to customer orders, manufacturing orders, and purchase orders. Regarding customer orders, order management includes order promising, order entry, order pick, pack and ship, billing, and reconciliation of the customer account. Regarding manufacturing orders, order management includes order release, routing, manufacture, monitoring, and receipt into stores or finished goods inventories. Regarding purchasing orders, order management includes order placement, monitoring, receiving, acceptance, and payment of supplier.

**Order Management Costs:** One of the elements comprising a company's total supply-chain management costs. These costs consist of the following:

1. New Product Release Phase-In and Maintenance: This includes costs associated with releasing new products to the field, maintaining released products, assigning product ID, defining configurations and packaging, publishing availability schedules, release letters and updates, and maintaining product databases.

2. Create Customer Order: This includes costs associated with creating and pricing configurations to order and preparing customer order documents.

3. Order Entry and Maintenance: This includes costs associated with maintaining the customer database, credit check, accepting new orders, and adding them to the order system as well as later order modifications.

4. Contract/Program and Channel Management: This includes costs related to contract negotiation, monitoring progress, and reporting against the customer's contract, including administration of performance or warranty related issues.

5. Installation Planning: This includes costs associated with installation engineering, scheduling and modification, handling cancellations, and planning the installation.

6. Order Fulfillment: This includes costs associated with order processing, inventory allocation, ordering from internal or external suppliers, shipment scheduling, order status reporting, and shipment initiation.

7. Distribution: This includes costs associated with warehouse space and management, finished goods receiving and stocking, processing shipments, picking and consolidating, selecting carrier, and staging products/systems.

8. Transportation, Outbound Freight and Duties: This includes costs associated with all company paid freight duties from point-of-manufacture to end-customer or channel.

9. Installation: This includes costs associated with verification of site preparation, installation, certification, and authorization of billing.

10. Customer Invoicing/Accounting: This includes costs associated with invoicing, processing customer payments, and verification of customer receipt.

**Order Picking:** Selecting or "picking" the required quantity of specific products for movement to a packaging area (usually in response to one or more shipping orders) and documenting that the material was moved from one location to shipping. *Also see: Batch Picking, Discrete Order Picking, Zone Picking*

**Order Point – Order Quantity System:** The inventory method that places an order for a lot whenever the quantity on hand is reduced to a predetermined level known as the order point. *Also see: Fixed Reorder Quantity Inventory Model, Hybrid system*

**Order Processing:** Activities associated with filling customer orders.

**Order Promising:** The process of making a delivery commitment, i.e., answering the question, When can you ship? For make-to-order products, this usually involves a check of uncommitted material and availability of capacity, often as represented by the master schedule available-to-promise. *Also see: Available-to-Promise*

**Order Receipt to Order Entry Complete:** Average lead-time from receipt of a customer order to the time that order entry is complete, including the following sub-elements: order revalidation, product configuration check, credit check, and order scheduling.

Note: Determined separately for Make-to-Order, Configure/Package-to-Order, Engineer-to-Order, and Make-to-Stock products.

**Origin:** The place where a shipment begins its movement.

**Original Equipment Manufacturer (OEM):** A manufacturer that buys and incorporates another supplier's products into its own products. Also, products supplied to the original equipment manufacturer or sold as part of an assembly. For example, an engine may be sold to an OEM for use as that company's power source for its generator units.

**OS&D:** *See Over, Short and Damaged*

**Oscar Mike:** The letters o (oscar) and m (mike) of the military phonetic alphabet which when used together indicates that a unit is "On the Move" or sometimes, "On Mission."

**OTIF:** *See On Time In Full*

**Out Of Stock:** The state of not having inventory at a location and available for distribution or for sell to the consumer (zero inventory).

**Out of Stocks:** *See Stock Outs*

**Outbound Consolidation:** Consolidation of a number of small shipments for various customers into a larger load. The large load is then shipped to a location near the customers where it is broken down and then the small shipments are distributed to the customers. This can reduce overall shipping charges where many small packet or parcel shipments are handled each day. *Also see: Break Bulk*

**Outbound Logistics:** The process related to the movement and storage of products from the end of the production line to the end user.

**Outlier:** A data point that differs significantly from other data for a similar phenomenon. For example, if the average sales for a product were 10 units per month, and one month the product had sales of 500 units, this sales point might be considered an outlier. *Also see: Abnormal Demand*

**Outpartnering:** The process of involving the supplier in a close partnership with the firm and its operations management system. Outpartnering is characterized by close working relationships between buyers and suppliers, high levels of trust, mutual respect, and emphasis on joint problem solving and cooperation. With outpartnering, the supplier is viewed not as an alternative source of goods and services (as observed under outsourcing) but rather as a source of knowledge, expertise, and complementary core competencies. Outpartnering is typically found during the early stages of the product life cycle when dealing with products that are viewed as critical to the strategic survival of the firm. *Also see: Customer-Supplier Partnership*

**Outsource:** To utilize a third-party provider to perform services previously performed in-house. Examples include manufacturing of products and call center/customer support.

**Outsourced Cost of Goods Sold:** Operations performed on raw material outside of the responding entity's organization that would typically be considered internal to the entity's manufacturing cycle. Outsourced cost of goods sold captures the value of all outsourced activities that roll up as cost of goods sold. Some examples of commonly outsourced areas are assembly by subcontract houses, test, metal finishing or painting, and specialized assembly process.

**Overpack:** The practice of using a large box or carton to contain multiple smaller packages which are all going to the same destination in order to achieve a reduced overall shipping cost vs. the individual packages.

**Over, short and damaged (OS&D):** This is typically a report issued at warehouse when goods are damaged. Used to file claim with carrier.

**Over-the-road**: A motor carrier operation that reflects long-distance, intercity moves; the opposite of local operations.

**Overall Equipment Effectiveness (OEE):** A measure of overall equipment effectiveness that takes into account machine availability & performance as well as output quality.

**Owner-Operator:** A trucking operation in which the opener of the truck is also the driver.


# P

**P2P:** *See Peer to Peer*

**Pack Out:** In a fulfillment environment this refers to the operations involved in packaging and palletizing individual units of product for introduction into the warehouse distribution environment. For example, a contract 3PL may received or assemble units of product which need to be placed into retail packaging, then over-packed with a carton and then palletized.

**Package to Order:** A production environment in which a good or service can be packaged after receipt of a customer order. The item is common across many different customers; packaging determines the end product.

**Packing and Marking:** The activities of packing for safe shipping and unitizing one or more items of an order, placing them into an appropriate container, and marking and labeling the container with customer shipping destination data, as well as other information that may be required.

**Packing List**: List showing merchandise packed and all particulars. Normally prepared by shipper but not required by carriers. Copy is sent to consignee to help verify shipment received. The physical equivalent of the electronic Advanced Ship Notice (ASN).

**Pallet:** The platform which cartons are stacked on and then used for shipment or movement as a group. Pallets may be made of wood or composite materials.

**Pallet Jack:** Material handling equipment consisting of two broad parallel pallet forks on small wheels used in the warehouse to move pallets of product, but not having the lifting capability of a forklift. It may be a motorized unit guided by an operator who stands on a platform; or it may be a motorized or manual unit guided by an operator who is walking behind or beside it. Comes as a "single" (one pallet) or "double" (two pallets).

**Pallet Rack:** A single or multi-level structural storage system that is utilized to support high stacking of single items or palletized loads.

**Pallet Tag:** The bar coded sticker that is placed on a unit load or partial load, typically at receiving. The pallet tag can be scanned with an RF gun.

**Pallet Ticket:** A label to track pallet-sized quantities of end items produced to identify the specific sub lot with specifications determined by periodic sampling and analysis during production.

**Pallet Wrapping Machine:** A machine that wraps a pallet's contents in stretch-wrap to ensure safe shipment.

**Parcel Shipment:** Parcels include small packages like those typically handled by providers such as UPS and FedEx.

**Pareto:** A means of sorting data for example. For example, number of quality faults by frequency of occurrence. An analysis that compares cumulative percentages of the rank ordering of costs, cost drivers, profits or other attributes to determine whether a minority of elements have a disproportionate impact. Another example, identifying that 20 percent of a set of independent variables is responsible for 80 percent of the effect. *Also see: 80/20 Rule*

**Part Period Balancing (PPB):** In forecasting, a dynamic lot-sizing technique that uses the same logic as the least total cost method, but adds a routine called look ahead/look back. When the look ahead/look back feature is used, a lot quantity is calculated, and before it is firmed up, the next or the previous period's demands are evaluated to determine whether it would be economical to include them in the current lot. *Also see: Discrete Order Quantity, Dynamic lot sizing*

**Part Standardization:** A program for planned elimination of superficial, accidental, and deliberate differences between similar parts in the interest of reducing part and supplier proliferation. A typical goal of part standardization is to reduce costs by reducing the number of parts that the company needs to manage.

**Passenger-Mile:** A measure of output for passenger transportation; it reflects the number of passengers transported and the distance traveled; a multiplication of passengers hauled and distance traveled.

**Password:** A private code required to gain access to a computer, an application program, or service.

**Path to Profitability (P2P):** The step-by-step model to generate earnings.

**Pay-on-Use:** Pay-on-Use is a process where payment is initiated by product consumption, i.e., consignment stock based on withdrawal of product from inventory. This process is popular with many European companies.

**Payment:** The transfer of money, or other agreed upon medium, for provision of goods or services.

**Payroll:** Total of all fully burdened labor costs, including wage, fringe, benefits, overtime, bonus, and profit sharing.

**PBIT:** *See Profit Before Interest and Tax*

**PBL:** *See Performance Based Logistics*

**P & D**: Pickup and delivery.

**PDA:** *See Personal Digital Assistant*

**PDCA:** *See Plan-Do-Check-Action*

**Peak Demand:** The time period during which the quantity demanded is greater than during any other comparable time period.

**Peer to Peer (P2P):** A computer networking environment which allows individual computers to share resources and data without passing through an intermediate network server.

**Pegged Requirement:** An MRP component requirement that shows the next-level parent item (or customer order) as the source of the demand.

**Pegging:** A technique in which a ERP system traces demand for a product by date, quantity, and warehouse location.

**Pareto analysis:** Is a statistical technique in decision making that is used for selection of a limited number of tasks that produce significant overall effect. It uses the Pareto principle – the idea that by doing 20% of work, 80% of the advantage of doing the entire job can be generated. Or in terms of quality improvement, a large majority of problems (80%) are produced by a few key causes (20%). Pareto analysis is a formal technique useful where many possible courses of action are competing for attention. In essence, the problem-solver estimates the benefit delivered by each action, then selects a number of the most effective actions that deliver a total benefit reasonably close to the maximal possible one.

**Pareto chart:** named after Vilfredo Pareto, is a type of chart that contains both bars and a line graph, where individual values are represented in descending order by bars, and the cumulative total is represented by the line.

**Percent of Fill:** Number of lines or quantity actually shipped as a percent of the original order. Synonym: Customer Service Ratio.

**Per Diem:** 1) The rate of payment for use by one railroad of the cars of another. 2) A daily rate of reimbursement for expenses.

**Performance-Based Logistics (PBL):** A U.S. Government program that describes the purchase of services and support as an integrated, affordable, performance package designed to optimize system readiness and meet performance goals for a weapon system through long-term support arrangements with clear lines of authority and responsibility.

**Performance and Event Management Systems:** The systems that report on the key measurements in the supply chain – inventory days of supply, delivery performance, order cycle times, capacity use, etc. Using this information to identify causal relationships to suggest actions in line with the business goals.

**Performance Measures:** Indicators of the work performed and the results achieved in an activity, process, or organizational unit. Performance measures should be both non-financial and financial. Performance measures enable periodic comparisons and benchmarking. For example, a common performance measure for a distribution center is % of order fill rate. *Also see: Performance Measurement Program* Attributes of good performance measurement include the following:

1. Measures only what is important: The measure focuses on key aspects of process performance

2. Can be collected economically: Processes and activities are designed to easily capture the relevant information

3. Are visible: The measure and its causal effects are readily available to everyone who is measured

4. Is easy to understand: The measure conveys at a glance what it is measuring and how it is derived

5. Is process oriented: The measure makes the proper trade-offs among utilization, productivity and performance

6. Is defined and mutually understood. The measure has been defined and mutually understood by all key parties (internal and external)

7. Facilitates trust: The measure validates the participation among various parties and discourages "game playing"

8. Are usable: The measure is used to show progress and not just data that is "collected". Indicated performance vs. data

**Performance Measurement Program:** A performance measurement program goes beyond just having performance metrics in place. Many companies do not realize the full benefit of their performance metrics because they often do not have all of the necessary elements in place that support their metrics. *Also see: Performance Measures, Dashboard, Scorecard, Key Performance Indicator* Typical characteristics of a good performance measurement program include the following:

• Metrics that are aligned to strategy and linked to the "shop floor" or line level workers

• A process and culture that drives performance and accountability to delivery performance against key performance indicators.

• An incentive plan that is tied to performance goals, objectives and metrics

• Tools/technology in place to support easy data collection and use. This often includes the use of a "dashboard" or "scorecard" to allow for ease of understanding and reporting against key performance indicators.

**Period Order Quantity:** A lot-sizing technique under which the lot size is equal to the net requirements for a given number of periods, e.g., weeks into the future. The number of periods to order is variable, each order size equalizing the holding costs and the ordering costs for the interval. *Also see: Discrete Order Quantity, Dynamic Lot Sizing*

**Periodic Review System:** *See Fixed Reorder Cycle Inventory Model*

**Permit:** A grant of authority to operate as a contract carrier.

**Perpetual Inventory:** An inventory record keeping system where each transaction in and out is recorded and a new balance is computed. Perpetual inventory records may be kept manually on paper logs or stock cards, or in a computer database.

**Personal Digital Assistant (PDA):** A computer term for a handheld device that combines computing, telephone/fax, and networking features. PDA examples include the Palm and Pocket PC devices. A typical PDA can function as a cellular phone, fax sender, and personal organizer. Unlike portable computers, most PDAs are pen-based, using a stylus rather than a keyboard for input. This means that they also incorporate handwriting recognition features. Some PDAs can also react to voice input by using voice recognition technologies. Some PDAs and networking software allow companies to use PDAs in their warehouses to support wireless transaction processing and inquiries.

**Personal Discrimination:** Charging different rates to shippers with similar transportation characteristics, or vice versa.

**Phantom Bill of Material:** A bill-of-material coding and structuring technique used primarily for transient (non stocked) subassemblies. For the transient item, lead time is set to zero and the order quantity to lot-for-lot. A phantom bill of material represents an item that is physically built, but rarely stocked, before being used in the next step or level of manufacturing. This permits MRP logic to drive requirements straight through (blowthrough) the phantom item to its components, but the MRP system usually retains its ability to net against any occasional inventories of the item. This technique also facilitates the use of common bills of material for engineering and manufacturing. *Synonym: Pseudo Bill of Material. Also see: blowthrough*

**Physical Distribution:** The movement and storage functions associated with finished goods from manufacturing plants to warehouses and to customers; also, used synonymously with business logistics.

**Physical Supply**: The movement and storage functions associated with raw materials from supply sources to the manufacturing facility.

**Pick-by-Light:** A laser identifies the bin for the next item in the rack; when the picker completes the pick, the bar code is scanned and the system then points the laser at the next bin.

**Pick/Pack:** Picking of product from inventory and packing into shipment containers.

**Pick List:** A list of items to be picked from stock in order to fill an order; the pick list generation and the picking method can be quite sophisticated.

**Pick on Receipt:** Product is receipted and picked in one operation (movement); therefore the product never actually touches the ground within the warehouse. It is unloaded from one vehicle and re-loaded on an outbound vehicle. *Related to Cross Docking*

**Pick-to-Clear:** A method often used in warehouse management systems that directs picking to the locations with the smallest quantities on hand.

**Pick-to-Carton:** Pick-to-carton logic uses item dimensions/weights to select the shipping carton prior to the order picking process. Items are then picked directly into the shipping carton.

**Pick-to-Light:** Pick-to light systems consist of lights and LED displays for each pick location. The system uses software to light the next pick and display the quantity to pick.

**Pick-to-Trailer:** Order-picking method where the order picker transports the materials directly from the pick location to the trailer without any interim checking or staging steps.

**Pick-Up Order:** A document indicating the authority to pick up cargo or equipment from a specific location.

**Picking:** The operations involved in pulling products from storage areas to complete a customer order.

**Picking by Aisle:** A method by which pickers pick all needed items in an aisle regardless of the items' ultimate destination; the items must be sorted later.

**Picking by Source:** A method in which pickers successively pick all items going to a particular destination regardless of the aisle in which each item is located.

**Piggyback:** Terminology used to describe a truck trailer being transported on a railroad flatcar.

**Pin Lock:** A hard piece of iron, formed to fit on a trailer's pin, that locks in place with a key to prevent an unauthorized person from moving the trailer.

**Place Utility:** A value created in a product by changing its location. Transportation creates place utility.

**Plaintext:** Data before it has been encrypted or after it has been decrypted, e.g., an ASCII text file.

**Plan Deliver:** The development and establishment of courses of action over specified time periods that represent a projected appropriation of supply resources to meet delivery requirements.

**Plan-Do-Check-Action (PDCA):**In quality management, a four-step process for quality improvement. In the first step (plan), a plan to effect improvement is developed. In the second step (do), the plan is carried out, preferably on a small scale. In the third step (check), the effects of the plan are observed. In the last step (action), the results are studied to determine what was learned and what can be predicted. The plan-do-check-act cycle is sometimes referred to as the Shewhart cycle (because Walter A. Shewhart discussed the concept in his book Statistical Method from the Viewpoint of Quality Control) and as the Deming circle (because W. Edwards Deming introduced the concept in Japan; the Japanese subsequently called it the Deming circle). *Synonyms: Shewhart Cycle. Also see: Deming Circle*

**Plan Make:** The development and establishment of courses of action over specified time periods that represent a projected appropriation of production resources to meet production requirements.

**Plan Source:** The development and establishment of courses of action over specified time periods that represent a projected appropriation of material resources to meet supply chain requirements.

**Plan Stability:** The difference between planned production and actual production, as a percentage of planned production.

**Planned Date:** The date an operation, such as a receipt, shipment, or delivery of an order is planned to occur.

**Planned Order:** A suggested order quantity, release date, and due date created by the planning system's logic when it encounters net requirements in processing MRP. In some cases, it can also be created by a master scheduling module. Planned orders are created by the computer, exist only within the computer, and may be changed or deleted by the computer during subsequent processing if conditions change. Planned orders at one level will be exploded into gross requirements for components at the next level. Planned orders, along with released orders, serve as input to capacity requirements planning to show the total capacity requirements by work center in future time periods. *Also see: Planning Time Fence, Firm Planned Order*

**Planned Receipt:** An anticipated receipt against an open purchase order or open production order.

**Planning Bill:** *See Planning Bill of Material*

**Planning Bill of Material:** An artificial grouping of items or events in bill-of-material format used to facilitate master scheduling and material planning. It may include the historical average of demand expressed as a percentage of total demand for all options within a feature or for a specific end item within a product family and is used as the quantity per in the planning bill of material. *Synonym: Planning Bill. Also see: Hedge Inventory, Production Forecast, Pseudo Bill of Material*

**Planning Calendar:** *See Manufacturing Calendar*

**Planning Fence:** *See Planning Time Fence*

**Planning Horizon:** The amount of time a plan extends into the future. For a master schedule, this is normally set to cover a minimum of cumulative lead time plus time for lot sizing low-level components and for capacity changes of primary work centers or of key suppliers. For longer term plans the planning horizon must be long enough to permit any needed additions to capacity. *Also see: Cumulative Lead Time, Planning Time Fence*

**Planning Time Fence:** A point in time denoted in the planning horizon of the master scheduling process that marks a boundary inside of which changes to the schedule may adversely affect component schedules, capacity plans, customer deliveries, and cost. Outside the planning time fence, customer orders may be booked and changes to the master schedule can be made within the constraints of the production plan. Changes inside the planning time fence must be made manually by the master scheduler. *Synonym: Planning Fence. Also see: Cumulative Lead Time, Demand Time Fence, Firm Planned Order, Planned Order, Planning Horizon, Time Fence.*

**Planogram:** The end result of analyzing the sales data of an item or group of items to determine the best arrangement of products on a store shelf. The process determines which shelf your top-selling product should be displayed on, the number of facings it gets, and what best to surround it with. It results in graphical picture or map of the allotted shelf space along with a specification of the facing and deep.

**Plant Finished Goods:** Finished goods inventory held at the end manufacturing location.

**PLU:** *See Price Look-Up*

**PM:** *See Preventative Maintenance*

**PO:** *See Purchase Order*

**POD:** *See Proof of Delivery*

**Point-of-Purchase (POP):** A retail sales term referring to the area where a sale occurs, such as the checkout counter. POP is also used to refer to the displays and other sales promotion tools located at a checkout counter.

**Point of Sale (POS):** 1) The time and place at which a sale occurs, such as a cash register in a retail operation, or the order confirmation screen in an on-line session. Supply chain partners are interested in capturing data at the POS, because it is a true record of the sale rather than being derived from other information such as inventory movement. 2) Also a national network of merchant terminals, at which customers can use client cards and personal security codes to make purchases. Transactions are directed against client deposit accounts. POS terminals are sophisticated cryptographic devices, with complex key management processes. POS standards draw on ABM network experiences and possess extremely stringent security requirements.

**Point of Sale Information:** Price and quantity data from retail locations as sales transactions occur.

**Point-of-Use Inventory:** Material used in production processes that is physically stored where it is consumed.

**Poka Yoke (mistake-proof):** The application of simple techniques that prevent process quality failure. A mechanism that either prevents a mistake from being made or makes the mistake obvious at a glance.

**Police Powers:** The United States constitutionally granted right or the states to establish regulations to protect the health and welfare of its citizens; truck weight, speed, length, and height laws are examples.

**Pooling:** A shipping term for the practice of combining shipment from multiple shippers into a truckload in order to reduce shipping charges.

**POP:** *See Point-of-Purchase*

**Port:** A harbor where ships will anchor.

**Port Authority:** A state or local government that owns, operates, or otherwise provides wharf, dock, and other terminal investments at ports.

**Port of Discharge:** Port where vessel is off loaded.

**Port of Entry:** A port at which foreign goods are admitted into the receiving country.

**Port of Loading:** Port where cargo is loaded aboard the vessel.

**Portal:** Websites that serve as starting points to other destinations or activities on the Internet. Initially thought of as a "home base" type of web page, portals attempt to provide all Internet needs in one location. Portals commonly provide services such as e-mail, online chat forums, shopping, searching, content, and news feeds.

**POS:** *See Point of Sale*

**Possession Utility:** The value created by marketing's effort to increase the desire to possess a good or benefit from a service.

**Post-Deduct Inventory Transaction Processing:** A method of inventory bookkeeping where the book (computer) inventory of components is reduced after issue. When compared to a real-time process, this approach has the disadvantage of a built-in differential between the book record and what is physically in stock. Consumption can be based on recorded actual use, or calculated using finished quantity received times the standard BOM quantity (backflush). *Also see: Backflush*

**Postponement:** The delay of final activities (i.e., assembly, production, packaging, etc.) until the latest possible time. A strategy used to eliminate excess inventory in the form of finished goods which may be packaged in a variety of configurations.

**Po To PoP:** Purchase Order to Point of Purchase visibility in the supply chain.

**PPB:** *See Part Period Balancing*

**Pre-Deduct Inventory Transaction Processing:** A method of inventory bookkeeping where the book (computer) inventory of components is reduced before issue, at the time a scheduled receipt for their parents or assemblies is created via a bill-of-material explosion. When compared to a real-time process, this approach has the disadvantage of a built-in differential between the book record and what is physically in stock.

**Pre-Expediting:** The function of following up on open orders before the scheduled delivery date, to ensure the timely delivery of materials in the specified quantity.

**Prepaid:** A freight term, which indicates that charges are to be paid by the shipper. Prepaid shipping charges may be added to the customer invoice, or the cost may be bundled into the pricing for the product.

**Present Value:** Today's value of future cash flows, discounted at an appropriate rate.

**Predictive Maintenance:** Practices that seek to prevent unscheduled machinery downtime by collecting and analyzing data on equipment conditions. The analysis is then used to predict time-tofailure, plan maintenance, and restore machinery to good operating condition. Predictive maintenance systems typically measure parameters on machine operations, such as vibration, heat, pressure, noise, and lubricant condition. In conjunction with computerized maintenance management systems (CMMS), predictive maintenance enables repair-work orders to be released automatically, repair-parts inventories checked, or routine maintenance scheduled.

**Preventative Maintenance (PM):** Regularly scheduled maintenance activities performed in order to reduce or eliminate unscheduled equipment failures and downtime.

**Price Erosion:** The decrease in price point and profit margin for a product or service, which occurs over time due to the effect of increased competition or commoditization.

**Price Look-Up (PLU):** Used for retail products sold loose, bunched or in bulk (to identify the different types of fruit, say). As opposed to UPC (Universal Product Codes) for packaged, fixed weight retail items. A PLU code contains 4-5 digits in total. The PLU is entered before an item is weighed to determine a price.

**Primary-Business Test:** A test used by the ICC to determine if a trucking operation is bona fide private transportation; the private trucking operation must be incidental to and in the furtherance of the primary business of the firm.

**Primary highways:** Highways that connect lesser populated cities with major cities.

**Primary Manufacturing Strategy:** Your company's dominant manufacturing strategy. The Primary Manufacturing Strategy generally accounts for 80-plus % of a company's product volume. According to a study by Pittiglio Rabin Todd & McGrath (PRTM), approximately 73% of all companies use a make-to-stock strategy.

**PRIME QR:** Product Replenishment and Inventory Management Edge for Quick Response.

**Private carrier:** A carrier that provides transportation service to the firm and that owns or leases the vehicles and does not charge a fee. Private motor carriers may haul at a fee for wholly-owned subsidiaries.

**Private Label:** Products that are designed, produced, controlled by, and which carry the name of the store or a name owned by the store; also known as a store brand or dealer brand. An example would be Wal-Mart's "Sam's Choice" products.

**Private Warehouse:** A warehouse that is owned by the company using it.

**Pro Number:** Any progressive or serialized number applied for identification of freight bills, bills of lading, etc.

**Proactive:** The strategy of understanding issues before they become apparent and presenting the solution as a benefit to the customer, etc.

**Process:** A series of time-based activities that are linked to complete a specific output.

**Process Benchmarking:** Benchmarking a process (such as the pick, pack, and ship process) against organizations known to be the best in class in this process. Process benchmarking is usually conducted on firms outside of the organization's industry. *Also see: Benchmarking, Best-in-Class, Competitive Benchmarking*

**Process Flow Diagram:** Graphical representation of physical activities associated with a supply chain platform.

**Process Improvement:** Designs or activities, which improve quality or reduce costs, often through the elimination of waste or non-value-added tasks.

**Process Manufacturing:** Production that adds value by mixing, separating, forming, and/or performing chemical reactions. It may be done in a batch, continuous, or mixed batch/continuous mode. Products in this manufacturing group include: foods, petrochemicals, bottling, chemicals, etc. Process manufacturing frequently generates co-products and by-products as an outcome in addition to the primary product being manufactured. An example would be the manufacture of petroleum products, where multiple grades of lubricants and fuels are produced from a single run as well as nonusable by-products such as sludge.

**Process Yield:** The resulting output from a process. An example would be a quantity of finished product output from manufacturing processes.

**Procurement:** The business functions of procurement planning, purchasing, inventory control, traffic, receiving, incoming inspection, and salvage operations. *Synonym: Purchasing*

**Procurement Services Provider (PSP):** A services firm that integrates procurement technologies with product, sourcing, and supply management expertise, to provide outsourced procurement solutions. A PSP serves as an extension of an organization's existing procurement infrastructure, managing the processes and spending categories and procurement processes that the organization feels it has opportunities for improvement but lacks the internal expertise to manage effectively.

**Product:** Something that has been or is being produced.

**Product Characteristics:** All of the elements that define a product's character, such as size, shape, weight, etc.

**Product Configurator:** A system, generally rule-based, to be used in design-to-order, engineer-to-order, or make-to-order environments where numerous product variations exist. Product configurators perform intelligent modeling of the part or product attributes and often create solid models, drawings, bills of material, and cost estimates that can be integrated into CAD/CAM and MRP II systems as well as sales order entry systems.

**Product ID:** A method of identifying a product without using a full description. These can be different for each document type and must, therefore, be captured and related to the document in which they were used. They must then be related to each other in context (also known as SKU, Item Code or Number, or other such name).

**Product Family:** A group of products with similar characteristics, often used in production planning (or sales and operations planning).

**Production Calendar:** *See Manufacturing Calendar*

**Production Capacity:** Measure of how much production volume may be experienced over a set period of time.

**Production Forecast:** A projected level of customer demand for a feature (option, accessory, etc.) of a make-to-order or an assemble-to-order product. Used in two-level master scheduling, it is calculated by netting customer backlog against an overall family or product line master production schedule and then factoring this product's available-to-promise by the option percentage in a planning bill of material. *Also see: Assemble-to-Order, Planning Bill of Material, Two-Level Master Schedule*

**Production Line:** A series of pieces of equipment dedicated to the manufacture of a specific number of products or families.

**Production Planning and Scheduling:** The systems that enable creation of detailed optimized plans and schedules taking into account the resource, material, and dependency constraints to meet the deadlines.

**Production-Related Material:** Production-related materials are those items classified as material purchases and included in Cost of Goods Sold as raw material purchases.

**Productivity:** A measure of efficiency of resource utilization; defined as the sum of the outputs divided by the sum of the inputs.

**Profit Ratio:** The percentage of profit to sales—that is, profit divided by sales.

**Profit Before Interest and Tax (PBIT):** The financial profit generated prior to the deduction of taxes and interest due on loans. Also called operating profit.

**Profitability Analysis:** The analysis of profit derived from cost objects with the view to improve or optimize profitability. Multiple views may be analyzed, such as market segment, customer, distribution channel, product families, products, technologies, platforms, regions, manufacturing capacity, etc.

**Profitable to Promise:** This is effectively a promise to deliver a certain order on agreed terms, including price and delivery. Profitable-to-Promise (PTP) is the logical evolution of Available-to-Promise (ATP) and Capable-to-Promise (CTP). While the first two are necessary for profitability, they are not sufficient. For enterprises to survive in a competitive environment, profit optimization is a vital technology.

**Pro-Forma:** A type of quotation or offer that may be used when first negotiating the sales of goods or services. If the pro-forma is accepted, then the terms and conditions of the pro-forma may become the request.

**Pro Forma Invoice:** An invoice, forwarded by the seller of goods prior to shipment, that advises the buyer of the particulars and value of the goods. Usually required by the buyer in order to obtain an import permit or letter of credit.

**Pro Number:** Any progressive or serialized number applied for identification of freight bills, bills of lading, etc.

**Profitability Analysis:** The analysis of profit derived from cost objects with the view to improve or optimize profitability. Multiple views may be analyzed, such as market segment, customer, distribution channel, product families, products, technologies, platforms, regions, manufacturing capacity, etc.

**Promotion:** The act of selling a product at a reduced price, or a buy one - get one free offer, for the purpose of increasing sales.

**Proof of Delivery (POD):** Information supplied by the carrier containing the name of the person who signed for the shipment, the time and date of delivery, and other shipment delivery related information. POD is also sometimes used to refer to the process of printing materials just prior to shipment (Print on Demand).

**Proportional Rate:** A rate lower than the regular rate for shipments that have prior or subsequent moves; used to overcome competitive disadvantages of combination rates.

**Protocol:** Communication standards that determine message content and format, enabling uniformity of transmissions.

**Pseudo Bill of Materials:** *See Phantom Bill of Materials*

**PSP:** *See Procurement Services Provider*

**Public Warehouse:** A business that provides short or long-term storage to a variety of businesses usually on a month-to-month basis. A public warehouse will generally use their own equipment and staff however agreements may be made where the client either buys or subsidizes equipment. Public warehouse fees are usually a combination of storage fees (per pallet or actual square footage) and transaction fees (inbound and outbound). Public warehouses are most often used to supplement space requirements of a private warehouse. See also Contract warehouse and 3PL.

**Public Warehouse Receipt:** The basic document issued by a public warehouse manager that is the receipt for the goods given to the warehouse manager. The receipt can be either negotiable or nonnegotiable.

**Pull Signal:** A signal from a using operation that triggers the issue of raw material.

**Pull or Pull-through distribution:** Supply-chain action initiated by the customer. Traditionally, the supply chain was pushed; manufacturers produced goods and "pushed" them through the supply chain, and the customer had no control. In a pull environment, a customer's purchase sends replenishment information back through the supply chain from retailer to distributor to manufacturer, so goods are "pulled" through the supply chain.

**Pull Ordering System:** A system in which each warehouse controls its own shipping requirements by placing individual orders for inventory with the central distribution center. A replenishment system where inventory is "pulled" into the supply chain (or "demand chain" by POS systems, or ECR programs). Associated with "build to order" systems.

**Purchase Order (PO):** The purchaser's authorization used to formalize a purchase transaction with a supplier. The physical form or electronic transaction a buyer uses when placing order for merchandise.

**Purchase Price Discount:** A pricing structure in which the seller offers a lower price if the buyer purchases a larger quantity.

**Purchasing:** The functions associated with buying the goods and services required by the firm.

**Pure Raw Material:** A raw material that does not lose weight in processing.

**Push Back Rack:** Utilizing wheels in the rack structure, this rack system allows palletized goods and materials to be stored by being pushed up a gently graded ramp. Stored materials are allowed to flow down the ramp to the aisle. This rack configuration allows for deep storage on each rack level.

**Push Distribution:** The process of building product and pushing it into the distribution channel without receiving any information regarding requirements. *Also see: Pull or Pull-Through Distribution*

**Push Ordering System:** A situation in which a firm makes inventory deployment decisions at the central distribution center and ships to its individual warehouses accordingly.

**Push Technology:** Webcasting (push technology) is the prearranged updating of news, weather, or other selected information on a computer user's desktop interface through periodic and generally unobtrusive transmission over the World Wide Web (including the use of the Web protocol on Intranet). Webcasting uses so-called push technology in which the Web server ostensibly "pushes" information to the user rather than waiting until the user specifically requests it.

**Put Away:** Removing the material from the dock (or other location of receipt), transporting the material to a storage area, placing that material in a staging area, and then moving it to a specific location and recording the movement and identification of the location where the material has been placed.

**Put-to-Light:** A method that uses lights to direct the placement of materials. Most often used in batch picking to designate the tote to place picked item into.

# Q

**QC:** *See Quality Control*
**QFD:** *See Quality Function Deployment*
**QR:** *See Quick Response*

**Qualifier:** A data element, which identifies or defines a related element, set of elements or a segment. The qualifier contains a code from a list of approved codes.

**Qualitative Forecasting Techniques:** In forecasting, an approach that is based on intuitive or judgmental evaluation. It is used generally when data are scarce, not available, or no longer relevant. Common types of qualitative techniques include: personal insight, sales force estimates, panel consensus, market research, visionary forecasting, and the Delphi method. Examples include developing long-range projections and new product introduction.

**Quality:** Conformance to requirements or fitness for use. Quality can be defined through five principal approaches:

1. Transcendent quality is an ideal, a condition of excellence
2. Product-based quality is based on a product attribute
3. User-based quality is fitness for use
4. Manufacturing-based quality is conformance to requirements
5. Value-based quality is the degree of excellence at an acceptable price. Also, quality has two major components: a. quality of conformance—quality is defined by the absence of defects, and b. quality of design—quality is measured by the degree of customer satisfaction with a product's characteristics and features.

**Quality Circle:** In quality management, a small group of people who normally work as a unit and meet frequently to uncover and solve problems concerning the quality of items produced, process capability, or process control. *Also see: Small Group Improvement activity*

**Quality Control (QC):** The management function that attempts to ensure that the foods or services manufactured or purchased meet the product or service specifications

**Quality Function Deployment (QFD):** A structured method for translating user requirements into detailed design specifications using a continual stream of 'what-how' matrices. QFD links the needs of the customer (end user) with design, development, engineering, manufacturing, and service functions. It helps organizations seek out both spoken and unspoken needs, translate these into actions and designs, and focus various business functions toward achieving this common goal.

**Quantitative Forecasting Techniques:** An approach to forecasting where historical demand data is used to project future demand. Extrinsic and intrinsic techniques are typically used. *Also see: Extrinsic Forecasting Method, Intrinsic Forecasting Method*

**Quantity Based Order System:** *See Fixed Reorder Quantity Inventory Model*

**Quarantine:** In quality management, the setting aside of items from availability for use or sale until all required quality tests have been performed and conformance certified. In a best practice process, items in quarantine are tagged, logged, and kept in a secure area pending disposition.

**Quick Response (QR):** A strategy widely adopted by general merchandise and soft lines retailers and manufacturers to reduce retail out-of-stocks, forced markdowns and operating expenses. These goals are accomplished through shipping accuracy and reduced response time. QR is a partnership strategy in which suppliers and retailers work together to respond more rapidly to the consumer by sharing point-of-sale scan data, enabling both to forecast replenishment needs.

# R

**Rack:** A storage device for handling material in pallets. A rack usually provides storage for pallets arranged in vertical sections with one or more pallets to a tier. Some racks accommodate more than one-pallet-deep storage. Some racks are static, meaning that the rack contents remain in a fixed position until physically moved. Some racks are designed with a sloped shelf to allow products to "flow" down as product in the front is removed. Replenishment of product on a flow rack may be from the rear, or the front in a "push back" manner.

**Racking:** A function performed by a rack-jobber, a full-function intermediary who performs all regular warehousing functions and some retail functions, typically stocking a display rack. Also a definition that is applied to the hardware which is used to build racks.

**Radio Frequency (RF):** A form of wireless communications that lets users relay information via electromagnetic energy waves from a terminal to a base station, which is linked in turn to a host computer. The terminals can be place at a fixed station, mounted on a forklift truck, or carried in the worker's hand. The base station contains a transmitter and receiver for communication with the terminals. RF systems use either narrow-band or spread-spectrum transmissions. Narrow-band data transmissions move along a single limited radio frequency, while spread-spectrum transmissions move across several different frequencies. When combined with a bar-code system for identifying inventory items, a radio-frequency system can relay data instantly, thus updating inventory records in so-called "real time."

**Radio Frequency Identification (RFID):** The use of radio frequency technology including RFID tags and tag readers to identify objects. Objects may include virtually anything physical, such as equipment, pallets of stock, or even individual units of product. RFID tags can be active or passive. Active tags contain a power source and emit a signal constantly. Passive tags receive power from the radio waves sent by the scanner / reader. The inherent advantages of RFID over bar code technology are: 1) the ability to be read over longer distances, 2) the elimination of requirement for "line of sight" reads, 3) added capacity to contain information, and 4) RFID tag data can be updated / changed.

**Ramp Rate:** A statement which quantifies how quickly you grow or expand an operation Growth trajectory. Can refer to sales, profits or margins.

**Random-Location Storage:** A storage technique in which parts are placed in any space that is empty when they arrive at the storeroom. Although this random method requires the use of a locator file to identify part locations, it often requires less storage space than a fixed-location storage method. *Also see: Fixed-Location Storage*

**Rate-Based Scheduling:** A method for scheduling and producing based on a periodic rate, e.g., daily, weekly, or monthly. This method has traditionally been applied to high-volume and process industries. The concept has recently been applied within job shops using cellular layouts and mixed model level schedules where the production rate is matched to the selling rate.

**Rate Basis Number:** The distance between two rate basis points.

**Rate Basis Point:** The major shipping point in a local area; all points in the local area are considered to be the rate basis point.

**Rate Bureau:** A group of carriers that get together to establish joint rates, to divide joint revenues and claim liabilities, and the publish tariffs. Rate bureaus have published single line rates, which were prohibited in 1984.

**Rationing:** The allocation of product among customers during periods of short supply. When price is used to allocate product, it is allocated to those willing to pay the most.

**Raw Materials (RM):** Crude or processed material that can be converted by manufacturing, processing, or combination into a new and useful product.

**Real-Time:** The processing of data in a business application as it happens - as contrasted with storing data for input at a later time (batch processing).

**Reasonable Rate:** A rate that is high enough to cover the carrier's cost but not too high to enable the carrier to realize monopolistic profits.

**Recapture Clause:** A provision of the 1920 Transportation Act that provided for self-help financing for railroads. Railroads that earned more than the prescribed return contributed one-half of the excess to the fund from which the ICC made loans to less profitable railroads. The Recapture Clause was repealed in 1933.

**Receiving:** The function encompassing the physical receipt of material, the inspection of the incoming shipment for conformance with the purchase order (quantity and damage), the identification and delivery to destination, and the preparation of receiving reports.

**Receiving Dock:** Distribution center location where the actual physical receipt of the purchased material from the carrier occurs.

**Reconsignment:** A carrier service that permits changing the destination and/or consignee after the shipment has reached its originally billed destination and paying the through rate from origin to final destination.

**Refrigerated Carriers:** Truckload carriers designed to keep perishables good refrigerated. The food industry typically uses this type of carrier.

**Reefer:** A term used for refrigerated vehicles.

**Reengineering:** 1) A fundamental rethinking and radical redesign of business processes to achieve dramatic improvements in performance. 2) A term used to describe the process of making (usually) significant and major revisions or modifications to business processes. 3) Also called Business Process Reengineering.

**Regeneration MRP:** An MRP processing approach where the master production schedule is totally Re-exploded down through all bills of material, to maintain valid priorities. New requirements and planned orders are completely recalculated or "regenerated" at that time.

**Regional Carrier:** A for-hire air carrier, usually certificated, that has annual operating revenues of less than $74 million; the carrier usually operates within a particular region of the country.

**Regular-Route Carrier:** A motor carrier that is authorized to provide service over designated routes.

**Relay Terminal:** A motor carrier terminal designed to facilitate the substitution of one driver for another who has driven the maximum hours permitted.

**Release-to-Start Manufacturing:** Average time from order release to manufacturing to the start of the production process. This cycle time may typically be required to support activities such as material movement and line changeovers.

**Released-Value Rates:** Rates based upon the value of the shipment; the maximum carrier liability for damage is less than the full value, and in return the carrier offers a lower rate.

**Reliability:** A carrier selection criterion that considers the variation in carrier transit time; the consistency of the transit time provided.

**Reorder Point:** A predetermined inventory level that triggers the need to place an order. This minimum level provides inventory to meet anticipated demand during the time it takes to receive the order.

**Reparation:** The ICC could require railroads to repay users the difference between the rate charged and the maximum rate permitted when the ICC found the rate to be unreasonable or too high.

**Re-plan Cycle:** Time between the initial creation of a regenerated forecast and the time its impact is incorporated into the Master Production Schedule of the end-product manufacturing facility. (An element of Total Supply Chain Response Time)

**Replenishment:** The process of moving or re-supplying inventory from a reserve (or upstream) storage location to a primary (or downstream) storage or picking location, or to another mode of storage in which picking is performed.

**Request for Information (RFI):** A document used to solicit information about vendors, products, and services prior to a formal RFQ/RFP process.

**Request for Proposal (RFP):** A document, which provides information concerning needs and requirements for a manufacturer. This document is created in order to solicit proposals from potential suppliers. For, example, a computer manufacturer may use a RFP to solicit proposals from suppliers of third party logistics services.

**Request for Quote (RFQ):** A document used to solicit vendor responses when a product has been selected and price quotations are needed from several vendors.

**Resellers:** Organizations intermediate in the manufacturing and distribution process, such as wholesalers and retailers.

**Resource Driver**: In cost accounting, the best single quantitative measure of the frequency and intensity of demands placed on a resource by other resources, activities, or cost objects. It is used to assign resource costs to activities, and cost objects, or to other resources.

**Resources:** Economic elements applied or used in the performance of activities or to directly support cost objects. They include people, materials, supplies, equipment, technologies and facilities. *Also see: Resource Driver, Capacity*

**Retailer:** A business that takes title to products and resells them to final consumers. Examples include Wal-Mart, Best Buy, and Safeway, but also include the many smaller independent stores.

**Return Disposal Costs:** The costs associated with disposing or recycling products that have been returned due to End-of-Life or Obsolescence.

**Return Goods Handling:** Processes involved with returning goods from the customer to the manufacturer. Products may be returned because of performance problems or simply because the customer doesn't like the product.

**Return Material Authorization or Return Merchandise Authorization (RMA):** A number usually produced to recognize and give authority for a faulty, perhaps, good to be returned to a distribution centre of manufacturer. A form generally required with a Warranty/ Return, which helps the company identify the original product, and the reason for return. The RPA number often acts as an order form for the work required in repair situations, or as a reference for credit approval.

**Return on Assets (ROA):** Financial measure calculated by dividing profit by assets.

**Return on Net Assets:** Financial measure calculated by dividing profit by assets net of depreciation.

**Return on Sales:** Financial measure calculated by dividing profit by sales.

**Return Product Authorization (RPA):** Also called Return Material or Goods Authorization (RMA or RGA). A form generally required with a Warranty/Return, which helps the company identify the original product, and the reason for return. The RPA number often acts as an order form for the work required in repair situations, or as a reference for credit approval.

**Return to Vendor (RTV):** Material that has been rejected by the customer or the buyer's inspection department and is awaiting shipment back to the supplier for repair or replacement.

**Returns Inventory Costs:** The costs associated with managing inventory, returned for any of the following reasons: repair, refurbish, excess, obsolescence, End-of-Life, ecological conformance, and demonstration. Includes all applicable elements of the Level 2 component Inventory Carrying Cost of Total Supply Chain Management Cost

**Returns Material Acquisition, Finance, Planning and IT Costs:** The costs associated with acquiring the defective products and materials for repair or refurbishing items, plus any Finance, Planning and Information Technology cost to support Return Activity.. Includes all applicable elements of the Level 2 components Material Acquisition Cost (acquiring materials for repairs), Supply Chain Related Finance and Planning Costs and Supply Chain IT Costs of Total Supply Chain Management Cost.

**Returns Order Management Costs:** The costs associated with managing Return Product Authorizations (RPA). Includes all applicable elements of the Level 2 component Order Management Cost of Total Supply Chain Management Cost. *See Order Management Costs*

**Returns Processing Cost:** The total cost to process repairs, refurbished, excess, obsolete, and Endof-Life products including diagnosing problems, and replacing products. Includes the costs of logistics support, materials, centralized functions, troubleshooting service requests, on-site diagnosis and repair, external repair, and miscellaneous. These costs are broken into Returns Order Management, Returns Inventory

Carrying, Returns Material Acquisition, Finance, Planning, IT, Disposal and Warranty Costs.

**Returns To Scale:** A defining characteristic of B2B. Bigger is better. It's what creates the winner takes all quality of most B2B hubs. It also places a premium on being first to market and first to achieve critical mass.

**Reverse Auction:** A type of auction where suppliers bid to sell products to a buyer (e.g. retailer). As bidding continues, the prices decline (opposite of a regular auction, where buyers are bidding to buy products).

**Reverse Engineering:** A process whereby competitors' products are disassembled & analyzed for evidence of the use of better processes, components & technologies

**Reverse Logistics**: A specialized segment of logistics focusing on the movement and management of products and resources after the sale and after delivery to the customer. Includes product returns for repair and/or credit.

**RF:** *See Radio Frequency*

**RFI:** *See Request for Information*

**RFID:** *See Radio Frequency Identification. Also see: Radio Frequency*

**RFP:** *See Request for Proposal*

**RFQ:** *See Request for Quote*

**RGA:** Return Goods Authorization. *See: Return Material Authorization*

**Rich Media:** An Internet advertising term for a Web page ad that uses advanced technology such as streaming video, downloaded applet (programs) that interact instantly with the user, and ads that change when the user's mouse passes over it.

**Rich Text Format (RFT):** A method of encoding text formatting and document structure using the ASCII character set. By convention, RTF files have an .rtf filename extension.

**Right of Eminent Domain:** A concept that permits the purchase of land needed for transportation right-of-way in a court of law; used by railroads and pipelines.

**RM:** *See Raw Materials*

**RMA**: Return Material Authorization. *See Return Product Authorization*

**ROA**: *See Return on Assets*

**ROI:** Return on Investment.

**Roll-On-Roll-Off (RO-RO):** A type of ship designed to permit cargo to be driven on at origin and off at destination; used extensively for the movement of automobiles.

**Root Cause Analysis:** Analytical methods to determine the core problem(s) of an organization, process, product, market, etc.

**Routing or Routing Guide:** 1) Process of determining how shipment will move between origin and destination. Routing information includes designation of carrier(s) involved, actual route of carrier, and estimated time enroute. 2) Right of shipper to determine carriers, routes and points for transfer shipments. 3) In manufacturing this is the document which defines a process of steps used to manufacture and/or assemble a product.

**Routing Accuracy:** When specified activities conform to administrative specifications, and specified resource consumptions (both man and machine) are detailed according to administrative specifications and are within ten percent of actual requirements.

**RPA:** *See Return Product Authorization*

**RTF:** *See Rich Text Format*

**RTV:** *See Return to Vendor*

**Rule of Eight:** Before the Motor Carrier Act of 1980, contract carriers requesting authority were restricted to eight shippers under contract. The number of shippers has been deleted as a consideration for granting a contract carrier permit.

**Rule of Rate Making:** A regulatory provision directing the regulatory agencies to consider the earnings necessary for a carrier to provide adequate transportation.


# S

**S&OP:** *See Sales and Operations Planning*

**SAE:** Society of Automotive Engineers.

**Safety Stock:** The inventory a company holds above normal needs as a buffer against delays in receipt of supply or changes in customer demand.

**Salable Goods:** A part or assembly authorized for sale to final customers through the marketing function.

**Sales and Operations Planning (SOP):** A strategic planning process that reconciles conflicting business objectives and plans future supply chain actions. S&OP Planning usually involves various business functions such as sales, operations and finance working together to agree on a single plan/forecast that can be used to drive the entire business.

**Sales Mix:** The proportion of individual product-type sales volumes that make up the total sales volume.

**Sales Plan:** A time-phased statement of expected customer orders anticipated to be received (incoming sales, not outgoing shipments) for each major product family or item. It represents sales and marketing management's commitment to take all reasonable steps necessary to achieve this level of actual customer orders. The sales plan is a necessary input to the production planning process (or sales and operations planning process). It is expressed in units identical to those used for the production plan (as well as in sales dollars). *Also see: Aggregate planning, Production Planning, Sales and Operations Planning*

**Sales Planning:** The process of determining the overall sales plan to best support customer needs and operations capabilities while meeting general business objectives of profitability, productivity, competitive customer lead times, and so on, as expressed in the overall business plan. *Also see: Production Planning, Sales and Operations Planning*

**Salvage Material:** Unused material that has a market value and can be sold.

**SaS:** *See Software as Services*

**Saw-Tooth Diagram:** A quantity-versus-time graphic representation of the order point/order quantity inventory system showing inventory being received and then used up and reordered.

**SBT:** *See Scan-Based Trading*

**SCAC/SCAC Code:** *See Standard Carrier Alpha Code*

**Scalability:** 1) How quickly and efficiently a company can ramp up to meet demand. See also uptime production flexibility. 2) How well a solution to some problem will work when the size of the problem increases. The economies to scale don't really kick in until you reach the critical mass, then revenues start to increase exponentially.

**Scan:** A computer term referring to the action of scanning bar codes or RF tags.

**Scan-Based Trading (SBT):** Scan-based trading is a method of using Point of Sale data from scanners and retail checkout to initiate invoicing between a manufacturer and retailer (pay on use), as well as generate re-supply orders.

**Scanlon Plan:** A system of group incentives on a companywide or plant-wide basis that sets up one measure that reflects the results of all efforts. The Scanlon plan originated in the 1930's by Joe Scanlon and MIT. The universal standard is the ratio of labor costs to sales value added by production. If there is an increase in production sales value with no change in labor costs, productivity has increased while unit cost has decreased.

**SCE:** *See Supply Chain Execution*

**SCEM:** *See Supply Chain Event Management*

**Scenario Planning:** A form of planning in which likely sets of relevant circumstances are identified in advance, and used to assess the impact of alternative actions.

**SCI:** *See Supply Chain Integration*

**SCM:** *See Supply Chain Management*

**SCOR:** *See Supply Chain Operations Reference Model*

**Scorecard:** A performance measurement tool used to capture a summary of the key performance indicators (KPIs)/metrics of a company. Metrics dashboards/scorecards should be easy to read and usually have "red, yellow, green" indicators to flag when the company is not meeting its targets for its metrics. Ideally, a dashboard/scorecard should be cross-functional in nature and include both financial and non-financial measures. In addition, scorecards should be reviewed regularly – at least on a monthly basis and weekly in key functions such as manufacturing and distribution where activities are critical to the success of a company. The dashboard/scorecards philosophy can also be applied to external supply chain partners such as suppliers to ensure that suppliers' objectives and practices align. *Synonym: Dashboard*

**Scrap Material:** Unusable material that has no market value.

**Seasonality:** A repetitive pattern of demand from year to year (or other repeating time interval) with some periods considerably higher than others. Seasonality explains the fluctuation in demand for various recreational products which are used during different seasons. *Also see: Base Series*

**Secondary Highways:** Highways that serve primarily rural areas.

**Secure Electronic Transaction (SET):** In e-commerce, a system for guaranteeing the security of financial transactions conducted over the Internet.

**Self Billing:** A transportation industry strategy which prescribes that a carrier will accept payment based on the tender document provided by the shipper.

**Self Correcting:** A computer term for an online process that validates data and won't allow the data to enter the system unless all errors are corrected.

**Sell In:** Units which are sold to retail stores by the manufacturer or distributor for re-sale to consumers. The period of time in a Product Life Cycle where the manufacture works with it's resellers to market and build inventory for sale. *Also see: Sell Through*

**Sell Through:** Units sold from retail stores to customers. The point in a Product Life Cycle where initial consumption rates are developed and demand established. *Also See: Sell In*

**Selling, General and Administrative (SG&A) Expenses:** Includes marketing, communication, customer service, sales salaries and commissions, occupancy expenses, unallocated overhead, etc. Excludes interest on debt, domestic or foreign income taxes, depreciation and amortization, extraordinary items, equity gains or losses, gain or loss from discontinued operations and extraordinary items.

**Separable Cost:** A cost that can be directly assignable to a particular segment of the business.

**Serial Number:** A unique number assigned for identification to a single piece that will never be repeated for similar pieces. Serial numbers are usually applied by the manufacturer but can be applied at other points, including by the distributor or wholesaler. Serial numbers can be used to support traceability and warranty programs.

**Serpentine Picking:** A method used for picking warehouse orders wherein the pickers are directed to pick from racks on both sides of an aisle as they move from one end to the other. A different method would be to pick from one side (front to back) then from the opposite side (back to front). Where used, serpentine picking can halve travel time and improve traffic flow down the aisles.

**Service Level:** A measure (usually expressed as a percentage) of satisfying demand through inventory or by the current production schedule in time to satisfy the customer's requested delivery dates and quantities.

**Service Oriented Architecture (SOA):** A computer system term which describes an software architectural concept that defines the use of services to support business requirements. In an SOA, resources are made available to other participants in the network as independent services that are accessed in a standardized way. Most definitions of SOA identify the use of web services (using SOAP and WSDL) in its implementation, however it is possible to implement SOA using any service-based technology.

**Service Parts Revenue:** The sum of the value of sales made to external customers and the transfer price valuation of sales within the company of repair or replacement parts and supplies, net of all discounts, coupons, allowances, and rebates.

**SET:** *See Secure Electronic Transaction*

**Setup Costs:** The costs incurred in staging the production line to produce a different item.

**SG&A:** *See Selling General & Administrative Expense*

**Shared Services:** Consolidation of a company's back-office processes to form a spinout (or a separate "shared services" unit, to be run like a separate business), providing services to the parent company and, sometimes, to external customers. Shared services typically lower overall cost due to the consolidation, and may improve support as a result of focus.

**Shareholder Value:** Combination of profitability (revenue and costs) and invested capital (working capital and fixed capital).

**Shelf Life:** The amount of time an item may be held in inventory before it becomes unusable. Shelf life is a consideration for food and drugs which deteriorate over time, and for high tech products which become obsolete quickly.

**Shewhart Cycle:** *See Plan-Do-Check-Action*

**Shingo's Seven Wastes:** Shigeo Shingo, a pioneer in the Japanese Just-in-Time philosophy, identified seven barriers to improving manufacturing. They are 1) waste of overproduction, 2) waste of waiting,

3) waste of transportation, 4) waste of stocks, 5) waste of motion, 6) waste of making defects, and 7) waste of the processing itself.

**Ship Agent:** A liner company or tramp ship operator representative who facilitates ship arrival, clearance, loading and unloading, and fee payment while at a specific port.

**Ship Broker:** A firm that serves as a go-between for the tramp ship owner and the chartering consignor or consignees.

**Shipper:** The party that tenders goods for transportation.

**Shipper-Carriers:** Shipper-carriers (also called private carriers) are companies with goods to be shipped that own or manage their own vehicle fleets. Many large retailers, particularly groceries and "big box" stores, are shipper-carriers.

**Shipper's Agent:** A firm that acts primarily to match up small shipments, especially single-traffic piggyback loads to permit use of twin-trailer piggyback rates.

**Shipper's Association:** A nonprofit, cooperative consolidator and distributor of shipments owned or shipped by member firms; acts in much the same was as for-profit freight forwarders.

**Shipping:** The function that performs tasks for the outgoing shipment of parts, components, and products. It includes packaging, marking, weighing, and loading for shipment.

**Shipping Lane:** A predetermined, mapped route on the ocean that commercial vessels tend to follow between ports. This helps ships avoid hazardous areas. In general transportation, the logical route between the point of shipment and the point of delivery used to analyze the volume of shipment between two points.

**Shipping Manifest:** A document that lists the pieces in a shipment. A manifest usually covers an entire load regardless of whether the load is to be delivered to a single destination or many destinations. Manifests usually list the items, piece count, total weight, and the destination name and address for each destination in the load.

**Shop Calendar:** *See Manufacturing Calendar*

**Shop Floor Production Control Systems:** The systems that assign priority to each shop order, maintaining work-in-process quantity information, providing actual output data for capacity control purposes and providing quantity by location by shop order for work-in-process inventory and accounting purposes.

**Short-Haul Discrimination:** Charging more for a shorter haul than for a longer haul over the same route, in the same direction, and for the same commodity.

**Short Shipment:** Piece of freight missing from shipment as stipulated by documents on hand.

**Shrinkage:** Reductions of actual quantities of items in stock, in process, or in transit. The loss may be caused by scrap, theft, deterioration, evaporation, etc.

**SIC:** *See Standard Industrial Classification*

**Sigma:** A Greek letter commonly used to designate the standard deviation of a population. Sigma is a statistical term that measures how much a process varies from perfection, based on the number of defects per million units.

One Sigma = 690,000 per million units

Two Sigma = 308,000 per million units

Three Sigma = 66,800 per million units

Four Sigma = 6,210 per million units

Five Sigma = 230 per million units

Six Sigma = 3.4 per million units

**Silo:** Also frequently called "Foxhole" or "Stovepipe", relates to a management / organization style where each functional unit operates independently, and with little or no collaboration between them on major business processes and issues.

**Simulation:** A mathematical technique for testing the performance of a system due to uncertain inputs and/or uncertain system configuration options. Simulation produces probability distributions for the behavior (outputs) of a system. A company may build a simulation model of its build plan process to evaluate the performance of the build plan under multiple scenarios on product demand.

**Single-Period Inventory Models:** Inventory models used to define economical or profit maximizing lot-size quantities when an item is ordered or produced only once, e.g., newspapers, calendars, tax guides, greeting cards, or periodicals, while facing uncertain demands.

**Single Sourcing:** When an organization deliberately chooses to use one supplier to provide a product or service, even though there are other suppliers available.

**Single Source Leasing:** Leasing both the truck and driver from one source.

**Six-Sigma Quality:** A term used generally to indicate that a process is well controlled, i.e., tolerance limits are ±6 sigma (3.4 defects per million events) from the centerline in a control chart. Six Sigma's goal is to define processes and manage those processes to obtain the lowest possible level of error— thus it can be applied to virtually any process, not just manufacturing. The term is usually associated with Motorola, which named one of its key operational initiatives Six-Sigma Quality.

**Skills Matrix:** A visible means of displaying people's skill levels in various tasks. Used in a team environment to identify the skills required by the team and which team members have those skills.

**SKU:** *See Stock Keeping Unit*

**Sleeper Team:** The use or two drivers to operate a truck equipped with a sleeper berth; while one driver sleeps in the berth to accumulate the mandatory off-duty time, the other driver operates the vehicle.

**Slip Seat Operation:** A term used to describe a motor carrier relay terminal operation where one driver is substituted for another who has accumulated the maximum driving time hours.

**Slip Sheet:** Similar to a pallet, the slip sheet, which is made of cardboard or plastic, is used to facilitate movement of unitized loads.

**Slot Based Production:** A lean manufacturing term used to describe a production system which has been level loaded (Heijunka) with a few slots held open for situations where demand must be met immediately.

**Slotting:** Inventory slotting or profiling is the process of identifying the most efficient placement for each item in a distribution center. Since each warehouse is different, proper slotting depends on a facility's unique product, movement, and storage characteristics. An optimal profile allows workers to pick items more quickly and accurately and reduces the risk of injuries.

**Slow Steaming:** operating a large steamship vessel at almost half capacity. Created in 2008 to reduce high bunker costs, and have a positive impact on operating a fleet of ships with less carbon footprint to have a positive impact on operational sustainability.

**Slurry:** Dry commodities that are made into a liquid form by the addition of water or other fluids to permit movement by pipeline.

**Small Group Improvement Activity:** An organizational technique for involving employees in continuous improvement activities. *Also see: Quality Circle*

**SMART:** *See Specific, Measurable, Achievable, Realistic, Time-Based*

**Smart and Secure Trade Lanes (SST):** Private initiative of the Strategic Council on Security Technology, an assembly of executives from port operators, major logistics technology providers, transportation consultancies, and former generals and public officials. Aims to enhance the safety, security and efficiency of cargo containers and their contents moving through the global supply chain into U.S. ports.

**Smart Label:** A label that has an RFID tag integrated into it.

**SMG:** Slow Moving Goods

**SNAFU:** is an *acronym* meaning *situation normal: all fucked up*. It is sometimes *bowdlerized* to *situation normal: all fouled up* or similar. In simple terms, it means that the normal situation is in a bad state, as it always is, therefore nothing unexpected.

**SOA:** *See Service Oriented Architecture*

**Social Media:** A type of online media, Twitter or Delicious, that expedites conversation as opposed to traditional media, which delivers content but doesn't allow readers/viewers/listeners to participate in the creation or development of the content.

**Social Network:** An association of people drawn together by platform (LinkedIn, Twitter, or Facebook), family, work or hobby. The term was first coined by professor J. A. Barnes in the 1950s.

**Social network fatigue:** The ennui induced by persistent solicitations to join new social networks. It is especially acute in those who are already members of more MySpaces and FaceBooks than they can remember.

**Society of Logistics Engineers:** A professional association engaged in the advancement of logistics technology and management.

**Software as Services (SaS):** A term which describes the use of computer systems provided by a remote third party, similar to what has traditionally been called a "Service Bureau" or "Application Service Provider (ASP)". In this setting the service provider maintains all of the computer hardware and software at their location, while the user accesses the systems via an internet connection and is charged a rate based on access time. Sometimes also referred to as "On Demand" services.

**SOP:** *See Sales and Operations Planning*

**SOW:** *See Statement of Work*

**Sole Sourcing:** When there is only one supplier for a product or service, and no alternate suppliers are available.

**Sortation:** Separating items (parcels, boxes, cartons, parts, etc.) according to their intended destination within a plant or for transit.

**Spam:** A computer industry term referring to the Act of sending identical and irrelevant postings to many different newsgroups or mailing lists. Usually this posting is something that has nothing to do with the particular topic of a newsgroup or of no real interest to the person on the mailing list.

**SPC:** *See Statistical Process Control*

**Special-Commodities Carrier:** A common carrier trucking company that has authority to haul a special commodity; there are 16 special commodities, such as household goods, petroleum products, and hazardous materials.

**Special-Commodity Warehouses:** A warehouse that is used to store products that require unique types of facilities, such as grain (elevator), liquid (tank), and tobacco (barn).

**Specific, Measurable, Achievable, Realistic, Time-Based (SMART):** A shorthand description of a way of setting goals and targets for individuals and teams.

**Splash Page:** A "first" or "front" page that you often see on some websites, usually containing a "click-through" logo or message, or a fancy Flash presentation, announcing that you have arrived. The main content and navigation on the site lie "behind" this page (a.k.a. the homepage or "welcome page").

**Split Case Order Picking:** A process used to fill orders for quantities less than a full case thereby requiring ordered items to be picked from a case or some similar container.

**Split Delivery:** A method by which a larger quantity is ordered on a purchase order to secure a lower price, but delivery is divided into smaller quantities and spread out over several dates to control inventory investment, save storage space, etc.

**Spot:** To move a trailer or boxcar into place for loading or unloading.

**Spot Demand:** Demand, having a short lead time that is difficult to estimate. Usually supply for this demand is provided at a premium price. An example of spot demand would be when there's a spiked demand for building materials as a result of a hurricane.

**Spur Track:** A railroad track that connects a company's plant or warehouse with the railroad's track; the cost of the spur track and its maintenance is borne by the user.

**SRFM:** Supply Chain Risk and Flexibility Management

**SST:** *See Smart and Secure Trade Lanes*

**Stable Demand:** Products for which demand does not fluctuate widely at specific points during the year.

**Staff Functions:** The support activities of planning and analysis provided to assist line managers with daily operations. Logistics staff functions include location analysis, system design, cost analysis, and planning.

**Staging:** 1) Pulling material for an order from inventory before the material is required. Staging is a means to ensure that all required materials are and will be available for use at time of assembly. The downside to staging is that it creates additional WIP inventory and reduces flexibility. 2) Placing trailers. *Also see: Accumulation Bin*

**Stakeholders:** People with a vested interest in a company or in a project, including managers, employees, stockholders, customers, suppliers, and others.

**Stand Up Fork Lift:** A forklift where the operator stands rather than sits. Most commonly used in case picking operations where the operator must get on and off the lift frequently.

**Standard Carrier Alpha Code (SCAC/SCAC Code):** A unique 2 to 4-letter code assigned to transportation companies for identification purposes. SCAC codes are required for EDI, and are printed on bills of lading and other transportation documents.

**Standard Components:** Components (parts) of a product, for which there is an abundance of suppliers. Not difficult to produce. An example would be a power cord for a computer.

**Standard Cost Accounting System:** A cost accounting system that uses cost units determined before production for estimating the cost of an order or product. For management control purposes, the standards are compared to actual costs, and variances are computed.

**Standard Deviation/Variance:** Measures of dispersion for a probability distribution. The variance is the average squared difference of a distribution from the distribution's mean (average) value. The standard deviation is defined mathematically as the square root of the variance, and is thereby expressed in the same units as the random variable that's described by the probability distribution. A distribution that varies widely about its mean value will have a larger standard deviation/variance than a distribution with less variation about its mean value.

**Standard Industrial Classification (SIC):** Classification codes that are used to categorize companies into industry groupings.

**Standing Order:** *See Blanket Purchase Order*

**STAR Process:** Leadership philosophy created by Michael J. Stolarczyk in late 20th century encompassing Speed, Trust, Accountability, and Relationships (now evolving into Rapport).

**Start Manufacture to Order Complete Manufacture:** Average lead-time from the time manufacturing begins to the time end products are ready for shipment, including the following supplements: order configuration verification, production scheduling, time to release order to manufacturing or distribution, and build or configure time. (An element of Order Fulfillment Lead Time)

**Statement of Work (SOW):** 1) A description of products to be supplied under a contract. A good practice is for companies to have SOWs in place with their trading partners – especially for all top suppliers. 2) In projection management, the first project planning document that should be prepared. It describes the purpose, history, deliverables, and measurable success indicators for a project. It captures the support required from the customer and identifies contingency plans for events that could throw the project off course. Because the project must be sold to management, staff, and review groups, the statement of work should be a persuasive document.

**Statistical Process Control (SPC):** A visual means of measuring and plotting process and product variation. Results are used to adjust variables and maintain product quality.

**Steamship Conferences:** Collective rate-making bodies for liner water carriers.

**Stickering:** Placing customer-specific stickers on boxes of product. An example would be where a retailer has a request for their own product codes to be applied to retail boxes prior to shipment.

**Stochastic Models:** Models where uncertainty is explicitly considered in the analysis.

**Stock Keeping Unit (SKU):** A category of unit with unique combination of form, fit, and function (i.e. unique components held in stock). To illustrate: If two items are indistinguishable to the customer, or if any distinguishing characteristics visible to the customer are not important to the customer, so that the customer believes the two items to be the same, these two items are part of the same SKU. As a further illustration consider a computer company that allows customers to configure a product from a standard catalogue components, choosing from three keyboards, three monitors, and three CPUs. Customers may also individually buy keyboards, monitors, and CPUs. If the stock were held at the configuration component level, the company would have nine SKUs. If the company stocks at the component level, as well as at the configured product level, the company would have 36 SKUs. (9 component SKUs + 3*3*3 configured product SKUs. If as part of a promotional campaign the company also specially packaged the products, the company would have a total of 72 SKUs.

**Stock Out:** A term used to refer to a situation where no stock was available to fill a request from a customer or production order during a pick operation. Stock outs can be costly, including the profit lost for not having the item available for sale, lost goodwill, substitutions. *Also referred to Out of Stock (OOS)*

**Stockchase:** Moving shipments through regular channels at an accelerated rate; to take extraordinary action because of an increase in relative priority. *Synonym: Expediting*

**Stockless Purchasing:** A practice whereby the buyer negotiates a price for the purchases of annual requirements of MRO items and the seller holds inventory until the buyer places an order for individual items.

**Stockout Cost:** The opportunity cost associated with not having sufficient supply to meet demand.

**Stovepipe:** *See Silo*

**Straight Truck:** A truck which has the driver's cab and the trailer combined onto a single frame. Straight trucks do not have a separate tractor and trailer. The driving compartment, engine and trailer are one unit.

**Strategic Alliance:** Business relationship in which two or more independent organizations cooperate and willingly modify their business objectives and practices to help achieve long-term goals and objectives. *Also see: Marquee Partners*

**Strategic Planning:** Looking one to five years into the future and designing a logistical system (or systems) to meet the needs of the various businesses in which a company is involved.

**Strategic Sourcing:** The process of determining long-term supply requirements, finding sources to fulfill those needs, selecting suppliers to provide the services, negotiating the purchase agreements and managing the suppliers' performance. Focuses on developing the most effective relationships with the right suppliers, to ensure that the right price is paid and that lifetime product costs are minimized. It also assesses whether services or processes would provide better value if they were outsourced to specialist organizations.

**Strategic Variables:** The variables that effect change in the environment and logistics strategy. The major strategic variables include economics, population, energy, and government.

**Strategy:** A specific action to achieve an objective.

**Stretch Wrap:** Clear plastic film that is wrapped around a unit load or partial load of product to secure it. The wrap is elastic.

**Stores:** The function associated with the storage and issuing of items that are frequently used. Also frequently seen as an alternative term for warehouse.

**Sub-Optimization:** Decisions or activities in a part made at the expense of the whole. An example of sub-optimization is where a manufacturing unit schedules production to benefit its cost structure without regard to customer requirements or the effect on other business units.

**Subcontracting:** Sending production work outside to another manufacturer. This can involve specialized operations such as plating metals, or complete functional operations. *Also see: Outsource*

**Substitutability:** The ability of a buyer to substitute the products of different sellers.

**Sunk Cost:** 1) The unrecovered balance of an investment. It is a cost, already paid, that is not relevant to the decision concerning the future that is being made. Capital already invested that for some reason cannot be retrieved. 2) A past cost that has no relevance with respect to future receipts and disbursements of a facility undergoing an economic study. This concept implies that since a past outlay is the same regardless of the alternative selected, it should not influence the choice between alternatives.

**Surrogate [item] Driver:** A substitute for the ideal driver, but is closely correlated to the ideal driver, where [item] is Resource, Activity, Cost Object. A surrogate driver is used to significantly reduce the cost of measurement while not significantly reducing accuracy. For example, the number of production runs is not descriptive of the material disbursing activity, but the number of production runs may be used as an activity driver if material disbursements correlate well with the number of production runs.

**Supermarket Approach:** An inventory management and picking technique used in lean enterprises. This concept was conceived by Taiichi Ohno of Toyota after a visit to the US in 1956 where he was impressed by how consumers could pick whatever they need from the shelf, and the store would simply replenish what was taken. This became the basis for the "pull system".

**Supplier:** 1) A provider of goods or services. *Also see: Vendor* 2) A seller with whom the buyer does business, as opposed to vendor, which is a generic term referring to all sellers in the marketplace.

**Supplier Certification:** Certification procedures verifying that a supplier operates, maintains, improves, and documents effective procedures that relate to the customer's requirements. Such requirements can include cost, quality, delivery, flexibility, maintenance, safety, and ISO quality and environmental standards.

**Supplier-Owned Inventory:** A variant of Vendor-Managed Inventory and Consignment Inventory. In this case, the supplier not only manages the inventory, but also owns the stock close to or at the customer location until the point of consumption or usage by the customer.

**Supplemental Carrier:** A for-hire air carrier subject to economic regulations; the carrier has no time schedule or designated route; service is provided under a charter or contract per plane per trip.

**Supply Chain:** 1) starting with unprocessed raw materials and ending with the final customer using the finished goods, the supply chain links many companies together. 2) the material and informational interchanges in the logistical process stretching from acquisition of raw materials to delivery of finished products to the end user. All vendors, service providers and customers are links in the supply chain.

**Supply Chain Council:** A non-profit organization dedicated to improving the supply chain efficiency of its members. The Supply-Chain Council's membership consists primarily practitioners representing a broad cross section of industries, including manufacturers, services, distributors, and retailers. It is the organization responsible for the SCOR standards.

**Supply Chain Design:** The determination of how to structure a supply chain. Design decisions include the selection of partners, the location and capacity of warehouse and production facilities, the products, the modes of transportation, and supporting information systems.

**Supply Chain Execution (SCE):** The ability to move the product out the warehouse door. This is a critical capacity and one that only brick-and-mortar firms bring to the B2B table. Dot-coms have the technology, but that's only part of the equation. The need for SCE is what is driving the Dot-coms to offer equity partnerships to the wholesale distributors.

**Supply Chain Event Management (SCEM):** SCEM is an application that supports control processes for managing events within and between companies. It consists of integrated software functionality that supports five business processes: monitor, notify, simulate, control and measure supply chain activities.

**Supply Chain Integration (SCI):** Likely to become a key competitive advantage of selected e-marketplaces. Similar concept to the Back-End Integration, but with greater emphasis on the moving of goods and services.

**Supply Chain Inventory Visibility:** Software applications that permit monitoring events across a supply chain. These systems track and trace inventory globally on a line-item level and notify the user of significant deviations from plans. Companies are provided with realistic estimates of when material will arrive.

**Supply Chain Management (SCM)** as defined by the Council of Supply Chain Management Professionals (CSCMP): "Supply Chain

Management encompasses the planning and management of all activities involved in sourcing and procurement, conversion, and all logistics management activities. Importantly, it also includes coordination and collaboration with channel partners, which can be suppliers, intermediaries, third-party service providers, and customers. In essence, supply chain management integrates supply and demand management within and across companies. Supply Chain Management is an integrating function with primary responsibility for linking major business functions and business processes within and across companies into a cohesive and high-performing business model. It includes all of the logistics management activities noted above, as well as manufacturing operations, and it drives coordination of processes and activities with and across marketing, sales, product design, finance and information technology."

**Supply Chain Network Design Systems:** The systems employed in optimizing the relationships among the various elements of the supply chain manufacturing plants, distribution centers, points-of-sale, as well as raw materials, relationships among product families, and other factors-to synchronize supply chains at a strategic level.

**Supply Chain Operations Reference Model (SCOR):** This is the model developed by the Supply-Chain Council SCC and is built around six major processes: plan, source, make, deliver, return and enable. The aim of the SCOR is to provide a standardized method of measuring supply chain performance and to use a common set of metrics to benchmark against other organizations.

**Supply Chain-Related Finance and Planning Cost Element:** One of the elements comprising a company's total supply-chain management costs. These costs consist of the following:

1. Supply-Chain Finance Costs: Costs associated with paying invoices, auditing physical counts, performing inventory accounting, and collecting accounts receivable. Does NOT include customer invoicing/accounting costs (see Order Management Costs).

2. Demand/Supply Planning Costs: Costs associated with forecasting, developing finished goods, intermediate, subassembly or end item inventory plans, and coordinating Demand/Supply

**Supply Chain-Related IT Costs:** Information Technology (IT) costs (in US dollars) associated with major supply-chain management processes as described below. These costs should include: Development costs

(costs incurred in process reengineering, planning, software development, installation, implementation, and training associated with new and/or upgraded architecture, infrastructure, and systems to support the described supply-chain management processes), Execution costs (operating costs to support supply-chain process users, including computer and network operations, EDI and telecommunications services, and amortization/depreciation of hardware, Maintenance costs (costs incurred in problem resolution, troubleshooting, repair, and routine maintenance associated with installed hardware and software for described supply-chain management processes. Include costs associated with data base administration, systems configuration control, release planning and management. These costs are associated with the following processes:

- PLAN

1. Product Data Management - Product phase-in/phase-out and release; post introduction support & expansion; testing and evaluation; end-of-life inventory management. Item master definition and control.

2. Forecasting and Demand/Supply Manage and Finished Goods - Forecasting; end-item inventory planning, DRP, production master scheduling for all products, all channels.

- SOURCE

1. Sourcing/Material Acquisition - Material requisitions, purchasing, supplier quality engineering, inbound freight management, receiving, incoming inspection, component engineering, tooling acquisition, accounts payable.

2. Component and Supplier Management - Part number cross-references, supplier catalogs, approved vendor lists.

3. Inventory Management - Perpetual and physical inventory controls and tools.

- MAKE

1. Manufacturing Planning - MRP, production scheduling, tracking, mfg. engineering, mfg. documentation management, inventory/obsolescence tracking.

2. Inventory Management - Perpetual and physical inventory controls and tools.

3. Manufacturing Execution - MES, detailed and finite interval scheduling, process controls and machine scheduling.

- DELIVER

1. Order Management - Order entry/ maintenance, quotes, customer database, product/price database, accounts receivable, credits and collections, invoicing.
2. Distribution and Transportation Management - DRP shipping, freight management, traffic management.
3. Inventory Management - Perpetual and physical inventory controls and tools.
4. Warehouse Management - Finished goods, receiving and stocking, pick/pack.
5. Channel Management - Promotions, pricing and discounting, customer satisfaction surveys.
6. Field Service/Support - Field service, customer and field support, technical service, service/call management, returns and warranty tracking.

- EXTERNAL ELECTRONIC INTERFACES

Plan/Source/Make/Deliver - Interfaces, gateways, and data repositories created and maintained to exchange supply-chain related information with the outside world. E-Commerce initiatives. Includes development and implementation costs.

Note: Accurate assignment of IT-related cost is challenging. It can be done using Activity-Based-Costing methods, or using other approaches such as allocation based on user counts, transaction counts, or departmental headcounts. The emphasis should be on capturing all costs. Costs for any IT activities that are outsourced should be included.

**Supply Chain Resiliency:** A term describing the level of hardening of the supply chain against disasters.

**Supply Chain Strategy Planning:** The process of process of analyzing, evaluating, defining supply chain strategies, including network design, manufacturing and transportation strategy and inventory policy.

**Supply Chain Vulnerability:** Of equal importance to Variability, Velocity and Volume in the elements of the Supply Chain. The term evaluates the supply chain based on the level of acceptance of the five steps of disaster logistics being planning, detection, mitigation, response and recovery.

**Supply Planning:** The process of identifying, prioritizing, and aggregating, as a whole with constituent parts, all sources of supply that are required and add value in the supply chain of a product or service at the appropriate level, horizon and interval.

**Supply Planning Systems:** The process of identifying, prioritizing, and aggregating, as a whole with constituent parts, all sources of supply that are required and add value in the supply chain of a product or service at the appropriate level, horizon and interval.

**Supply Warehouse:** A warehouse that stores raw materials. Goods from different suppliers are picked, sorted, staged, or sequenced at the warehouse to assemble plant orders.

**Support Costs:** Costs of activities not directly associated with producing or delivering products or services. Examples are the costs of information systems, process engineering and purchasing. *Also see: Indirect Cost*

**Surcharge:** An add-on charge to the applicable charges; motor carriers have a fuel surcharge, and railroads can apply a surcharge to any joint rate that does not yield 110% of variable cost.

**Sustaining Activity:** An activity that benefits an organizational unit as a whole, but not any specific cost object.

**SWAS:** Store-Within-A-Store.

**Switch Engine:** A railroad engine that is used to move rail cars short distances within a terminal and plant.

**Switching Company:** A railroad that moves rail cars short distances; switching companies connect two mainline railroads to facilitate through movement of shipments.

**SWOT:** *See SWOT Analysis*

**SWOT Analysis:** An analysis of the strengths, weaknesses, opportunities, and threats of and to an organization. SWOT analysis is useful in developing strategy.

**Synchronization:** The concept that all supply chain functions are integrated and interact in real time; when changes are made to one area, the effect is automatically reflected throughout the supply chain.

**Syntax:** The grammar or rules which define the structure of the EDI standard.

**System:** A set of interacting elements, variables, parts, or objects that are functionally related to each other and form a coherent group.

**Systems concept:** A decision-making strategy that emphasizes overall system efficiency rather than the efficiency of the individual part of the system.

# T

**Tact Time:** *See Takt Time*

**Tactical Planning:** The process of developing a set of tactical plans (e.g., production plan, sales plan, marketing plan, and so on). Two approaches to tactical planning exist for linking tactical plans to strategic plans—production planning and sales and operations planning. *See: Sales and operational planning, strategic planning.*

**Taguchi Method:** A concept of off-line quality control methods conducted at the product and process design stages in the product development cycle. This concept, expressed by Genichi Taguchi, encompasses three phases of product design: system design, parameter design, and tolerance design. The goal is to reduce quality loss by reducing the variability of the product's characteristics during the parameter phase of product development.

**Takt Time:** Sets the pace of production to match the rate of customer demand and becomes the heartbeat of any lean production system. It is computed as the available production time divided by the rate of customer demand. For example, assume demand is 10,000 units per month, or 500 units per day, and planned available capacity is 420 minutes per day. The takt time = 420 minutes per day/500 units per day = 0.84 minutes per unit. This takt time means that a unit should be planned to exit the production system on average every 0.84 minutes.

**Tally Sheet:** A printed form on which companies record, by making an appropriate mark, the number of items they receive or ship. In many operations, tally sheets become a part of the permanent inventory records.

**Tandem:** A truck that has two drive axles or a trailer that has two axles.

**Tank Cars:** Rail cars that are designed to haul bulk liquids or gas commodities.

**Tapering Rate:** A rate that increases with distance but not in direct proportion to the distance the commodity is shipped.

**Tare Weight:** The weight of a substance, obtained by deducting the weight of the empty container from the gross weight of the full container.

**Target Costing:** A target cost is calculated by subtracting a desired profit margin from an estimated or a market-based price to arrive at a desired production, engineering, or marketing cost. This may not be the initial production cost, but one expected to be achieved during the mature production stage. Target costing is a method used in the analysis of product design that involves estimating a target cost and then designing the product/service to meet that cost. *Also see: Value Analysis*

**Tariff:** A tax assessed by a government on goods entering or leaving a country. The term is also used in transportation in reference to the fees and rules applied by a carrier for its services.

**Tasks:** The breakdown of the work in an activity into smaller elements.

**Task Interleaving:** A method of combining warehouse picking and put-away. Warehouse Management Systems (WMS) use logic to direct (typically with an RF terminal) a lift truck operator to put away a pallet en route to the next pick. The idea is to reduce "deadheading" or driving empty material handling equipment around the warehouse.

**T's & C's**: *See Terms and Conditions*

**TCO:** *See Total Cost of Ownership*

**Technical Components:** Component (part) of a product for which there is a limited number of suppliers. These parts are hard to make, and require much more lead time and expertise on the part of the supplier to produce than standard components do.

**Temporary authority:** The ICC may grant a temporary operating authority as a common carrier for up to 270 days.

**Ten Principles:** A principle is a general rule, fundamental, or other statement of an observed truth. Over time certain fundamental truths of material handling have been found to exist. The "principles" of material handling are often useful in analyzing, planning and managing material handling activities and systems. At the very least they form a basic foundation upon which one can begin building expertise in material handling. These principles, serve as a starting point to identifying potential problems and assessing need, are:

1. Planning
2. Standardization
3. Work
4. Ergonomic
5. Unit Load
6. Space Utilization
7. System
8. Automation
9. Environment
10. Life Cycle Cost

**Tender:** The document which describes a business transaction to be performed.

**Terminal Delivery Allowance:** A reduced rate offered in return for the shipper of consignee tendering or picking up the freight at the carrier's terminal.

**Terms and conditions (T's & C's):** All the provisions and agreements of a contract.

**TEU:** *See Twenty-foot Equivalent Unit*

**Theoretical Cycle Time:** The back-to-back process time required for a single unit to complete all stages of a process without waiting, stoppage, or time lost due to error.

**Theory of Constraints (TOC):** A production management theory which dictates that volume is controlled by a series of constraints related to work center capacity, component availability, finance, etc. Total throughput cannot exceed the capacity of the smallest constraint, and any inventory buffers or excess capacity at non-related work centers is waste.

**Third-Party Logistics (3PL):** Outsourcing all or much of a company's logistics operations to a specialized company. The term "3PL" was first used in the early 1970s to identify intermodal marketing companies (IMCs) in transportation contracts. Up to that point, contracts for transportation had featured only two parties, the shipper and the carrier. When IMCs entered the picture—as intermediaries that accepted shipments from the shippers and tendered them to the rail carriers—they became the third party to the contract, the 3PL. But over the years, that definition has broadened to the point where these days, every company that offers some kind of logistics service for hire calls itself a 3PL

**Third Party Logistics Provider:** A firm which provides multiple logistics services for use by customers. Preferably, these services are integrated, or "bundled" together by the provider. These firms facilitate the movement of parts and materials from suppliers to manufacturers, and finished products from manufacturers to distributors and retailers. Among the services which they provide are transportation, warehousing, cross-docking, inventory management, packaging, and freight forwarding.

**Third-Party Warehousing:** The outsourcing of the warehousing function by the seller of the goods.

**Three-layer Framework:** A basic structure and operational activity of a company; the three layers include operational systems, control and administrative management, and master planning.

**Throughput:** A measure of volume through a process such as warehousing output volume (weight, number of units). Also, the total amount of units received plus the total amount of units shipped, divided by two.

**Time Based Order System:** *See Fixed Reorder Cycle Inventory Model*

**Time Bucket:** A number of days of data summarized into a columnar display. A weekly time bucket would contain all of the relevant data for an entire week. Weekly time buckets are considered to be the largest possible (at least in the near and medium term) to permit effective MRP.

**Time Fence:** A policy or guideline established to note where various restrictions or changes in operating procedures take place. For example, changes to the master production schedule can be accomplished easily beyond the cumulative lead time, while changes inside the cumulative lead time become increasingly more difficult to a point where changes should be resisted. Time fences can be used to define these points.

**Time-Definite Services:** Delivery is guaranteed on a specific day or at a certain time of the day.

**Time/Service Rate:** A rail rate that is based upon transit time.

**Time-to-Product:** The total time required to receive, fill, and deliver an order for an existing product to a customer, timed from the moment that the customer places the order until the customer receives the product.

**Time Utility:** A value created in a product by having the product available at the time desired. Transportation and warehousing create time utility.

**Timetables:** Time schedules of departures and arrivals by origin and destination; typically used for passenger transportation by air, bus, and rail.

**TL:** *See Truckload Carrier*

**TMS:** *See Transportation Management System*

**TOC:** *See Theory of Constraints*

**TOFC:** *See Trailer-on-Flat Car, Piggyback*

**Ton-Mile:** A measure of output for freight transportation; it reflects the weight of the shipment and the distance it is hauled; a multiplication of tons hauled and distance traveled.

**Total Annual Material Receipts:** The dollar amount associated with all direct materials received from Jan 1 to Dec 31.

**Total Annual Sales:** Total Annual Sales are Total Product Revenue plus post-delivery revenues (e.g., maintenance and repair of equipment, system integration) royalties, sales of other services, spare parts revenue, and rental/lease revenues.

**Total Average Inventory:** Average normal use stock, plus average lead stock, plus safety stock.

**Total Cost Analysis:** A decision-making approach that considers minimization of total costs and recognizes the interrelationship among system variables such as transportation, warehousing, inventory, and customer service.

**Total Cost Curve**: 1) In cost-volume-profit (breakeven) analysis, the total cost curve is composed of total fixed and variable costs per unit multiplied by the number of units provided. Breakeven quantity occurs where the total cost curve and total sales revenue curve intersect. *See: Break-even chart, Break-even point.* 2) In inventory theory, the total cost curve for an inventory item is the sum of the costs of acquiring and carrying the item. *Also see: Economic Order Quantity*

**Total Cost of Ownership (TCO):** Total cost of a computer asset throughout its lifecycle, from acquisition to disposal. TCO is the combined hard and soft costs of owning networked information assets. 'Hard' costs include items such as the purchase price of the asset, implementation fees, upgrades, maintenance contracts, support contracts, and disposal costs, license fees that may or may not be upfront or charged annually. These costs are considered 'hard costs' because they are tangible and easily accounted for.

**Total Cumulative Manufacture Cycle Time:** The average time between commencement of upstream processing and completion of final packaging for shipment operations as well as release approval for shipment. Do not include WIP storage time.

*Calculation:* [Average # of units in WIP] / [Average daily output in units] – WIP days of supply

**Total Inventory Days of Supply:** Total gross value of inventory at standard cost before reserves for excess and obsolescence. Includes only inventory that is on the books and currently owned by the business entity. Future liabilities such as consignments from suppliers are not included.

*Calculation:* [5 Point Annual Average Gross Inventory] / [Cost of Goods Sold/365]

**Total Make Cycle Time:** The average total processing time between commencement of upstream processing and completion of all manufacturing process steps up to, but NOT including, packaging and labeling operations (i.e. from start of manufacturing to final formulated product ready for primary packaging). Do not include hold or test and release times.

*Calculation:* [Average # of units in active manufacturing] / [Average daily output in units]

**Total Package and Label Cycle Time:** The average total processing time between the commencement of the primary packaging and labeling steps to completion of the final packaging steps for shipment.

*Calculation:* [Average # of units in packaging and labeling WIP] / [Average daily output in units]

**Total Product Revenue:** The total value of sales made to external customers plus the transfer price valuation of intra-company shipments, net of all discounts, coupons, allowances, and rebates. Includes only the intra-company revenue for product transferring out of an entity, installation services if these services are sold bundled with end products, and recognized leases to customers initiated during the same period as revenue shipments, with revenue credited at the average selling price.

Note: Total Product Revenue excludes post-delivery revenues (maintenance and repair of equipment, system integration), royalties, sales of other services, spare parts revenue, and rental/lease revenues.

**Total Productive Maintenance (TPM):** Team based maintenance process designed to maximize machine availability and performance and product quality.

**Total quality management (TQM):** A management approach in which managers constantly communicate with organizational stakeholders to emphasize the importance of continuous quality improvement.

**Total Sourcing Lead Time (95% of Raw Material Dollar Value):** Cumulative lead time (total average combined inside-plant planning, supplier lead time [external or internal], receiving, handling, etc., from demand identification at the factory until the materials are available in the production facility) required to source 95% of the dollar value (per unit) of raw materials from internal and external suppliers.

**Total Supply-Chain Management Cost (5 elements):** Total cost to manage order processing, acquire materials, manage inventory, and manage supply-chain finance, planning, and IT costs, as represented as a percent of revenue. Accurate assignment of IT-related cost is challenging. It can be done using Activity-Based-Costing methods, or based on more traditional approaches. Allocation based on user counts, transaction counts, or departmental headcounts are reasonable approaches. The emphasis should be on capturing all costs, whether incurred in the entity completing the survey or incurred in a supporting organization on behalf of the entity. Reasonable estimates founded in data were accepted as a means to assess overall performance. All estimates reflected fully burdened actual inclusive of salary, benefits, space and facilities, and general and administrative allocations.

*Calculation:* [Order Management Costs + Material Acquisition Costs + Inventory Carrying Costs + Supply-Chain-Related Finance and Planning Costs + Total Supply-Chain-Related IT Costs] / [Total Product Revenue]

**Total Supply Chain Response Time:** The time it takes to rebalance the entire supply chain after determining a change in market demand. Also, a measure of a supply chain's ability to change rapidly in response to marketplace changes.

**Total Test and Release Cycle Time:** The average total test and release time for all tests, documentation reviews, and batch approval processes performed from start of manufacturing to release of final packaged product for shipment.

**Calculation:** *[Average # of units in test and release] / [Average daily output in units]*

**Toto Authority:** A private motor carrier receiving operating authority as a common carrier to haul freight for the public over the private carrier's backhaul; this type of authority was granted to the Toto Company in 1978.

**Touch Labor:** The labor that adds value to the product - assemblers, welders etc. This does not include indirect resources such as material handlers (mover and stage product, mechanical and electrical technicians responsible for maintaining equipment.

**Touches:** The number of times a labor action is taken during a manufacturing or assembly process. Touches are typically used to measure efficiency or for costing and pricing purposes.

**TPM:** *See Total Productive Maintenance*

**TQM:** *See Total Quality Management*

**Tracing:** Determining where a shipment is during the course of a move.

**Traceability:** 1) The attribute allowing the ongoing location of a shipment to be determined. 2) The registering and tracking of parts, processes, and materials used in production, by lot or serial number.

**Tracing:** The practice of relating resources, activities and cost objects using the drivers underlying their cost causal relationships. The purpose of tracing is to observe and understand how costs are arising in the normal course of business operations. *Synonym: Assignment*

**Tracking and Tracing:** Monitoring and recording shipment movements from origin to destination.

**Tracking Signal:** The ratio of the cumulative algebraic sum of the deviations between the forecasts and the actual values to the mean absolute deviation. Used to signal when the validity of the forecasting model might be in doubt.

**Tractor:** The tractor is the driver compartment and engine of the truck. It has two or three axles.

**Trading Partner:** Companies that do business with each other via EDI (e.g., send and receive business documents, such as purchase orders).

**Trading Partner Agreement:** The written contract that spells out agreed upon terms between EDI trading partners.

**Traffic:** A department or function charged with the responsibility for arranging the most economic classification and method of shipment for both incoming and outgoing materials and products.

**Traffic Management:** The management and controlling of transportation modes, carriers and services.

**Trailer:** The part of the truck that carries the goods.

**Trailer Drops:** When a driver drops off a full truck at a warehouse and picks up an empty one.

**Trailer on a Flatcar (TOFC):** A specialized form of containerization in which motor and rail transport coordinate. *Synonym: Piggyback*

**Tramp:** An international water carrier that has no fixed route or published schedule; a tramp ship is chartered for a particular voyage or a given time period.

**Transaction:** A single completed transmission, e.g., transmission of an invoice over an EDI network. Analogous to usage of the term in data processing, in which a transaction can be an inquiry or a range of updates and trading transactions. The definition is important for EDI service operators, who must interpret invoices and other documents.

**Transaction Set:** Commonly used business transactions (e.g. purchase order, invoice, etc.) organized in a formal, structured manner, consisting of a Transaction Set header control segment, one or more Data Segments, and a Transaction Set trailer Control Data Segment.

**Transaction Set ID:** A three digit numerical representation that identifies a transaction set.

**Transactional Acknowledgement:** Specific Transaction Sets, such as the Purchase Order Acknowledgement (855), that both acknowledges receipt of an order and provides special status information such as reschedules, price changes, back order situation, etc.

**Transfer Pricing:** The pricing of goods or services transferred from one segment of a business to another. Transfer pricing generally includes the costs associated with performing the transfer and therefore item costs will be incrementally higher than when received through normal channels.

**Transit Inventory:** Inventory in transit between manufacturing and stocking locations, or between warehouses in a distributed warehousing model. *Also see: In-transit Inventory*

**Transit Privilege:** A carrier service that permits the shipper to stop the shipment in transit to perform a function that changes the commodity's physical characteristics but to pay the through rate.

**Transit Time:** The total time that elapses between a shipment's pickup and delivery.

**Translation Software:** Software the converts or "translates" business application data into EDI standard formats, and vice versa.

**Transmission Acknowledgment:** Acknowledgment that a total transmission was received with no errors detected

**Transparency:** The ability to gain access to information without regard to the systems landscape or architecture. An example would be where an online customer could access a vendor's web site to place an order and receive availability information supplied by a third party outsourced manufacturer or shipment information from a third party logistics provider. *See also: Visibility*

**Transportation Association of America:** An association that represents the entire U.S. Transportation system, carriers, users, and the public; now defunct.

**Transportation Management System (TMS):** A computer system designed to provide optimized transportation management in various modes along with associated activities, including managing shipping units, labor planning and building, shipment scheduling through inbound, outbound, intra-company shipments, documentation management (especially when international shipping is involved), and third party logistics management.

**Transportation Mode:** The method of transportation: land, sea, or air shipment.

**Transportation Planning:** The process of defining an integrated supply chain transportation plan and maintaining the information which characterizes total supply chain transportation requirements, and the management of transporters both inter and intra company.

**Transportation Planning Systems:** The systems used in optimizing of assignments from plants to distribution centers, and from distribution centers to stores. The systems combine "moves" to ensure the most economical means are employed.

**Transportation Requirements Planning (TRP):** Utilizing computer technology and information already available in MRP and DRP databases to plan transportation needs based on field demand.

**Transportation Research Board**: A division of the National Academy of Sciences which pertains to transportation research.

**Transportation Security Administration (TSA):** TSA was created in response to the attacks of September 11th and signed into law in November 2001. TSA was originally in the Department of Transportation but was moved to the Department of Homeland Security in March 2003. TSA's mission is to protect the nation's transportation systems by ensuring the freedom of movement for people and commerce.

**Transit Privilege:** A carrier service that permits the shipper to stop the shipment in transit to perform a function that changes the commodity's physical characteristics, but to pay the through rate.

**Transit Time:** The total time that elapses from pickup to delivery of a shipment.

**Transportation Association of America:** An association that represents the entire U.S. transportation system—carriers, users, and the public; now defunct.

**Transportation Method:** A linear programming technique that determines the least-cost allocation of shipping goods from plants to warehouses of from warehouses to customers.

**Transportation Research Forum:** A professional association that provides a forum for the discussion of transportation ideas and research techniques.

**Transshipment Problem:** A variation of the transportation method of linear programming that considers consolidating shipments to one destination and reshipping from that destination.

**Travel Agent:** A firm that provides passenger travel information; air, rail, and steamship ticketing; and hotel reservations. The travel agent is paid a commission by the carrier and hotel.

**Trend:** General upward or downward movement of a variable over time such as demand for a product. Trends are used in forecasting to help anticipate changes in consumption over time.

**Trend Forecasting Models:** Methods for forecasting sales data when a definite upward or downward pattern exists. Models include double exponential smoothing, regression, and triple smoothing.

**Trojan Mice**: are a small group of well focused change agents, which introduce, on an ongoing basis, in an inconspicuous way, changes. The concepts are small enough to be understood and owned by all concerned but their effects can be far-reaching.

**TRP:** *See Transportation Requirements Planning*

**Truckload Carriers (TL):** Trucking companies, which move full truckloads of freight directly from the point of origin to destination.

**Truckload Lot:** A truck shipment that qualifies for a lower freight rate because it meets a minimum weight and/or volume.

**Trunk Lines:** Oil pipelines that are used for the long-distance movement of crude oil, refined oil, or other liquid products.

**TSA:** *See Transportation Security Administration*

**Turnover:** 1) Typically refers to Inventory Turnover. 2) In the United Kingdom and certain other countries, turnover refers to annual sales volume. *Also see: Inventory Turns*

**Twenty-foot Equivalent Unit (TEU):** Standard unit for counting containers of various capacities and for describing the capacities of container ships or terminals. One 20 Foot ISO container equals 1 TEU. One 40 Foot ISO container equals two TEU.

**Two-Level Master Schedule:** A master scheduling approach in which a planning bill of material is used to master schedule an end product or family, along with selected key features (options and accessories). *Also see: Production Forecast*

**Two-Bin System:** An inventory ordering system in which the time to place an order for an item is indicated when the first bin is empty. The second bin contains sufficient supply until the order is received.

# U

**Ubiquity:** Existence or apparent existence everywhere at the same time. A raw material that is found at all locations.

**UCC***: GS1*

**UCS:** *See Uniform Communication Standard*

**UI:** User Interface.

**ULD:** *See Unit Load Device*

**Umbrella Rate:** An ICC rate-making practice that held rates to a particular level to protect the traffic of another mode.

**Unbundled Payment/Remittance:** The process where payment is delivered separately from its associated detail.

**Uncertainty Principle:** states by precise inequalities that certain pairs of physical properties, such as position and momentum, cannot be simultaneously known to arbitrarily high precision. That is, the more precisely one property is measured, the less precisely the other can be measured. Published by Werner Heisenberg in 1927

**Uniform Code Council (UCC):** *See GS1*

**Uniform Communication Standard (UCS):** A set of standard transaction sets for the grocery industry that allows computer-to-computer, paperless exchange of documents between trading partners. Using Electronic Data Interchange, UCS is a rapid, accurate and economical method of business communication; it can be used by companies of all sizes and with varying levels of technical sophistication.

**Uniform Product Code (UPC):** A standard product numbering and bar coding system used by the retail industry. UPC codes are administered by the Uniform Code Council; they identify the manufacturer as well as the item, and are included on virtually all retail packaging. *Also see: Uniform Code Council*

**Uniform Resource Locator (URL):** A string that supplies the Internet address of a website or resource on the World Wide Web, along with the protocol by which the site or resource is accessed. The most common URL type is http://, which gives the Internet address of a web page. Some other URL types are gopher://, which gives the Internet address of a Gopher directory, and ftp:;//, which gives the network location of an FTP resource.

**Uniform Warehouse Receipts Act:** The act that sets forth the regulations governing public warehousing. The regulations define the legal responsibility of a warehouse manager and define the types of receipts issued.

**Unit Cost:** The cost associated with a single unit of product. The total cost of producing a product or service divided by the total number of units. The cost associated with a single unit of measure underlying a resource, activity, product or service. It is calculated by dividing the total cost by the measured volume. Unit cost measurement must be used with caution as it may not always be practical or relevant in all aspects of cost management.

**Unit of Driver Measure:** The common denominator between groupings of similar activities. Example: 20 hours of process time is performed in an activity center. This time equates to a number of common activities varying in process time duration. The unit of measure is a standard measure of time such as a minute or an hour.

**Unit Load Device (ULD):** Refers to airfreight containers and pallets.

**Unit of Measure (UOM):** The unit in which the quantity of an item is managed, e.g., pounds, each, box of 12, package of 20, or case of 144. Various UOMs may exist for a single item. For example, a product may be purchased in cases, stocked in boxes and issued in single units.

**Unit-of-Measure Conversion:** A conversion ratio used whenever multiple units-of-measure are used with the same item. For example, if you purchased an item in cases (meaning that your purchase order stated a number of cases rather than a number of pieces) and then stocked the item in eaches, you would require a conversion to allow your system to calculate how many eaches are represented by a quantity of cases. This way, when you received the cases, your system would automatically convert the case quantity into an each quantity.

**Unit Train:** An entire, uninterrupted locomotive, care, and caboose movement between an origin and destination.

**United Nations Standard Product and Service Code (UN/SPSC):** - developed jointly between the UN and Dun & Bradstreet (D&B). Has a five level coding structure (segment, family, class, commodity, business function) for nearly 9000 products.

**United States Railway Association:** The planning and funding agency for Conrail; created by the 3-R Act of 1973.

**Unitize:** To consolidate a number of packages into one unit; the several packages are strapped, banded, or otherwise attached together.

**Unitization:** In warehousing, the consolidation of several units into larger units for fewer handlings.

**Unplanned Order:** Orders which are received that do not fit into the volumes prescribed by the plans developed from forecasts.

**UN/SPSC:** *See United Nations Standard Product and Service Code*

**UOM:** *See Unit of Measure*

**UPC:** *See Uniform Product Code*

**Upcharges:** Charges added to a bill, particularly a freight bill, to cover additional costs that were not envisioned when a contract was written. These might include costs related to rapidly increasing fuel charges or costs related to government mandates. *See also: Accessorial Charges*

**Upsell:** The practice of attempting to sell a higher-value product to the customer.

**Upside Production Flexibility:** The number of days required to complete manufacture and delivery of an unplanned sustainable 20% increase in end product supply of the predominant product line. The one constraint that is estimated to be the principal obstacle to a 20% increase in end product supply, as represented in days, is Upside Flexibility: Principal Constraint. Upside Flexibility could affect three possible areas: direct labor availability, internal manufacturing capacity, and key components or material availability.

**Upstream:** Refers to the supply side of the supply chain. Upstream partners are the suppliers who provide goods and services to the organization needed to satisfy demands which originate at point of demand or use, as well as other flows such as return product movements, payments for purchases, etc. Opposite of downstream.

**Urban Mass Transportation Administration:** An agency of the U.S. Department of Transportation responsible for developing comprehensive mass transport systems for urban areas and for providing financial aid to transit systems.

**URL:** *See Uniform Resource Locator*

**Usage Rate:** Measure of demand for product per unit of time (e.g., units per month, etc.).

# V

**Validation:** To check whether a document is the correct type for a particular EDI system, as agreed upon by the trading partners, in order to determine whether the document is going to or coming from an authorized EDI user.

**Value Added:** Increased or improved value, worth, functionality or usefulness.

**Value-Added Network (VAN):** A company that acts as a clearinghouse for electronic transactions between trading partners. A third-party supplier that receives EDI transmissions from sending trading partners and holds them in a "mailbox" until retrieved by the receiving partners.

**Value-Added Productivity Per Employee:** Contribution made by employees to total product revenue minus the material purchases divided by total employment. Total employment is total employment for the entity being surveyed. This is the average full-time equivalent employee in all functions, including sales and marketing, distribution, manufacturing, engineering, customer service, finance, general and administrative, and other. Total employment should include contract and temporary employees on a full-time equivalent (FTE) basis.

*Calculation:* Total Product Revenue-External Direct Material / [FTE's]

**Value-Adding/Nonvalue-Adding:** Assessing the relative value of activities according to how they contribute to customer value or to meeting an organization's needs. The degree of contribution reflects the influence of an activity's cost driver(s).

**Value Analysis:** A method to determine how features of a product or service relate to cost, functionality, appeal and utility to a customer (i.e., engineering value analysis). *Also see: Target Costing*

**Value Based Return (VBR):** A measure of the creation of value. It is the difference between economic profit and capital charge.

**Value Chain:** A series of activities, which combined, define a business process; the series of activities from manufacturers to the retail stores that define the industry supply chain.

**Value Chain Analysis:** A method to identify all the elements in the linkage of activities a firm relies on to secure the necessary materials and services, starting from their point of origin, to manufacture, and to distribute their products and services to an end user.

**Value-of-Service Pricing:** Pricing according to the value of the product being transported; thirddegree price discrimination; demand-oriented pricing; charging what the traffic will bear.

**Value of Transfers:** The total dollar value (for the calendar year) associated with movement of inventory from one "bucket" into another, such as raw material to work-in-process, work-in-process to finished goods, plant finished goods to field finished goods or customers, and field finished goods to customers. Value of Transfers is based on the value of inventory withdrawn from a certain category and is often approached from a costing perspective, using cost accounts. For example, Raw Materials Value of Transfers is the value of transfers out of the raw material cost accounts (you may have cost centers associated with inventory locations, but all "raw ingredients" usually share common cost accounts or can be rolled up into one financial view). The same goes for WIP. Take the manufacturing cost centers and look at the total value of withdrawals from those cost centers. While Average Gross Inventory represents the value of the inventory in the cost center at any given time, the Value of Transfers is the total value of inventory leaving the cost center during the year. The value of transfers for Finished Goods is, in theory, equivalent to COGS.

**Value Proposition:** What the supply chain member offers to other members. To be truly effective, the value proposition has to be two-sided; a benefit to both buyers and sellers.

**Value stream**: All activities, both value added and non-value added, required to bring a product from raw material state into the hands of the customer, bring a customer requirement from order to delivery and bring a design from concept to launch.

**Value Stream Mapping:** A pencil and paper tool used in two stages: 1. Follow a product's production path from beginning to end and draw a visual representation of every process in the material and information flows. 2. Then draw a future state map of how value should flow. The most important map is the future state map.

**VAN:** *See Value-Added Network*

**Variable Cost:** A cost that fluctuates with the volume or activity level of business.

**VBR:** *See Value Based Return*

**Velocity:** Rate of product movement through a warehouse

**Vendor:** The manufacturer or distributor of an item or product line. *Also see: Supplier*

**Vendor Code:** A unique identifier, usually a number and sometimes the company's DUNS number, assigned by a Customer for the Vendor it buys from. Example; a Grocery Store Chain buys Oreo's from Nabisco. The Grocery Store Chain, for accounting purposes, identifies Nabisco as Vendor #76091. One company can have multiple vendor codes. Example; Welch's Foods sells many different products. Frozen grape juice concentrate, chilled grape juice, bottled grape juice, and grape jelly. Because each of these items is a different type of product, frozen food, chilled food, beverages, dry food, they may have a different buyer at the Grocery Store Chain, requiring a different vendor code for each product line.

**Vendor-Managed Inventory (VMI):** The practice of retailers making suppliers responsible for determining order size and timing, usually based on receipt of retail POS and inventory data. Its goal is to increase retail inventory turns and reduce stock outs. Its goal is to increase retail inventory turns and reduce stock outs. It may or may not involve consignment of inventory (supplier ownership of the inventory located at the customer).

**Vendor Owned Inventory (VOI):** *See Consignment Inventory*

**Vertical Hub/Vertical Portal:** Serving one specific industry. Vertical portal websites that cater to consumers within a particular industry. Similar to the term "vertical industry", these websites are industry specific, and like a portal, they make use of Internet technology by using the same kind of personalization technology. In addition to industry specific vertical portals that cater to consumers, another definition of a vertical portal is one that caters solely to other businesses.

**Vertical Integration:** The degree to which a firm has decided to directly produce multiple value-adding stages from raw material to the sale of the product to the ultimate consumer. The more steps in the sequence, the greater the vertical integration. A manufacturer that decides to begin producing parts, components, and materials that it normally purchases is said to be backward integrated. Likewise, a manufacturer that decides to take over distribution and perhaps sale to the ultimate consumer is said to be forward integrated.

**Vested Collaboration:** Creating empathetic, mutually successful partnerships, not zero-sum relationships

**Vested Outsourcing:** A collaborative business model that creates transformational value to both the firm outsourcing and its service provider. Kate Vitasek, is the founder and lead researcher of this concept.

**Vessel:** A floating structure designed for transport.

**VICS:** Voluntary Inter-industry Commerce Standards. The retail industry standards body responsible for the CPFR standard, among other things.

**Vigorish:** or simply *the vig*, also known as *juice* or *the take*, is the amount charged by a bookmaker for his services. In the United States it also means the interest on a shark's loan. The term is Yiddish slang originating from the Russian word for *winnings*. Bookmakers use this concept to make money on their wagers regardless of the outcome.

Because of the vigorish concept, bookmakers should not have an interest in either side winning in a given sporting event. They are interested, instead, in getting equal action on each side of the event. In this way, the bookmaker minimizes his risk and always collects a small commission from the vigorish. The concept is also sometimes referred to as the *overround*, although this is technically different, being the percentage the event book is above 100% whereas the vigorish is the bookmaker's percentage profit on the total stakes made on the event. For example, 20% overround is vigorish of $16\,^2/_3\%$. The connecting formulae are $v = {}^o/_{(1+o)}$ and $o = {}^v/_{(1-v)}$ where $o$ is overround.

**Viral Marketing:** The concept of embedding advertising into web portals, pop-ups and as e-mail attachments to spread the word about products or services that the target audience may not otherwise have been interested in.

**Virtual Corporation:** The logical extension of outpartnering. With the virtual corporation, the capabilities and systems of the firm are merged with those of the suppliers, resulting in a new type of corporation where the boundaries between the suppliers' systems and those of the firm seem to disappear. The virtual corporation is dynamic in that the relationships and structures formed change according to the changing needs of the customer.

**Virtual Factory:** A changed transformation process most frequently found under the virtual corporation. It is a transformation process that involves merging the capabilities and capacities of the firm with those of its suppliers. Typically, the components provided by the suppliers are those that are not related to a core competency of the firm, while the components managed by the firm are related to core competencies. One advantage found in the virtual factory is that it can be restructured quickly in response to changing customer demands and needs.

**Visibility:** The ability to access or view pertinent data or information as it relates to logistics and the supply chain, regardless of the point in the chain where the data exists.

**Vision:** The shared perception of the organization's future—what the organization will achieve and a supporting philosophy. This shared vision must be supported by strategic objectives, strategies, and action plans to move it in the desired direction. *Syn: vision statement*

**VMI:** *See Vendor Managed Inventory*

**VOI:** *See Vendor Owned Inventory*

**Voice Activated or Voice Directed:** Systems which guide users such as warehouse personnel via voice commands

**Voice of the Customer:** The expressed requirements and expectations of customers relative to products or services, as documented and disseminated to the members of the providing organization.

# W

**Wagner-Whitin Algorithm:** A mathematically complex, dynamic lot-sizing technique that evaluates all possible ways of ordering to cover net requirements in each period of the planning horizon to arrive at the theoretically optimum ordering strategy for the entire net requirements schedule. *Also see: Discrete Order Quantity, Dynamic Lot Sizing*

**Wall-to-Wall Inventory:** An inventory management technique in which material enters a plant and is processed through the plant into finished goods without ever having entered a formal stock area.

**WAN:** *See Wide Area Network*

**Warehouse:** Storage place for products. Principal warehouse activities include receipt of product, storage, shipment, and order picking.

**Warehousing:** The storing (holding) of goods.

**Warehouse Management System (WMS):** The systems used in effectively managing warehouse business processes and direct warehouse activities, including receiving, put-away, picking, shipping, and inventory cycle counts. Also includes support of radio-frequency communications, allowing real time data transfer between the system and warehouse personnel. They also maximize space and minimize material handling by automating put-away processes.

**Warranty Costs:** Includes materials, labor, and problem diagnosis for products returned for repair or refurbishment.

**Waste:** 1) In Lean and Just-in-Time, any activity that does not add value to the good or service in the eyes of the consumer. 2) A by-product of a process or task with unique characteristics requiring special management control. Waste production can usually be planned and controlled. Scrap is typically not planned and may result from the same production run as waste.

**Waterway Use Tax:** A per-gallon tax assessed barge carriers for use of the waterways.

**Wave Picking:** A method of selecting and sequencing picking lists to improve the efficiency of picking and minimize the waiting time of the delivered material. Shipping orders may be picked in waves combined by a common product, common carrier or destination, and manufacturing orders in waves related to work centers. Picked materials would then be consolidated by ship location during the packaging / shipping process.

**Waybill:** Document containing description of goods that are part of common carrier freight shipment. Show origin, destination, consignee/consignor, and amount charged. Copies travel with goods and are retained by originating/delivering agents. Used by carrier for internal record and control, especially during transit. Not a transportation contract.

**Web:** A computer term used to describe the global Internet. *Synonym: World Wide Web*

**Web Browser:** A client application that fetches and displays web pages and other World Wide Web resources to the user.

**Web Services:** A computer term for information processing services that are delivered by third parties using internet portals. Standardized technology communications protocols; network services as collections of communication formats or endpoints capable of exchanging messages.

**Web Site:** A location on the Internet.

**Weight Break:** The shipment volume at which the LTL charges equal the TL charges at the minimum weight.

**Weight Confirmation:** The practice of confirming or validating receipts or shipments based on the weight.

**Weight-losing raw material:** A raw material that loses weight in processing

**Weighted-Point Plan:** A supplier selection and rating approach that uses the input gathered in the categorical plan approach and assigns weights to each evaluation category. A weighted sum for each supplier is obtained and a comparison made. The weights used should sum to 100% for all categories. *Also see: Categorical Plan*

**What You See Is What You Get (WYSIWYG):** An editing interface in which a file created is displayed as it will appear to an end-user.

**Wholesaler:** *See Distributor*

**Wide Area Network (WAN):** A public or private data communications system for linking computers distributed over a large geographic area.

**Will Call:** The practice of taking orders that will be picked up at the selling facility by the buyer. An area where buyers can pick up an order at the selling facility. This practice is widely used in the service parts business.

**Windows Meta File (WMF):** A vector graphics format for Windows-compatible computers used mostly or word processing clip art.

**WIP:** *See Work in Process*

**WMS:** *See Warehouse Management System*

**Work-in-Process (WIP):** Parts and subassemblies in the process of becoming completed finished goods. Work in process generally includes all of the material, labor and overhead charged against a production order which has not been absorbed back into inventory through receipt of completed products.

**World Trade Organization (WTO):** An organization established on January 1, 1995 replacing the previous General Agreement on Tariffs and Trade GATT that forms the cornerstone of the world trading system.

**World Wide Web (WWW):** A "multimedia hyper linked database that spans the globe" and lets you browse through lots of interesting information. Unlike earlier Internet services, the 'Web' combines text, pictures, sounds, and even animations, and it lets you move around with a click of your computer mouse.

**WTO:** *See World Trade Organization*

**WWW:** *See World Wide Web*

**WYSIWYG:** *See What You See Is What You Get*

# X Y X

**X12:** The ANSI standard for inter-industry electronic interchange of business transactions.

**XML:** *See Extensible Markup Language*

**YAA:** Yes Another Acronym

**Yard Management System (YMS):** A system which is designed to facilitate and organize the coming, going and staging of trucks and trucks with trailers in the parking "yard" that serves a warehouse, distribution or manufacturing facility.

**Yield:** The ratio of usable output from a process to its input.

**YMS:** *See Yard Management System*

**Zone of Rate Flexibility:** Railroads are permitted to raise rates by a percentage increase in the railroad cost index determined by the ICC; rates may be raised by 6% per year through 1984 and 4% thereafter.

**Zone of Rate Freedom:** Motor carriers are permitted to raise or lower rates by 10% in one year without ICC interference; if the rate change is within the zone of freedom, the rate is presumed to be reasonable.

**Zone of Reasonableness:** A zone or limit within which air carriers are permitted to change rates without regulatory scrutiny; if the rate change is within the zone, the new rate is presumed to be reasonable.

**Zone Picking:** A method of subdividing a picking list by areas within a storeroom for more efficient and rapid order picking. A zone-picked order must be grouped to a single location and the separate pieces combined before delivery or must be delivered to different locations, such a work centers. *Also see: Batch Picking*

**Zone Price:** The constant price of a product at all geographic locations within the zone.

**Zone Skipping:** For shipments via the US Postal Service, depositing mail at a facility one or more zones closer to the destination. This option would benefit customers operating in close proximity to a zone border or shipping sufficient volumes to offset additional transportation costs. Bellevue, Washington

# Numbers

**14 Points:** W. Edwards Deming's 14 management practices to help companies increase their quality and productivity:

1. create constancy of purpose for improving products and services,
2. adopt the new philosophy,
3. cease dependence on inspection to achieve quality,

4. end the practice of awarding business on price alone; instead, minimize total cost by working with a single supplier,

5. improve constantly and forever every process for planning, production and service,

6. institute training on the job,

7. adopt and institute leadership,

8. drive out fear,

9. break down barriers between staff areas,

10. eliminate slogans, exhortations and targets for the workforce,

11. eliminate numerical quotas for the workforce and numerical goals for management,

12. remove barriers that rob people of pride of workmanship, and eliminate the annual rating or merit system,

13. institute a vigorous program of education and self-improvement for everyone and

14. put everybody in the company to work to accomplish the transformation.

**24-hour Manifest Rule (24-hour Rule):** U.S. Customs rule requiring carriers to submit a cargo declaration 24 hours before cargo is laden aboard a vessel at a foreign port.

**24/7:** Referring to operations that are conducted 24 hours a day, 7 days a week

**24/7/365:** Referring to operations that are conducted 24 hours a day, 7 days a week, 365 days per year, with no breaks for holidays, etc

**3D Loading:** 3D loading is a method of space optimizing designed to help quickly and easily plan the best compact arrangement of any 3D rectangular object set (boxes) within one or more larger rectangular enclosures (containers). It's based on three-dimensional, most-dense packing algorithms

**3PL:** *See Third Party Logistics*

**4PL:** *See Forth Party Logistics*

**5-Point Annual Average:** Method frequently used in PMG studies to establish a representative average for a one year period. **Calculation:** *[12/31/98 + 3/31/98 + 6/30/99 + 9/30/99 + 12/31/99] / 5*

**5-S Program:** A program for organizing work areas. Sometimes referred to as elements, each of the five components of the program begins with the letter "S." They include sort, systemize, shine or sweep, standardize, and sustain. In the UK, the concept is converted to the 5-C program comprising five comparable components: clear out, configure, clean and check, conformity, and custom and practice.

- Sort—get rid of clutter; separate out what is needed for the operations.
- Systemize/Set in Order—organize the work area; make it easy to find what is needed.
- Shine—clean the work area; make it shine.
- Standardize—establish schedules and methods of performing the cleaning and sorting.
- Sustain—implement mechanisms to sustain the gains through involvement of people, integration into the performance measurement system, discipline, and recognition.

The 5-S program is frequently combined with precepts of the Lean Manufacturing Initiative. Even when used separately, however, the 5-S (or 5-C) program is said to yield excellent results.

Implementation of the program involves introducing each of the five elements in order, which reportedly generates multiple benefits, including product diversification, higher quality, lower costs, reliable deliveries, improved safety, and higher availability rate.

**10+2:** U.S. Customs and Border Protection's (CBP) Security Filing regulation, requires that importers and vessel operating carriers provide additional advance information on non-bulk cargo shipments arriving into the United States by vessel. Enforcement of 10+2 went into effect on January 26, 2010.

**80-20 Rule:** A term referring to the Pareto principle. The principle suggests that most effects come from relatively few causes; that is, 80% of the effects (or sales or costs) come from 20% of the possible causes (or items). *Also see: ABC Classification, Pareto*

# Michael J. Stolarczyk
# Bio

In December 2009, Michael J. Stolarczyk joined the team at Kontane Logistics in Charleston, South Carolina, as president. Kontane Logistics is an industry leader in third-party logistics. Kontane Logistics was established in 1995 as a separate operating division of Kontane Inc., the Southeast's premier packaging designer and builder, based in Hickory, North Carolina. The logistics division was originally formed as a dedicated third-party logistics provider involved with packaging and exporting to several countries around the globe. Since 1997, Kontane Logistics has expanded to include warehousing and distribution, cross-docking, freight consolidation, import material receipt, line sequencing, parts distribution, development of logistics information systems, subassembly, and foreign trade zones services.

Prior to joining Kontane Logistics, Stolarczyk served as CEO of the Toledo-Lucas County Port Authority in Toledo, Ohio. Founded in 1955, the TLCPA was the first port authority in Ohio and operates the Port of Toledo, Toledo Express Airport, and Toledo Executive Airport.

From 2005–2009, Michael worked as senior director for Exel, a leader in supply-chain management that provides customer-focused solutions to a wide range of manufacturing, retail, and consumer industries. Mike supported the strategic growth of Exel's retail customer roster. Prior to Exel, Michael founded FourPointStar (FPS-Ronin LLC) to establish a forum where people could stimulate collaboration and achievement.

Michael was with the A.P. Moller/Maersk Group from 1988 until 2004 and held various management positions within Maersk, ranging from manager, international accounts, with Maersk Hong Kong Limited, to director, US Flag Liner Operations, for Maersk Line Limited, located in their Arlington, Virginia, office.

In 2002, Michael's efforts led to the organization's quantum growth in Central Europe, and he was named to *Fast Company* magazine's debut list of "Fast 50: Global Innovators Whose Achievements Helped Change Their Company or Society."

In 1999, Michael was transferred to Prague to accept the managing director post within the Maersk Agency SRO, administrating all business activities in the Central European countries of the Czech Republic and Slovak Republic. He was also chairman of the board for both Maersk Logistics Czech Republic SRO and Maersk Intermodal Europe SRO.

## Board Positions

In 2003, Michael was elected as vice chairman of the Ceske Pristavy A.S. (Czech ports) board of directors by the shareholders of the company. He was also appointed to the board of advisors for West Virginia University's School of Business and Economics that same year. Additionally, Michael serves on the board of governors at West Liberty University in Wheeling, West Virginia and is currently a board member for Navismart Hungary Limited.

*He can be contacted at* michael@kontanelogistics.com.

*You can follow him on Twitter at* http://twitter.com/mjstolarczyk.

Michael has been featured in these newspapers and magazines:

*Fast Company Magazine*
*Wall Street Journal*
*USA Today*
*Containerization International*
*New World Magazine*
*Journal of Commerce*
*American Shipper*
*Toledo Blade*
*Charleston Post and Courier*
*Prague Post*
*Prague Business Journal*
*Marion Star*
*Columbus Dispatch*
*Toledo Free Press*
*Cleveland Plain Dealer*
*Inbound Logistics*
*Dailey Athenaeum*
*Dominion Post*
*The Bottom Line Newsletter*

*Ad astra per aspera*

*Montani semper liberi*

# INDEX

China market 222-3
China Strategy 221, 223
Chinese economy 57-8
clients 3, 15, 44-5, 48, 94-5,
    188, 202, 211, 222
collaboration 18-19, 21, 23, 27,
    31, 33, 39, 56, 75, 165,
    222
  vested 19, 23
communications 6, 21, 31, 51-2,
    55-6, 83, 119, 142, 193
companies
  big-box 199
  drayage 192
  influence 203
companies scatter inventory 199
complexity 46, 48, 61, 107,
    129, 207, 209, 228
compliance 82, 188-9, 213
component 11, 45, 77, 81, 101
computers 13, 15, 59, 105,
    175
conference-room pilots 35
consolidate 198, 200
consumers 2-3, 105-6, 141, 201
container security device 145,
    147-8
containers 130, 146, 148
contracts 20, 85, 197-8, 217
  multiyear 22
cost savings 156, 169, 213,
    218
costs 13-14, 21-2, 26, 46-7,
    56, 83, 90-1, 93, 95,
    118, 134-6, 155-6, 169,
    198-202, 207-9, 217-19
  incremental 134, 137

reduced 212, 222
  reducing 48, 163
creativity 30, 163
crisis 117-19
CSD 147-8
cube 181, 184
culture 63, 65, 69, 214
  changing organizational 114
customer service 20-1, 33, 197,
    212
Customs-Trade Partnership 145,
    148
cycle time 164, 166
  compressing 163
Czech Republic 60, 228

**D**

data exchange 187-8
data standards 187-8
DC 179, 184, 227
DC managers 179-81
deliveries, timed 47
delivery benchmarks, time-definite
    48
demand conditions 134-6
demand outcomes 134-6
demand planning 102, 104,
    191
demands, time-definite 45
Department of Homeland
    Security 146-7
departments 21, 30, 34, 164,
    179
devices 147-9, 192
disruptions 111, 117
distribute 48, 145, 149, 228
distribution 45, 89-91

Made in the USA
San Bernardino, CA
27 June 2013